*SHAKESPEARE'S*
*100 GREATEST*
*DRAMATIC IMAGES*

# SHAKESPEARE'S
# 100 GREATEST
## DRAMATIC IMAGES

Chosen and introduced by
*Claire and John Saunders*

Pari
Publishing

*For*
*Reggie Alton and Harvey Hallsmith*
*whose love of Shakespeare*
*and of word-play*
*inspired this book.*

A catalogue record for this book is available from the British Library.
ISBN 978-88-95604-01-5

Printed and bound in the United States of America.

Book and cover design by Andrea Barbieri
Cover image © Andrea Barbieri

**Pari Publishing**

*Via Tozzi 7, 58045 Pari, Grosseto, Italy*
*www.paripublishing.com*

# TABLE OF CONTENTS

# Introduction

This book is centred on one hundred of Shakespeare's greatest images—at least one taken from each of his plays. Although every image is essentially dramatic, presenting a picture which should be experienced both on the stage and in the mind, many can be enjoyed as short poems in their own right. They deal with the enduring subjects of poetry—love, loss, loveliness, folly, injustice—in voices which range from witty to tender, from indignant to resigned. Taken together they eloquently demonstrate why Shakespeare is generally considered to be not only the greatest dramatist, but also the greatest poet.

In Section 1 the images are introduced to the reader through "Word-Play"—ten short sub-sections which can be enjoyed individually or in a group. If the lines are spoken aloud several times (and they should be, since sound is often an integral part of meaning) readers will find themselves well on the way to appreciating some of Shakespeare's richest poetry and prose.

Section 2, 'Images in Context', consists of 37 short essays. Here each image is placed within its dramatic context and serves as a window into the play from which it has been taken. Where appropriate, historical and theatrical perspectives as well as modern interpretations and controversies are explored.

Aimed at 'the great variety of readers', the book is intended to be versatile. It can be dipped-into at random, taken a section at a time or read from start to finish as a short but original introduction to Shakespeare's plays.

# SECTION I
# *Word-Play*

*Page references in square brackets show where
each quotation is discussed in Section 2*

## *A. Last Words*

**Complete each of the following quotations from the three
alternatives offered:**

1  Dost thou think because thou art virtuous there shall be
no more cakes and —— ?                               [p. 67]

  (a) ices
  (b) crumpet
  (c) ale

2             We are such stuff
As dreams are made on; and our little life
Is rounded with a —— .                               [p. 76]

  (a) sleep
  (b) sheep
  (c) nightmare

3 Men have died from time to time, and worms have eaten them, but not for —— . [p. 48]

(a) fun
(b) love
(c) diet

4 As flies to wanton boys are we to th' gods, They kill us for their —— . [p. 88]

(a) dinner
(b) sport
(c) experiments

5 If you prick us, do we not bleed? If you tickle us, do we not laugh? If you poison us, do we not die? And if you wrong us, shall we not —— ? [p. 53]

(a) revenge
(b) forgive
(c) sue

6 Those are pearls that were his eyes: Nothing of him that doth fade, But doth suffer a sea-change Into something rich and —— . [p. 74]

(a) delicate
(b) wise
(c) strange

7 On her left breast A mole cinque-spotted, like the crimson drops I' th' bottom of a —— . [p. 68]

(a) shrew
(b) toadstool
(c) cowslip

8     When didst thou see me heave up my leg and make water against a gentlewoman's farthingale? Didst thou ever see me do such a —— ?

[p. 36]

(a) trickle
(b) trick
(c) treat

9
        Young boys and girls
Are level now with men; the odds is gone,
And there is nothing left remarkable
Beneath the visiting —— .           [p. 104]

(a) stars
(b) comet
(c) moon

10     I charge and command that, of the city's cost, the pissing-conduit run nothing but claret wine this first year of our —— .

[p. 123]

(a) rain
(b) rein
(c) reign

***Answers to 'Last Words' are on p. 48***

# B. Deaths and Entrances

**Complete each of the following quotations from the three words on offer:**

1 Thou met'st with things ——— , I with things new born.  [p. 71]

    (**a**) crying
    (**b**) dying
    (**c**) sighing

2 Thou must be patient; we came crying hither.
Thou know'st, the first time that we smell the air
We ——— and cry.  [p. 91]

    (**a**) crawl
    (**b**) mewl
    (**c**) wawl

3 A terrible child-bed hast thou had, my dear,
No light, no fire. Th' unfriendly ———
Forgot thee utterly.  [p. 67]

    (**a**) elephants
    (**b**) weather
    (**c**) elements

4 Some report a sea-maid ——— him; some, that he was begot between two stock-fishes. But it is certain that when he makes water his urine is congeal'd ice.  [p. 59]

    (**a**) begot
    (**b**) spawn'd
    (**c**) pawn'd

5 Give me my robe, put on my —— , I have
Immortal longings in me.                                    [p. 105]

    (a) gown
    (b) crown
    (c) wig

6 Death, that hath suck'd the honey of thy —— ,
Hath had no power yet upon thy beauty.                      [p. 80]

    (a) health
    (b) breath
    (c) wealth

7         Yet I'll not shed her blood,
Nor scar that whiter skin of hers than snow,
And smooth as monumental —— .                              [p.87]

    (a) mayhem
    (b) masonry
    (c) alabaster

8         She looks like sleep,
As she would —— another Antony
In her strong toil of grace.                               [p.106]

    (a) scratch
    (b) catch
    (c) place

9         Last scene of all,
That ends this strange eventful history,
Is second childishness, and mere —— ,
Sans teeth, sans eyes, sans taste, sans everything.         [p.47]

    (a) oblivion
    (b) senility
    (c) obligation

10 Ay, but to die, and go we know not where;
To lie in cold obstruction, and to rot;
This sensible warm motion to become
A kneaded ——— .                              [p.61]

(a) sod
(b) loaf
(c) clod

ANSWERS TO 'DEATHS AND ENTRANCES' ARE ON P. 57

# C. The Bestiary

**Place the following animals in their correct quotations:**

(a) swallow(s)        (b) steed (s)        (c) crow(s)

(d) dog(s)            (e) butterfly/flies  (f) toad(s)

(g) horse(s)          (h) worm(s)          (i) ape(s)

(j) whale(s)

1 Think, when we talk of ——— , that you see them
Printing their proud hoofs i'th' receiving earth.        [p.120]

2 Why should a ——— , a horse, a rat, have life,
And thou no breath at all?                               [p.92]

3 Light thickens and the ———
Makes wing to th' rooky wood.                            [p.93]

**4**
                    Daffodils,
That come before the —— dares, and take
The winds of March with beauty.                    [p.72]

**5**
                    Man, proud man,
Dress'd in a little brief authority,
Most ignorant of what he's most assured
(His glassy essence), like an angry ——
Plays such fantastic tricks before high heaven
As makes the angels weep.                          [p.59]

**6**
But there, where I have garner'd up my heart,
Where either I must live or bear no life;
The fountain from the which my current runs
Or else dries up: to be discarded thence!
Or keep it as a cistern for foul ——
To knot and gender in!                             [p.87]

**7**
          Civil dissension is a viperous ——
That gnaws the bowels of the commonwealth.         [p.122]              **19**

**8**
I saw him run after a gilded —— , and when he caught it, he let
it go again, and after it again, and over and over he comes, and
up again; catch'd it again: or whether his fall enrag'd him, or how
'twas, he did so set his teeth and tear it. O, I warrant, how he
mammock'd it!                                      [p.107]

**9**
          The belching ——
And humming water must o'erwhelm thy corpse,
Lying with simple shells.                          [p.67]

**10**
Steed threatens —— , in high and boastful neighs
Piercing the night's dull ear; and from the tents
The armourers, accomplishing the knights,
With busy hammers closing rivets up,
Give dreadful note of preparation.                 [p.121]

*ANSWERS TO 'THE BESTIARY' ARE ON P. **62***

# D. Lost Verbs

**Which of the three alternatives do you think is Shakespeare's?**

1 Now, afore God, I am so vex'd that every part about me ——— .
[p.80]

   (a) shivers
   (b) rumbles
   (c) quivers

2 They say many young gentlemen flock to him everyday, and ———
the time carelessly, as they did in the golden world.     [p.46]

   (a) beat
   (b) fleet
   (c) pass

3
           Not poppy, nor mandragora,
   Nor all the drowsy syrups of the world
   Shall ever ——— thee to that sweet sleep
   Which thou ow'st yesterday.                    [p.86]

   (a) sing
   (b) medicine
   (c) fatten

4
           The gods are just, and of our pleasant vices
   Make instruments to ——— us:
   The dark and vicious place where thee he got
   Cost him his eyes.                             [p.89]

   (a) plague
   (b) blind
   (c) teach

5 My mother cried, but then there was a star —— , and under that
was I born. [p.44]

    (a) danced
    (b) exploded
    (c) shone

6 And many a man there is (even at this present,
Now, while I speak this) holds his wife by th' arm,
That little thinks she has been —— in 's absence,
And his pond fish'd by his next neighbour—by
Sir Smile, his neighbour. [p.70]

    (a) seduced
    (b) sluiced
    (c) spruced

7 Come, make him stand upon this molehill here
That —— at mountains with outstretched arm. [p.124]

    (a) caught
    (b) fought
    (c) raught

8 If one good deed in all my life I did,
I do —— it from my very soul. [p.99]

    (a) repent
    (b) invent
    (c) refute

9 O for a Muse of fire, that would ——
The brightest heaven of invention. [p.120]

    (a) climb
    (b) ascend
    (c) amend

10 Now get you to my Lady's chamber, and tell her, let her —— an inch thick, to this favour she must come; make her laugh at that. [p.85]

(a) pad
(b) pinch
(c) paint

ANSWERS TO 'LOST VERBS' ARE ON P. 77

# E. Love and Lust

**Complete each of the following quotations from the three words on offer:**

1 If music be the food of love, play on,
Give me excess of it, that surfeiting,
The appetite may —— and so die. [p.65]

(a) quicken
(b) sicken
(c) thicken

2 'If it be love indeed, tell me how much.'
There's beggary in the love that can be reckon'd.
'I'll set a bourn how far to be belov'd.'
Then must thou needs find out new —— , new earth. [p.102]

(a) heaven
(b) sea
(c) islands

3 He capers, he dances, he has eyes of youth, he writes verses, he speaks —— , he smells April and May.  [p. 43]

   (a) Esperanto
   (b) fun
   (c) holiday

4 No, the world must be —— . When I said I would die a bachelor, I did not think I should live till I were married.  [p.45]

   (a) inhabited
   (b) rabbited
   (c) peopled

5                    One that cares for thee;
   And for thy maintenance, commits his body
   To painful labour both by sea and land,
   To watch the night in storms, the day in cold,
   Whilst thou liest —— at home, secure and safe.  [p. 50]

   (a) still
   (b) cool
   (c) warm

6 The moon methinks looks with a wat'ry eye;
   And when she weeps, weeps every little —— ,
   Lamenting some enforced chastity.  [p. 40]

   (a) spider
   (b) spinster
   (c) flower

**7** What a devil hast thou to do with the time of day? Unless hours were cups of sack, and minutes capons, and clocks the tongues of bawds, and dials the signs of leaping-houses, and the blessed sun himself a fair hot —— in flame coloured taffata. [p. 114]

    **(a)** goose
    **(b)** wench
    **(c)** day

**8** Thou rascal —— , hold thy bloody hand!
Why dost thou lash that whore? Strip thy own back,
Thou hotly lusts to use her in that kind
For which thou whip'st her. [p. 91]

    **(a)** beagle
    **(b)** beadle
    **(c)** officer

**9**                Our natures do pursue,
Like rats that ravin down their proper bane,
A —— evil; and when we drink we die. [p. 58]

    **(a)** thirsty
    **(b)** dirty
    **(c)** devilish

**10**              This is it
That makes the wappen'd widow wed again;
She, whom the spittle-house and ulcerous sores
Would cast the gorge at, this embalms and ——
To th'April day again. [p. 108]

    **(a)** entices
    **(b)** spices
    **(c)** splices

**ANSWERS TO 'LOVE AND LUST' ARE ON P. 81**

# F. Epiphanies

## Complete the following quotations

1 Yet who would have thought the old man to have had so much
—— in him? [p. 95]

   (a) food
   (b) blood
   (c) good

2 This thing of —— I acknowledge mine. [p.75]

   (a) wickedness
   (b) darkness
   (c) beastliness

3 Had I but serv'd my God with half the zeal
I serv'd my king, he would not in mine age
Have left me —— to mine enemies. [p.126]

   (a) donated
   (b) naked
   (c) abandoned

4 If —— hath a soul, this is not she. [p.55]

   (a) duty
   (b) chastity
   (c) beauty

5    Thou hast nor youth nor age,
But as it were an after-dinner's —— ,
Dreaming on both. [p.60]

   (a) sleep
   (b) ague
   (c) speech

6   Do you see this? Look on her! Look her —— ,
    Look there, look there!                              [p. 92]

    **(a)** hair
    **(b)** hips
    **(c)** lips

7   What a piece of work is a man, how noble in reason, how infinite in
    faculties, in form and moving how express and admirable, in action
    how like an angel, in apprehension how like a god! the beauty
    of the world, the paragon of animals; and yet to me what is this
    quintessence of —— ?                                [p. 84]

    **(a)** life
    **(b)** lust
    **(c)** dust

8   And pity, like a naked new-born babe,
    Striding the blast, or heaven's cherubin, hors'd
    Upon the sightless couriers of the air,
    Shall blow the horrid deed in every eye,
    That —— shall drown the wind.                        [p.95]

    **(a)** seas
    **(b)** tears
    **(c)** bears

9   Poor naked wretches, wheresoe'er you are,
    That bide the pelting of this pitiless storm,
    How shall your houseless heads and unfed sides,
    Your loop'd and window'd —— , defend you
    From seasons such as these?                          [p.89]

    **(a)** palaces
    **(b)** raggedness
    **(c)** vulnerability

10 Life's but a walking shadow, a poor player,
That struts and frets his hour upon the stage,
And then is heard no more. It is a tale,
Told by an —— , full of sound and fury,
Signifying nothing.                                    [p.96]

(a) artist
(b) ass
(c) idiot

ANSWERS TO 'EPIPHANIES' ARE ON P. *93*

# G. *Abstractions*

**Attempt to match these abstractions to the missing words in the quotations which follow.**

(a) mercy            (b) corruption          (c) fortune

(d) mind             (e) conscience          (f) grief

(g) time             (h) imagination         (i) virginity

(j) perturbation

1     The quality of —— is not strain'd;
It droppeth as the gentle rain from heaven
Upon the place beneath.                              [p. 52]

2   The lunatic, the lover, and the poet
Are of —— all compact.                              [p.41]

3 There is a tide in the affairs of men,
Which taken at the flood, leads on to —— ;
Omitted, all the voyage of their life
Is bound in shallows and in miseries.                [p.102]

4 Thus —— does make cowards of us all,
And thus the native hue of resolution
Is sicklied o'er with the pale cast of thought,
And enterprises of great pitch and moment
With this regard their currents turn awry,
And lose the name of action.                         [p.85 ]

5 —— fills the room up of my absent child,
Lies in his bed, walks up and down with me,
Puts on his pretty looks, repeats his words,
Remembers me of all his gracious parts.              [p.111]

6 —— breeds mites, much like a cheese, consumes itself to the very
paring, and so dies with feeding his own stomach.        [p. 57]

7 Injurious —— now with a robber's haste
Crams his rich thiev'ry up, he knows not how.
As many farewells as be stars in heaven,
With distinct breath and consign'd kisses to them,
He fumbles up into a loose adieu;
And scants us with a single famish'd kiss,
Distasted with the salt of broken tears.             [p.56]

8 Lay not that flattering unction to your soul,
That not your trespass but my madness speaks;
It will but skim and film the ulcerous place,
Whiles rank —— , mining all within,
Infects unseen.                                       [p. 83]

9        O polished —— ! golden care!
That keep'st the ports of slumber open wide
To many a watchful night.                            [p.117]

10 O, what a noble —— is here o'erthrown!
The courtier's, soldier's, scholar's, eye, tongue, sword,
Th' expectancy and rose of the fair state,
The glass of fashion and the mould of form,
Th' observ'd of all observers, quite, quite down!     [p.82]

*ANSWERS TO 'ABSTRACTIONS' ARE ON P. 97*

# H. Scapes

**There follow descriptions of settings (landscapes, seascapes, mindscapes etc). Attempt to match each description to one of the following 'places':**

**(a)** water          **(b)** isle          **(c)** bed

**(d)** court          **(e)** heaven          **(f)** land

**(g)** town          **(h)** blood          **(i)** bank

**(j)** world

1 I know a —— where the wild thyme blows,
Where oxlips and the nodding violet grows,
Quite over-canopied with luscious woodbine,
With sweet musk-roses and with eglantine.     [p.39]

2        Look how the floor of ——
Is thick inlaid with patens of bright gold.
There's not the smallest orb which thou behold'st
But in his motion like an angel sings,
Still quiring to the young-eye'd cherubins.     [p.51]

3 Disorder, horror, fear, and mutiny
Shall here inhabit, and this —— be call'd
The field of Golgotha and dead men's skulls.                    [p.113]

4 They say this —— is full of cozenage:
As nimble jugglers that deceive the eye,
Dark-working sorcerers that change the mind,
Soul-killing witches that deform the body,
Disguised cheaters, prating mountebanks,
And many such-like liberties of sin.                            [p.64]

5 The barge she sat in, like a burnish'd throne,
Burnt on the —— . The poop was beaten gold,
Purple the sails, and so perfumed that
The winds were love-sick with them.                             [p.103]

6 Be not afeard, the —— is full of noises,
Sounds and sweet airs, that give delight and hurt not.          [p.73]

7                          I am in ——
Stepp'd in so far that, should I wade no more,
Returning were as tedious as go o'er.                           [p.94]

8          He doth bestride the narrow ——
Like a Colossus, and we petty men
Walk under his huge legs, and peep about
To find ourselves dishonourable graves.                         [p.100]

9               For within the hollow crown
That rounds the mortal temples of a King
Keeps death his —— and there the antic sits,
Scoffing his state and grinning at his pomp.                    [p.112]

10                         Nay, but to live
In the rank sweat of an enseamed —— ,
Stew'd in corruption, honeying and making love
Over the nasty sty!                                             [p.83]

**ANSWERS TO 'SCAPES' ARE ON P. 106**

# I. Do It Yourself

**One word, is missing from each of the following ten quotations.**
**After reading the quotation, try to decide on the missing word.**

1   Not all the water in the rough rude sea
    Can wash the balm off from an anointed —— .        [p.112]

2   From forth the fatal loins of these two foes
    A pair of star-cross'd —— take their life.         [p.79]

3   And Crispin Crispian shall ne'er go by,
    From this day to the ending of the —— ,
    But we in it shall be remembered.                  [p.119]

4   To hold as 'twere the —— up to nature: to show virtue her
    own feature, scorn her own image, and the very age and
    body of the time his form and pressure.            [p.82]

5   Fear no more the heat o' th' sun,
    Nor the furious winter's rages,
    Thou thy worldly task has done,
    Home art gone, and ta'en thy wages.
    Golden lads and girls all must,
    As chimney-sweepers, come to —— .                  [p.69]

6   Why, I, in this weak, piping time of peace,
    Have no delight to pass away the time,
    Unless to spy my shadow in the —— ,
    And descant on mine own deformity.                 [p.125]

7               Peace, peace!
    Dost thou not see my —— at my breast,
    That sucks the nurse asleep?                        [p.105]

8 But if the cause be not good, the King himself hath a heavy reckoning to make, when all those legs and arms, and —— , chopp'd off in a battle, shall join together at the latter day and cry all, "We died at such a place." [p.119]

9 I have no way, and therefore want no —— ;
I stumbled when I saw. [p.88]

10 'Throca movousus, cargo, cargo, cargo'.
Cargo, cargo, cargo, villianda par corbo, —— . [p.58]

**ANSWERS TO 'DO IT YOURSELF' ARE ON P. 109**

# J. Plausible Misprints

**Find and correct the misprint in each of the following:**

1 Oh grave new world that has such people in it! [p. 74]

2 The best in this kind are but sadshows. [p.42]

3 The words of Mercury are hash after the songs of Apollo. [p.37]

4 There is a devil hunts thee in the likeness of an old fat man.
[p.115]

5     More than our brother is our charity.       [p. 60]

6     Satan and Venus this year in conjunction.       [p.117]

7     For the red blood reins in the winter's pale.       [p.72]

8     We have heard the crimes at midnight, Master Shallow.       [p.118]

9     Bash plump Jack, and bash all the world.       [p.116]

10     Take but degree away, untune that spring
And hark what discord follows.       [p.54]

*ANSWERS TO 'PLAUSIBLE MISPRINTS' ARE ON P. 122*

# SECTION 2
# *Images In Context*

## COMEDIES

Shakespearean comedy includes elements of farce, satire and romance. Usually the plot centres on mishaps in 'the course of true love' and climaxes in at least one wedding. The fact that female roles were played by boy actors may have added a frisson to some of the scenes and certainly made sense of heroines disguising themselves as young men. Songs, and often dancing, are important, both linked to the sense of 'festival' which underlies most of the plays.

The essays which follow take the plays in the probable order of their composition.

The Two Gentlemen of Verona  (1592)
Love's Labour's Lost  (1594)
A Midsummer Night's Dream  (1595-6)
The Merry Wives of Windsor  (1597)
Much Ado about Nothing  (1598-9)
As You Like It  (1599)

# The Two Gentlemen of Verona

**When didst thou ever see me heave up my leg and make**
**water against a gentlewoman's farthingale°?**          *skirt*
**Didst thou ever see me do such a trick?**          IV.iv. 37-9

Launce, a 'clownish servant' is addressing his dog, Crab. He reveals to the audience that Crab has a history of embarrassing misdemeanours. When presented as a gift to the lady Sylvia, Crab had responded by lifting his leg and urinating on her skirt. Then, ungenerous and weak of bladder, Crab disgraced himself and his master by gate-crashing the Duke's dinner party, 'thrusting himself into the company of three or four gentlemanlike dogs' and again lifting his leg. This last 'trick' almost destroyed Crab. When 'all the chamber smelt him', there was uproar in the polite assembly and a call for the dog to be whipped and hanged. However, in a moment of comic heroism, Launce had intervened to save Crab's life: 'Twas I that did the thing you wot of,' he told the man about to whip Crab. As a result Launce himself was whipped and banished from the dining hall. No wonder he addresses his dog with such reproachful indignation.

In a play centred on the idealism of courtly, romantic love, Launce's devotion to Crab provides an amusing contrast to the somewhat glib poetry and posturing of the 'two gentlemen', Valentine and Proteus. Proteus is shallow and inconstant. He leaves Verona professing passionate love for Julia, but the moment that he sees his friend Valentine's beloved, Sylvia, all thoughts of Julia and friendship are abandoned. Valentine, placing friendship above love, is quick to offer the surprised Sylvia to his fickle friend.

"What's in a name?" (Juliet asks this in *Romeo and Juliet*). In *The Two Gentlemen of Verona*, the answer would be 'plenty'. Valentine is a moody, melancholic lover; Proteus is an inconstant, changeable friend. Launce may be an abbreviation of Launcelot, the gallant Knight of Arthurian legend. And Crab? Crab is particularly well named—like the crab-apple, sour. What is more he is a serial offender, who kills geese and steals capons and puddings. Incapable of demonstrating any 'human' warmth or sympathy, he is quite unworthy of his master's devotion.

*The Two Gentlemen of Verona* anticipates Shakespeare's later comedies in a number of ways. Love is a central theme. Song and music are important motifs. Julia is the first of Shakespeare's heroines to disguise herself as a young man. As in later plays, the setting moves from scenes in the court to scenes in 'a forest' where, released from 'civilised' control, characters begin to reveal their true selves. The later plays treat these elements with greater subtlety and success but *The Two Gentlemen of Verona* is sufficiently varied and fast-moving to provide excellent entertainment. And, although there is a potentially comical dog-role to accompany Starveling's 'Moonshine' in *A Midsummer Night's Dream*, Launce and Crab remain a comic act unrivalled in later plays.

# Love's Labour's Lost

**The words of Mercury are harsh after the songs of Apollo.**

V.ii.930-1

This image, which concludes *Love's Labour's Lost*, may initially seem puzzling. The words are spoken by the absurd Spaniard, Don Adriano de Armado, a man whose linguistic affectation (he refers to 'the afternoon' as 'the posteriors of the day') provides a rich vein of comedy throughout the play. But this, his last line, has a sharpness and economy quite unlike his other utterances.

Why 'the songs of Apollo'? After a potentially serious opening scene, in which the King of Navarre persuades three of his lords to join him in a three-year period of intensive study (during which time no women will be allowed to enter his court), the Princess of France, accompanied by three ladies-in-waiting, arrives, and four love-suits commence. Intensive study gives way to the writing of poetry and an indulgence in dance, the four men dressing up as 'muscovites' to court their loved-ones in a masque. Clumsy courtship is then followed by pageant and song, provided by the villagers for the entertainment of the royal party. Apollo represents music and art and could be said to rule over this central section of the play.

Why Mercury? Mercury is the messenger of the gods and it is, surely, no accident that the messenger who enters to report the death of the Princess's father (thus ending the holiday interlude and the reign of Apollo) is named Mercade—a near echo of the mythic original. What is more, Mercade is not the only messenger to deliver 'harsh' words. Don Armado has just heard from his rival in love, that their beloved, Jaquenetta, is pregnant. As the courtship of the eight main lovers ends with a sobering announcement of death, the courtship of the comic lovers ends with the equally sobering promise of birth—and its ensuing responsibilities.

*Love's Labour's Lost* was almost certainly written between 1593 and 1595, when an epidemic of plague resulted in the closing of the London theatres. With the theatres closed, it is possible that this play was written to be performed by friends of Shakespeare's patron, the Earl of Southampton.[1] Love had been a central theme in earlier plays, but it is in *Love's Labour's Lost* that the concept of love is first expressed with real eloquence. As Berowne, the most witty and sceptical of the young lords, comes to realise, 'Love's feeling is more soft and sensible/ Than are the tender horns of cockled snails'.

*Love's Labour's Lost* is marked by a linguistic vitality only hinted at in Shakespeare's earlier plays. It is an exuberant satire and celebration focusing on both love and language. Don Adriano de Armado is one of a trio of minor characters (the other two are a schoolmaster and a curate) who parade their language and learning in an absurd attempt to impress the unlearned. 'They have been at a great feast of languages and stol'n the scraps,' says the young page-boy, Moth, who is unimpressed by both their 'little Latin' and their contorted English. The plays which follow *Love's Labour's Lost* are in various ways celebrations of the 'great feast'.

---

1. Shakespeare dedicated both of his long narrative poems, *Venus and Adonis* (published in 1593) and *The Rape of Lucrece* (published in 1594) to Henry Wriothesley, the third Earl of Southampton—a favourite at Queen Elizabeth's court.

# A Midsummer Night's Dream

**I know a bank where the wild thyme blows,**
**Where oxlips and the nodding violet grows,**
**Quite over-canopied with luscious woodbine,**
**With sweet musk-roses and with eglantine.**

II.ii.249-52

This image of a forest glade is provided by Oberon, the King of
the Fairies. Although the plants he lists are simple wildflowers of the
countryside, the combined effect is both rich and delicate. In this
enchanted setting will take place one of the most famous comic love-
encounters in all literature. Here, after she has been lulled to sleep by
'dances and delight', Oberon's consort, Titania, will have her eyes streaked
with 'love juice', so that when she wakes she will dote madly on the 'first
living creature' that she sees. This creature will be half-man, half-animal
—the weaver, Bottom, changed magically into an ass. The love match is
extraordinary for a number of reasons. Titania,[1] the queen of the fairies,
is delicate and ethereal; Bottom is, as his name suggests, low in the social
order, representing both physical grossness and animal crudity.

---

1. If, as seems likely, Queen Elizabeth was present at the first performance of *A Midsummer
Night's Dream*, she may well have been somewhat bewildered by the direct and indirect
references to herself within the play. When Oberon explains to Puck the origins of the
magical love-juice which plays havoc with the emotions of all the lovers, he is clearly paying
the Queen an elaborate compliment. Oberon remembers seeing Cupid aiming an arrow at
'a fair vestal'. It missed her and struck a small white flower which turned purple with the
wound, leaving 'the imperial vot'ress', to pass on 'in maiden meditation, fancy-free'. There
can be no doubt that the terms 'fair vestal' and 'imperial vot'ress' referred to Queen Elizabeth
who, having done much to encourage the cult of her own virginity, would have been pleased
by the image of herself as immune to love's passions. But Elizabeth was known among her
courtiers as 'The Fairy Queen', and had recently featured as the heroine of Spenser's allegory
of that name. What is more, 'Titania' was one of several nicknames given to her by admiring
courtiers. How might Queen Elizabeth have responded to Titania's predicament as she is
tricked into falling passionately in love with the ass/man, Bottom? Perhaps, as a recent critic
has argued, she would have seen the encounter as a symbolic representation of the union
between herself and her people (Bottom representing the lower classes). Perhaps.

Once, *A Midsummer Night's Dream* was considered to be an ideal introduction to Shakespeare for young children. In traditional productions, Titania and her train were invariably portrayed as genteel Victorian fairies—an extension of a young child's toy cupboard. Bottom in his ass's head would have been about as sexy as a teddy bear. When waking from the 'dream' of his encounter with Titania, on the line 'methought I had—', Bottom would have raised his hands tentatively to find out whether he had retained his ass's ears. Today's Bottom is likely to lower his eyes shyly. Some modern productions advise their audiences that the play contains scenes which are inappropriate for children. Why?

In his ground-breaking production of 1970, Peter Brook made a complete break with the Victorian tradition, presenting his forest as a place marked by dangerous eroticism. Some critics condemned this blatant sexuality as irresponsible sub-textual fantasy, telling us more about the minds of the director and his actors than about Shakespeare's play. But since 1970, few major productions have ignored the forest's latent sexuality.

So, what does the text itself suggest happens off-stage between Bottom and Titania's exit and their next entry? The scene of their first meeting concludes with these words spoken by Titania:

> Lead him to my bower.
> **The moon methinks looks with a wat'ry eye;**
> **And when she weeps, weeps every little flower,**
> **Lamenting some enforced° chastity.**  *violated*
> Tie up my lover's tongue, bring him silently.  III.ii.197-201

The delicacy of the poetry is characteristic of Titania, of the fairy kingdom and of the play itself. However, beneath the delicacy of the verse there are hints of an impending violation. Throughout the play the image of 'the moon', and particularly the old moon, is associated with chastity and virginal restraint. Now the moon has 'a wat'ry eye' and is about to weep. She and the flowers (the 'oxlips', the 'nodding violets', the 'eglantine') weep, we are told, when chastity is violated. Who, as Bottom and Titania leave for the bower, is the violator and who the violated? In Brook's production, a well-placed actor's arm and fist presented a rampant Bottom. But surely, a part of the comedy in this exit results from a reversal of expected roles. The language suggests that Titania (like Venus in Shakespeare's narrative poem, *Venus and Adonis*, written at about the same time) is to be the seducer. 'Tie up my lover's tongue,' she says to her fairies, implying that the distraught Bottom is neighing uncontrollably. 'Bring him silently', she continues, further suggesting that it is he who is about to be 'enforced'. A number of recent productions have tended to embroider such subtextual musings with an orgiastic energy.

There is a further dimension to this if, as often now happens, the roles of Oberon/ Theseus and Titania/ Hippolyta are doubled-up. Duke Theseus and Hippolyta Queen of the Amazons inhabit the daytime city of Athens and their story forms a surrounding frame for the 'night's dream' centre of the play. Though separate from the moonlit forest and fairy kingdom, there are strong parallels between their relationship and that of the fairy rulers. Actor-doubling brings the mad fantasies of the night uncomfortably close to everyday 'reality'.

Theseus, in particular, is more at ease in daytime Athens than in the darkness of the wood.

**The lunatic, the lover, and the poet**
**Are of imagination all compact⁰**                    *composed*
                                                       V.i.7-8


he says, reflectively dismissing the happenings in the wood as the products of over-lively imaginations. Back in Athens, the birthplace of western philosophy, Theseus speaks as a philosopher king in the platonic tradition, which set reason above imagination. Plato controversially banned poets and dramatists from his utopian 'Republic'. He banned them for two main reasons: they excited the emotions and they offered their audiences false representations of reality. Plato argued that most humans are like prisoners in a cave who can see only shadows of the real/ideal world and that artists of all kinds, including dramatists, produce only shadows of shadows. Sharing this mindset, Theseus watches amiably as Bottom and his men, the humble tradesmen (or 'rude mechanicals') of the city, present to the court the play of 'Pyramus and Thisbe'. In some ways the play mirrors the story of the principal lovers in *A Midsummer Night's Dream*.

Like Hermia and Lysander, Pyramus and Thisbe face parental opposition to their love and take refuge in a moonlit wood. But here any similarities between the main play and the rude mechanicals' performance ends: the script, the acting, the direction and the production turn a potential tragedy into a farce.

'Pyramus and Thisbe' has traditionally been presented as somewhat harmless 'fun'. However, just as freed from its Victorian heritage *A Midsummer Night's Dream* has emerged as a text which plays with dangerous eroticism, 'Pyramus and Thisbe' has taken on new meanings. Much hinges on an 18th century stage direction—'Wall holds up his fingers'—which usually creates the 'chink' through which the lovers address each other. If, as in some modern productions, Wall is so bound up with 'plaster', 'loam' and 'rough-cast' that the lovers are forced to communicate not between his fingers, but between his legs, much of the dialogue is rudely 'translated'. Phrases like Pyramus's, 'My cherry lips have often kiss'd thy stones' and Thisbe's, 'I kiss the wall's hole, not your lips at all' become outrageously bawdy. No wonder that Hippolyta is not amused. 'This is the silliest stuff that ever I heard,' she says, following the exit of 'Wall'.

### The best in this kind are but shadows                    V.i.211

Theseus replies, platonically dismissing both 'Pyramus and Thisbe' and *A Midsummer Night's Dream* as false representations. But, though his tone is magisterial, by the end of the play the audience have learned that drama can offer more than 'shadows' and that the fantasies of 'the lunatic, the lover and the poet' can serve to highlight the limitations of 'cool reason', together with Theseus's complacent, overbearingly masculine, view of the world.

# The Merry Wives of Windsor

**He capers, he dances, he has eyes of youth,
he writes verses, he speaks holiday, he smells
April and May.**                                    III.ii.67-9

With this image of freshness and festivity the Host of the Garter Inn describes Master Fenton, one of three suitors to Anne Page. Anne's 'pretty virginity', together with her potential wealth, make her a most desirable prize. However the Page family are in dispute over the merits of the competitors for her hand. Mr Page suspects Fenton (rightly) of fortune-hunting and favours a more solid match with Slender (who combines the solidity of the landed gentry with a slender physique and an even more slender intellect.) Mistress Page favours the suit of the choleric Dr Caius—a Frenchman who spends his time abusing God's patience and the Queen's English ('by gar, I will myself have Anne Page'.)

Not surprisingly, Anne is attracted to the youth, vitality and eloquence of Master Fenton. Theirs is the only successful match of the six clandestine meetings which make up the core of the play's plot. Falstaff's planned encounters with the 'merry wives' result in a near drowning, a beating and the humiliation of being publicly pinched by children pretending to be fairies. In the pinching scene, while Falstaff takes centre stage, both Slender and Dr Caius are duped into eloping with young men—the former with 'a great lubberly boy', the latter with 'un garcon, a boy, un payson, by gar'. Meanwhile, aided by the Host, Fenton has eloped with and married Anne, showing that true love, of a kind, will find out the way.

According to a theatrical tradition dating back to 1702, following the success of the *Henry IV* plays, Shakespeare created *The Merry Wives of Windsor* in response to a request from Queen Elizabeth that he write a play about 'Falstaff in love'. Regardless of the authenticity of the tradition, Falstaff is not motivated by love. Mistress Page sees lust as his prime mover, anticipating how 'the wicked fire of lust' will 'melt him in his own grease'. However, just as both Fenton (initially) and Slender are attracted to the solid wealth of the Page family, Falstaff anticipates that his affairs with the two merry wives will result in a much-needed boost to his private purse. In a succession of images which comically anticipate the extravagant speculations of metaphysical love poetry, he sees Mistress Page as 'a region in Guiana, all gold and bounty' and—after reflecting on the benefits of his relationships with her and with Mistress Ford—he further elaborates the idea: 'they shall be my East and West Indies, and I will trade to them both'. (Using almost the same images John Donne was later to delight not in his mistress's wealth, but in her body, seeing her as 'my America, my new found land' and as a 'myne of precious stones'.) Slightly less poetically, Fenton confesses that he was at first attracted to Anne's fortune, though wooing her he finds her of more value than 'gold or sums in sealed bags'.

# Much Ado About Nothing

**My mother cried, but then there was a star danc'd, and under that was I born.**                                    II.i.334-36

This astrological image of the moment of her nativity is provided for us by the play's heroine, Beatrice. It gives a charming, almost fairy-tale explanation of her relentlessly merry temperament at the start of the play. It is a self-caricature endorsed by her friends and relatives. 'She hath often dreamed of unhappiness and waked herself laughing,' says her uncle, admiringly. (There is no mention in the play of Beatrice's mother, who may well have died in childbirth!)

In the opening scenes of *Much Ado*, Beatrice is the mistress of mockery, the chief butt of her humour being Benedick, a young man as dedicatedly anti-love as his spirited adversary. Beatrice imagines herself as a spinster in heaven, sitting among the bachelors there and indulging in eternal merriment. Benedick sees himself as Cupid's arch-enemy, also an eternal bachelor, though his idea of heaven would be unlikely to include Beatrice, whom he speaks of as 'Lady Disdain'. However, in a world dominated by elaborate politeness, the exaggerated insults between the two suggest from the start that they are soul-mates and that their wit protects them from revealing their true feelings for each other. In contrast the play's second pair of lovers, Beatrice's cousin, Hero, and Benedick's best friend, Claudio, are conventional lovers who wear their hearts on their sleeves, and tend to speak in slightly sugared verse.

*Much Ado* is elegantly structured, its two plots revealing both the shallowness of Claudio's love for Hero and the self-deceptions integral to the witty battle between Beatrice and Benedick. Deception is central to both discoveries. Benedick, eavesdropping on a staged conversation, is easily trapped into believing that Beatrice's disdain is a pretence and that she is dying for love of him. His transformation from detached wit to committed lover is one of the great u-turns in Shakespearean comedy and is charmingly executed by Benedick himself. Making of his own predicament a universal statement about marriage and procreation, he declares to the audience:

**No, the world must be peopled. When I said I would die a bachelor, I did not think I should live till I were married.**

II.iii.242-4

Similarly unabashed Beatrice, on hearing that she is loved by Benedick, swiftly bids her 'maiden pride, adieu' and, in an outburst of rhyming verse, prepares to 'bind our loves up in a holy band'.

It takes the evil plotting of Don John, the play's villain, to provide Claudio with a visual 'proof' of Hero's infidelity. When, at her wedding ceremony, Hero is publicly shamed, Beatrice is quick to show her genuine feeling, immediately instructing her lover to 'Kill Claudio'. For some critics this is the line that nails the play to reality. Others will see Claudio's death at his best friend's hand as somewhat improbable, remembering that at the start of the play, when Benedick returned from the wars, Beatrice had promised to 'eat all of his killing'.

Misuse of language is integral to both love stories and it lies at the heart of the play's comic resolution. Don John's plot is improbably uncovered by Constable Dogberry and his Watch. The bumbling Dogberry is the play's arch misuser of language. For Dogberry, 'senseless' means 'sensible' and 'odorous', 'odious'. So, before making his final exit, who knows exactly what he means when he asks the assembled company 'not to forget to specify, when time and place shall serve, that I am an ass'?

# *As You Like It*

**They say many young gentlemen flock to him
every day, and fleet the time carelessly, as they
did in the golden world.**                              I.i.116-19

These lyrical words (spoken somewhat unexpectedly by Charles, the wicked Duke Frederick's wrestler) give the audience their first image of the Forest of Arden, the rural retreat of the play's virtuous characters. The lines also introduce the idea of 'time' as an important motif. The play's structure, which contrasts Duke Frederick's court (full of frenetic action, with rapid entrances and exits) and the Forest of Arden (marked by leisurely, reflective, 'careless' exchanges) accentuates two quite different attitudes to time.

The idea of 'a golden world' needs explanation. Shakespeare and his contemporaries were intrigued by the classical idea of a 'golden age'—a time which preceded the coming of towns and civilizations, a mythical age when shepherds and shepherdesses lived in harmony with nature and, unencumbered by work, were free to concentrate on love. In the Elizabethan mind the Arcadia of Greek and Roman poetry became fused with the Garden of Eden. It is no accident that the oldest character in *As You Like It* is called Adam. However, once the action of the play moves into Arden, it is clear that the forest combines mythical and realistic elements. In his opening speech Duke Senior (the good Duke, who has been usurped and exiled by Frederick, his younger brother) stresses that this pastoral setting is not caught in a perpetual, idealised spring. Here, even courtiers feel the 'icy fang' of winter winds. An appreciation of 'the golden world' requires not just an absence of flattering courtiers, but Duke Senior's optimistically meditative mind.

Much of the fleeting of time in Arden centres on a range of discussions on the nature of time itself. 'Time travels in divers paces with divers persons', Rosalind tells Orlando, illustrating her idea with witty examples of time's relativity (and in so doing anticipating Einstein). Throughout the play linear time is contrasted with seasonal time. The best-known illustrations of linear time come in the 'All the world's a stage' speech, where Jaques defines human existence through seven brief pictures representing the seven ages of man. Moving from the 'mewling and puking' infant, to the boy 'creeping like snail unwillingly to school', he goes on to capture each 'act' in vivid detail. As a satirist, Jaques emphasises the ridiculous or negative wherever possible and when he reaches the final age—senility—his image is very bleak:

> **Last scene of all,**
> **That ends this strange eventful history,**
> **Is second childishness, and mere oblivion,**
> **Sans° teeth, sans eyes, sans taste, sans everything.**  *without*
>
> II.vii.163-6

However, the play itself undermines Jaques' view as these sombre lines are the cue for the entry of Adam. He is indeed a toothless old man without some of his faculties and approaching 'oblivion', but the devoted care of his young master, Orlando, together with the generous welcome that they both receive from the exiled courtiers, provide a warmer, more optimistic image of old age.

Adam, himself, likens his old age to 'a lusty winter', one of many references to the seasons. With the arrival of young lovers, the Forest of Arden blossoms into a pastoral springtime, dominated by love, and much of the action centres on the courtships of the four couples whose marriages provide the climax of the play. These courtships explore a rich variety of attitudes to love, ranging from convenient lust to absurd Platonic idealism. The heroine, Rosalind, acts as mistress of ceremonies. 'Come, woo me, woo me; for now I am in a holiday humour, and like enough to consent,' she teasingly says to Orlando, expressing both the urgency of her love and an awareness, perhaps, that *As You Like It* is a festive play and that festive, holiday romances may not last forever. Their courtship takes the form of role-play, with Rosalind, (already in cross-gender disguise as 'Ganymede') pretending to be the Rosalind whom Orlando loves. When Rosalind/Ganymede playfully threatens to reject Orlando's suit, he claims that his response to rejection must be death. She then pours scorn on the idea of dying for love, wittily demolishing several great myths of tragic love, before concluding that:

> **men have died from time to time and worms**
> **have eaten them, but not for love.** IV.i.106-8

Rosalind's gaiety and the down-to-earth style—as evident in this image—give a refreshing solidity to her character and the love she professes; the other lovers may find that the magic exists only within the holiday world of Arden.

## ANSWERS TO 'LAST WORDS'

1. **(c)** ale Sir Toby Belch, *Twelfth Night,* II.iii.114-6
2. **(a)** sleep Prospero, *The Tempest* , IV.i.156-8
3. **(b)** love Rosalind, *As You Like It,* IV.i.106-8
4. **(b)** sport Gloucester, *King Lear,* IV.i.36-7
5. **(a)** revenge Shylock, *The Merchant of Venice,* III.i.64-7
6. **(c)** strange Ariel, *The Tempest,* I.ii.399-402
7. **(c)** cowslip Iachimo, *Cymbeline,* II.iii.37-9
8. **(b)** trick Launce, *The Two Gentlemen of Verona,* IV.iv. 16-20
9. **(c)** moon Cleopatra, *Antony and Cleopatra,* IV.xv, 65-8
10. **(c)** reign Jack Cade, *Henry VI, Part 2* , IV.vi.2-4.

# PROBLEM COMEDIES

For over a hundred years, *Troilus and Cressida*, *All's Well that Ends Well* and *Measure for Measure* have been grouped together as 'problem plays', though there has been much disagreement concerning the nature of the 'problem'. For some it has been Shakespeare's problem, the plays thought to reflect a period of the author's disillusionment with life in general and sex in particular. For others it has been more a question of theme, the plays dealing with serious moral issues of a kind generally not dealt with in comedy. Some Victorian commentators thought that the sexual content of the plays was so problematic that young minds might be damaged by reading them. Now, however, they are regularly set as school texts. It is two different plays which are sometimes seen as offensive to today's sensibilities. *The Taming of the Shrew* and *The Merchant of Venice* are classed here as 'problem comedies' because, being easily read as sexist and racist, respectively, they both require subtle handling when produced for the modern stage.

*Troilus and Cressida* presents a further 'problem', that of classification. Though not included in the Contents page of the First Folio, the text was squeezed into a space at the beginning of 'Tragedies'; it had already been printed separately—with a title-page calling it a History and an Epistle praising it as a Comedy!

The discussions which follow deal with the plays in order of their approximate dating.

The Taming of the Shrew  (1593)
The Merchant of Venice  (1596-7)
Troilus and Cressida  (1601-2)
All's Well that Ends Well  (1602 -3)
Measure for Measure  (1604)

# The Taming of the Shrew

One that cares for thee;
And for thy maintenance, commits his body
To painful labour both by sea and land,
To watch the night in storms, the day in cold,
Whilst thou liest warm at home, secure and safe.

V.iii.147-51

This image presents a striking contrast between the roles of husband and wife. Katherina, the tamed shrew, is addressing a pair of newly-married couples and presents a domestic/romantic view of marriage in which the husband endures pain and danger, cold and sleeplessness, so that the object of his care can relax in blissful warmth and security. Katherina's words are now a red rag to feminists or anyone with a more liberal philosophy of the relationship between the sexes. What to Elizabethans was the vice of shrewishness is, to modern audiences, the virtue of feisty independence.

In the play's opening scenes, Katherina (or Kate) is quite untamed. She has a verbal and physical energy which is in marked contrast to her milky sister, Bianca. Whereas suitors flock to the apparently docile Bianca, Kate is married-off, against her will, to Petruchio and endures misery and humiliation at his hands before he presents her, successfully 'tamed', at a dinner party. It is here that Petruchio charges her to 'tell these headstrong women / What duty they do owe their lords and husbands.' Instead of the defiance that we feel he deserves, she launches into what is by far the most eloquent speech of the play, concluding that wives owe abject obedience to their husbands. Shakespeare seems to have sacrificed Katherina on the altar of the male ego.

How seriously should we take the 'message' of the play? In the theatre it comes across as a fast-moving, earthy comedy, taking its energy from the crazy 'courtship' between the two protagonists. Yet despite its success on the stage, some critics have argued that *The Taming of the Shrew* represents attitudes which are now so offensive that it should have no place in the repertoire of a modern company. Other critics have been less judgemental. Juliet Dusinberre, in her pioneering study, *Shakespeare and the Nature of Women*, reminds us that the whole 'taming of the shrew' story is a play within a play, a part of a scheme to persuade a drunken tinker, Christopher Sly, that he is really a Lord. In this context, Katherina's transformation should be seen more as role-play than as reality. Anne Barton, in her short Introduction to the text in *The Riverside Shakespeare*, suggests that we should see Petruchio as something of a liberator, one who frees Katherina from her shrew's role, and enables her to integrate her 'unbroken spirit and gaiety' into a stable relationship—very unlike the relationships of the other two couples, whose marriages are built on sterile tangles of fortune-hunting and deception. Perhaps as the central feature of an early comedy, the battle between Kate and Petruchio is most interesting as a courtship which prefigures the more subtle and acceptable sparring between Beatrice and Benedick in *Much Ado About Nothing*.

# *The Merchant of Venice*

**Look how the floor of heaven**
**Is thick inlaid with patens° of bright gold.**        *discs*
**There's not the smallest orb which thou behold'st**
**But in his motion like an angel sings,**
**Still quiring° to the young-eye'd cherubins.**        *singing*
                                            V.i.158-62

This image, at the heart of the final scene of *The Merchant of Venice*, is built on the ancient concept of the music of the spheres (perfect harmony created by the combined notes of the revolving planets and stars). The setting is the fairy-tale world of Belmont, far removed from the troubled, mercantile city of Venice. The situation is made for romance: it is after dinner and two young lovers emerge into a moonlit garden; while waiting for the resident musicians to come and play to them, Lorenzo calls his bride to him—'Sit, Jessica'—and as they look up to a star-lit heaven he gives this lyrical account of celestial harmony. Unfortunately, as Lorenzo goes on to explain, the souls of human beings are enclosed by a 'muddy vesture of decay' (their mortal bodies made from the lower elements, 'earth' and 'water') so they cannot actually hear the music of the spheres and have to be content with a lesser harmony. This is a metaphor for the lovers' own situation, which is less romantic than the scene might suggest, since we are aware that Jessica has stolen (in both senses) from her father's house and faces an uncertain future among people of an alien culture. Shakespeare's comedies usually end in a celebration of love and marriage; this one has darker undertones which cannot be ignored.

Of all the comedies the plot of *The Merchant of Venice* is built on the most sombre foundations—the reciprocal hatred of two opposed groups, Christians and Jews. Antonio, the Merchant of the title, and all the wealthy Christian Venetians of his social group, call Jews 'unbelievers' and, while relying on them as money-lenders, despise them as 'usurers'. Shylock, father of Jessica, is a Jew who bears a tribal grudge, exacerbated by the routine humiliations he suffers from the Christians. Spat on and treated like a dog, it is not surprising that he is ready for revenge. When Antonio, forced to borrow money from Shylock, fails to honour his contract (or 'bond') and Shylock simultaneously discovers that Jessica has taken his money and has eloped with a Christian, he is determined to have the pound of Antonio's flesh which he had asked for as collateral against his loan. In the highly theatrical trial scene Shylock appears in court, armed with a pair of scales and a sharp knife, ready to take what the bond says is rightfully his. Justice would seem to be on his side, but can it be challenged?

It falls to the beautiful, rich, clever and Christian heroine, Portia, disguised as a lawyer, to defend Antonio. Shylock rejects her direction that he should be merciful: 'On what compulsion must I?' Portia replies:

**The quality of mercy is not strain'd;**
**It droppeth as the gentle rain from heaven**
**Upon the place beneath.**                    IV.i.184-6

The image of 'gentle rain' supports her point, that mercy comes as a gift, and adds a gracious, life-giving element. Portia continues in a powerful, ringing speech, to argue that mercy is an essentially religious concept, a God-given virtue which transcends human law and justice. Though Portia again urges Shylock to be merciful, he is unmoved by her rhetoric and her New Testament emphasis on compassion, demanding only 'justice'. But he has fallen into a trap. As he stands with well-sharpened knife poised to cut and scales on hand to weigh the flesh, Portia intervenes with a clever point of law. Shylock loses his lands and his goods as well as his daughter and is forced, by his enemy Antonio, to become a Christian. Moments after his anticipated triumph, Shylock leaves the stage a broken man: 'I pray you give me leave to go from hence,/ I am not well'. Antonio's friends are exultant. The Christians have triumphed legally, materialistically, and even morally (in allowing Shylock to live they have technically shown that very mercy which he had denied to Antonio).

So is *The Merchant of Venice* an essentially anti-semitic play? There was indeed plenty of anti-semitism in Elizabethan England and, although Jews had been driven out of the country several centuries earlier, there remained in the imagination a stereotypical bogey-man Jewish figure, available to be incorporated into popular drama; (Marlowe's *The Jew of Malta* had proved a theatrical success some years before Shakespeare's play). Unlike Marlowe, however, Shakespeare avoids the stereotype and gives Shylock an essential humanity which makes him more a tragic figure than a comic villain. His character is drawn with great subtlety and many fine touches—as when he laments Jessica's swapping of the ring given to him by his wife, Leah, for a pet monkey: 'I would not have given it for a wilderness of monkeys'. But, ironically, it is when he justifies his desire for revenge to two Christians who are baiting him, that he most eloquently demonstrates his humanity: 'Hath not a Jew hands, organs, dimensions, senses, affections, passions?' he asks.

**If you prick us do we not bleed? If you tickle us do we not laugh? If you poison us do we not die? And if you wrong us, shall we not revenge?** III.i.64-7

Until its uncompromising conclusion this image provides a moving plea for tolerance based on a shared experience of human life. It is a text to be quoted in the face of all forms of divisive prejudice—social, racial, religious. When the speaker of it finally exits at the end of Act IV, ruined and desolate, most modern audiences are left feeling very uncomfortable and much in need of that final scene, romantic and comic, set in Belmont.

## *Troilus and Cressida*

**Take but degree away, untune that string,**
**And hark what discord follows.** I.iii.109-10

Behind this image is the notion of the music of the spheres, a manifestation of harmony in a God-given universe. The speaker, Ulysses, proceeds to give powerful examples of the 'discord'—cosmic, social and psychological—which follows from an absence of order or 'degree'.[1] Ulysses (Odysseus in the Greek), famed in legend for his wisdom, is lecturing the assembled Greek generals on the dangers of the current quarrelling, which threatens to subvert their attempt to conquer Troy and recapture Helen. But however magnificent the rhetoric, the audience will feel that Ulysses' speech is futile. Within and beyond the play 'discord' already reigns. Agamemnon, the leader of the Greeks, wins little respect. The Trojan who refers to him as 'that god in office guiding men' is being heavily sarcastic, while in the Greek camp crude jokes about the leader are regarded as entertainment. ('Agamemnon, how if he had boils—full, all over, generally?')

If Ulysses' plea for order and harmony serves to highlight political disorder, the anguish of Troilus, a Trojan prince, provides a parallel of emotional chaos. Troilus, described by Ulysses as 'a prince of chivalry' and



1. Though ostensibly set in a mythical past, the play has been seen as mirroring the disintegration of values in a Renaissance world deprived of medieval certainties. By 1602, when the play was written, a range of Renaissance thinkers, including Copernicus, Machiavelli and Montaigne had effectively undermined the concepts of 'degree' and 'order' and the linked notion of the divine right of Kings—though King James I, who succeeded Queen Elizabeth in 1603, was later to champion 'divine right' on his own behalf.

'a true knight', begins the play as a teenage lover, luxuriating in clichés about love in general and Cressida in particular and attempting to see in her sexual allure an image of moral goodness. This is not how the more world-weary Ulysses sees her: 'There's language in her eye, her cheek, her lip,/ Nay her foot speaks,' he says, as he watches her flirt with the Greek generals moments after her forced separation from Troilus. And in the play's most disturbing scene Troilus, still idealistic and 'true', watches Cressida, the legendary epitome of falsehood, betray him with the Greek, Diomedes.

### If beauty hath a soul, this is not she          V.ii.138

Troilus exclaims as he is compelled to realise the limitations of the Platonic link between 'beauty' and 'the soul' which has so elevated his desire. Betrayed lovers down the ages will not need the framework of neo-Platonic philosophy to share in Troilus's anguish. But Shakespeare does not allow the audience to empathise too much. He sets the intimate scene within a framework of observers: as Troilus watches Cressida and Diomedes, he is in turn watched by Ulysses and, watching all of them, is the arch cynic, Thersites. This 'deformed and scurrilous slave' acts as an unacknowledged chorus throughout the play and here provides a typically leering commentary: 'How the devil luxury, with his fat rump and potato finger,/Tickles these two together!' For Thersites 'all war is lechery'. He pictures lechery ('luxury') as a fat-arsed devil, lewdly encouraging Cressida and Diomedes. (It is a verbal cartoon, reminiscent of the grotesque images of artists like Bosch, Hogarth, Daumier—or Steve Bell.) The play shows us enough of Helen, the cause of the Trojan War, to suggest that Thersites is an astute commentator. For Thersites the Trojan War is not about the world's most beautiful woman and a nation's honour, but about 'a whore and a cuckold', Diomedes' seduction of Cressida being a mirror-image of the 'rape' of Helen.

However the audience are unlikely to side totally with Thersites in his dismissal of Cressida or his mockery of Troilus. Shakespeare's portrayal of Cressida is ambiguous enough for her to gain some sympathy and for us the pain of Troilus's disillusion is heightened by our having so recently experienced something of the emotional depth of his feeling for her. In his great speech on parting from Cressida, the cliché-ridden language of his early infatuation gives way to a genuinely sensual and precise expression:

> **Injurious time now with a robber's haste**
> **Crams his rich thiev'ry up, he knows not how.**
> **As many farewells as be stars in heaven,**
> **With distinct breath and consign'd kisses to them,**
> **He fumbles up into a loose adieu;**
> **And scants us with a single famish'd kiss,**
> **Distasted with the salt of broken tears.**          IV.iv.42-8

In this extended image, Time is shown as a clumsy intruder, a robber with no appreciation of the value of his 'rich thiev'ry' and quite incapable of making distinctions between the farewell kisses of the multitude of lovers that he separates. Troilus, in contrast, describes his final kiss with a precision which conveys both his emotional distress and the exact physical sensation of the moment of parting. The lovers' kiss is 'famished' because it contains their desperate, unsatisfied hunger. It is 'distasted' by the very saltness of the tears which fall and break on their lips even while they are kissing.

Troilus's personification of 'Time' recalls an earlier image from the play. Ulysses, warning Achilles that his fame will not last, describes Time as an ungrateful beggar: 'Time hath, my lord, a wallet at his back/ Wherein he puts alms for oblivion'. In both these images Time is seen as a destroyer, contemptuous of human values such as 'love' and 'fame' and 'honour'. But it is a particularly nasty manifestation of time (not Time) which concludes the play as Pandarus (Cressida's guardian, the original pandar) steps forward to speak the epilogue. Evidently aging and anticipating his death from syphilis, Pandarus implicates us, the audience, in his end: 'Till then I'll sweat and seek about for eases/ And at that time bequeath you my diseases'.

Although *Troilus and Cressida* celebrates the power of myth to transcend time, Shakespeare treats the events and characters of the Trojan story with sustained irony, making it, perhaps, his most disturbing play.

1. **(b)** dying   Old Shepherd, *The Winter's Tale*, III.iii.113-4
2. **(c)** wawl   Lear, *King Lear*, IV.vi.178-80
3. **(c)** elements   Pericles, *Pericles*, III.i.56-8
4. **(b)** spawn'd   Lucio, *Measure for Measure*, III.ii.108-11
5. **(b)** crown   Cleopatra, *Antony and Cleopatra*, V.ii.280-1
6. **(b)** breath   Romeo, *Romeo and Juliet*, V.iii.92-3
7. **(c)** alabaster   Othello, *Othello*, V.ii.3-5
8. **(b)** catch   Caesar, *Antony and Cleopatra*, V.ii.346-8
9. **(a)** oblivion   Jaques, *As You Like It*, II.vii, 163-6
10. **(c)** clod   Claudio, *Measure for Measure*, III.i.117-20

---

# All's Well that Ends Well

**Virginity breeds mites, much like a cheese, consumes itself to the very paring, and so dies with feeding his own stomach.**

I.i.141-3

This image comes from a witty attack on virginity by Parolles, the cowardly braggart in *All's Well*. Parolles is talking to Helena, the play's heroine. Momentarily the audience might sense that this is no more than a comic set piece—the crude, worldly liar giving the idealistic young heroine a taste of his cynicism. But as the play's action unfolds, we discover that Helena has her own reservations about virginity, particularly her own virginity. Passionately in love with 'young Bertram', the Count of Roussilion, she finds that although she can trap him into a formal marriage, she cannot persuade him to consummate it. After much travel and travail, she manages the 'bed-trick'—substituting herself for Diana, an Italian beauty whom Bertram thinks he is seducing.

Parallel to this is a second plot, which focuses on Bertram's other life, that of a privileged young officer serving the King of France. In his budding career as a soldier he has taken the loud-mouthed Parolles as his role-model but fellow officers realise that this man is a fraud. In a hilarious scene they capture and blindfold Parolles and convince him that he is in enemy hands by pretending to speak in a foreign tongue:

> First Lord: **Throca movousus, cargo, cargo, cargo.**
> Other soldiers: **Cargo, cargo, cargo, villianda par corbo,**
> **cargo.** Etc. IV.i.65-6

This crazy invented language totally hoodwinks Parolles (ironically, because 'parolles' means 'words' and it is Parolles' words rather than deeds that have impressed Bertram and led him astray). As one of the officers pretends to be a translator, the frightened Parolles readily turns traitor and, in Bertram's presence, reveals 'all the secrets' of the French camp'. In a moment of truth he also volunteers his unflattering opinion of Bertram—'a dangerous and lascivious boy, who is a whale to virginity'.

The plots centred on Bertram are, as the play's title would suggest, comic; the prevailing atmosphere of the play is, however, rather sombre. Though Helena is seen as sensitive and courageous by almost all the characters who meet her, her actual behaviour can make her seem a manipulative adventuress. Bertram's exposure as a liar and seducer comes at the end of the play before a scene of apparent reconciliation but since we are uncertain as to whether Bertram deserves, or even wants, his wife, the audience are left with the feeling that All may not be Well after all.

## *Measure for Measure*

| | |
|---|---|
| **Our natures do pursue,** | |
| **Like rats that ravin down° their proper bane,** | *devour greedily* |
| **A thirsty evil; and when we drink we die.** | I.ii.128-30 |

Vienna is caught in the grip of sexual excess. Brothels have proliferated. Bawds and pimps walk the streets. Venereal disease is rife. It is left to the puritanical Angelo, deputy to the Duke of Vienna, to control the epidemic. He has revived an ancient law which enables him to sentence to death all sexual offenders—those who indulge in sexual intercourse outside marriage. The first to be sentenced is Claudio, the speaker of the above lines, whose fiancée's pregnancy cannot be hidden. In this image Claudio, a little unexpectedly, sees himself as a symptom of the diseased state of Vienna, linking his plight to that of a poisoned rat. 'Bane', or ratsbane, was a dual-action poison. It was a powder which induced in rats an uncontrollable thirst. When a rat drank to slake its thirst, the powder, reacting with the water, hardened in the rat's intestines, resulting in an agonizing death. In his startling simile, Claudio likens sexual desire to the thirst of the poisoned rat, an analogy which would have pleased Angelo, who approaches his task of cleaning up Vienna with the zeal of a rat-catcher delivering a city from plague.

Extreme attitudes to sexuality lie at the heart of *Measure for Measure*. The libertine Lucio, who regards promiscuous sex as sport ('A game of tick tack,' he says to Claudio), mockingly characterises Angelo as a very 'cold fish':

> **Some report a sea-maid spawn'd him; some that he was begotten between two stock-fishes. But it is certain that when he makes water his urine is congeal'd ice.**     III.ii.108-11

Lucio is a dedicated gossip-monger, but his caricature does capture the 'frozen' aspect of Angelo's personality. In the absence of the Duke, Angelo, as Deputy, has been tyrannical in his use of authority. When Isabella, Claudio's sister, is urged by Lucio to plead mercy for her brother, she shows great eloquence in condemning such tyranny:

> **Man, proud man,**
> **Dress'd in a little brief authority,**
> **Most ignorant of what he's most assured**
> **(His glassy essence), like an angry ape**
> **Plays such fantastic tricks before high heaven**
> **As makes the angels weep.**     II.ii.117-22

Isabella's soaring indignation presents an image which extends beyond Angelo and his punishment of her brother and stands as a more general plea for mercy. Her words have a biblical force, echoing the Gospel source of the play's title: 'Judge not that ye be not judged...For with what measure ye mete, it shall be measured to you again'. Ironically her passionate purity succeeds in unlocking Angelo's hitherto repressed sexuality, leaving him lusting uncontrollably for her—'a thirsty evil'.

When Angelo offers Isabella her brother's life in exchange for her own virginity, it becomes apparent that her own 'purity' is something of a problem. She is about to enter a nunnery (perhaps as a retreat from the sexual excesses of Vienna). Now, caught between her desire to save her brother and her abhorrence of Angelo's proffered 'remedy', she determines to cling to her honour:

> Then Isabel live chaste and brother die:
> **More than our brother is our chastity.**                    II.iv.184-5

Even though she is young, idealistic and a novice nun, modern audiences, particularly those who share Lucio's contempt for sexual restraint, are likely to find it difficult to sympathise with Isabella's decision. And Shakespeare's crafting of the above couplet tends to distance us from her in her predicament: the detachment implied in referring to herself in the third person, the formal use of 'our brother' (rather than 'my brother') and the glibness of the rhyme all tend to emphasise her cold insensitivity at this moment in the play. Sympathy for Claudio is further increased by his own anguish when facing death, and the dialogue which follows stands as Shakespeare's most eloquent exploration of this theme.

Before being visited by Isabella, Claudio had been prepared for death by the Duke, posing as a Friar. 'Be absolute for death' he had advised, in a powerfully measured but compassionate dismissal of human existence, culminating in a haunting image of the unlived life:

> **Thou hast nor youth nor age,**
> **But as it were an after-dinner's sleep,**
> **Dreaming on both.**                    III.i.31-3

Isabella arrives in Claudio's death cell, hoping that he will release her from the dilemma Angelo has forced upon her. Initially Claudio accepts his sentence stoically, almost lyrically, seeing death's 'darkness' as 'a bride' whom he will hug in his arms. Isabella, convinced of the afterlife of the soul (our 'glassy essence'), tells Claudio that the actual pain of dying is no worse for 'a giant' than for an accidentally crushed 'poor beetle'. But when she gives her brother a glimpse of hope, by telling him of Angelo's offer, Claudio allows himself to explore what it will be like to die in far stronger imagery:

**Ay, but to die, and go we know not where;**
**To lie in cold obstruction, and to rot;**
**This sensible° warm motion to become**          *full of feeling*
**A kneaded clod.**                                III.i.117-20

Though the first line here is composed of a succession of simple monosyllables, the long vowels and the internal rhyming of 'i' and 'o' sounds create a kind of wailing. The second line pictures the physical reality of the corpse which will 'lie' (chiming with the previous 'die') claustrophobically trapped—a claustrophobia emphasised by all those consonants in 'cold obstruction', as the 'sensible warm motion' of the living body finally becomes a 'kneaded clod'. The lines which follow explore the imagined sensations of purgatory and hell. This speech of Claudio's is one of the great expressions of the human fear of death. But the idealistic Isabella is moved to frenzy, not compassion. 'Thy sin's not accidental, but a trade,' she tells her brother; she, like Angelo, sees sexuality outside marriage as a kind of prostitution.

Brother and sister are caught in a dilemma from which there seems to be no escape. At this moment the Duke/Friar, who has been eavesdropping, intervenes. How should we see the Duke? Lucio comically describes him as 'the old fantastical Duke of dark corners'; Angelo as 'like power divine'. King James, who was possibly present at the play's first ever production, would probably have seen the Duke as a flattering image of

61

himself.[1] Regardless of how directors choose to interpret his character, from this moment he begins to control the action and the play moves from tragedy to comedy—though somewhat uneasily.

---

1. It is possible, or even probable, that the deep ambiguity inherent in the construction of the Duke's character and role was intentional, Shakespeare intending to flatter King James without totally compromising his own integrity.

## 🌿 Answers to 'The Bestiary'

1. **(g)** horses   Opening Chorus to Act 1, *Henry V*, 36-7
2. **(d)** dog   Lear, *King Lear*, V.iii. 307-8
3. **(c)** crow   Macbeth, *Macbeth*, III.ii.50-1
4. **(a)** swallow   Perdita, *The Winter's Tale* , IV.iv.118-20
5. **(i)** ape   Isabella, *Measure for Measure*, II.ii.117-22
6. **(f)** toads   Othello, *Othello*, IV.ii.57-62
7. **(h)** worm   Henry VI, *Henry VI, Part 1*, III.i.72-3
8. **(e)** butterfly   Valeria, *Coriolanus*, I.iii.60-5
9. **(j)** whale   Pericles, *Pericles*, III.i.62-4
10. **(b)** steed   Opening Chorus to Act IV, *Henry V*, 10-14

# TRAGI-COMEDIES

*Pericles, Cymbeline, The Winter's Tale* and *The Tempest*—Shakespeare's 'late plays'—share several features. All centre on father and daughter relationships. All deal with loss and renewal. All have themes, characters and situations which could be the stuff of tragedy. Potentially tragic situations are often averted through magical or supernatural interventions. Three have storms, two resulting in shipwreck. We have linked these four plays with two much earlier plays, *The Comedy of Errors* and *Twelfth Night*, in order to show that throughout his career Shakespeare was interested in the 'tempest' motif and that the themes of loss and renewal were explored again and again. *Twelfth Night* is often performed in an atmosphere of autumnal melancholy and although *The Comedy of Errors* is usually thought of as a brilliant farce, linking it with the other plays in this section does give it a further dimension.

The plays covered in this section are:

# The Comedy of Errors

They say this town is full of cozenage°:     *cheating*
As nimble jugglers that deceive the eye,
Dark-working sorcerers that change the mind,
Soul-killing witches that deform the body,
Disguised cheaters, prating mountebanks°,     *swindlers*
And many such-like liberties of sin.     I.ii.97-102

Antipholus of Syracuse, searching for his long-lost twin brother, has just arrived in Ephesus— a town with a reputation for witchcraft. Though his image of the town has provided ample scope for directors to play with mystery, menace and hallucination as elements of their productions, it soon becomes apparent that the bewilderment which he is experiencing stems not from sorcery but from a series of mistaken identities. In a brilliantly orchestrated succession of scenes, he and his servant Dromio are repeatedly mistaken for their twin brothers who, as established residents of Ephesus, have many acquaintances and complicated love lives. (Antipholus of Ephesus, the 'home' twin, is married to Adriana— Shakespeare's early, not unsympathetic, study of a discontented wife.)

Shakespeare took the central idea of *The Comedy of Errors* from the *Menaechmi*, a Latin play by Plautus, which he would almost certainly have read at the Grammar School in Stratford. In the *Menaechmi* the confusions are confined to a single pair of twins; by adding twin servants, Shakespeare increased the number of farcical situations. However, in the light of his later comedies and romances, other additions to the Latin play are more interesting. The crazy action of the play is framed by the more sombre story of Egeon, the father of the Antipholus twins. In the opening scene he, also a traveller from Syracuse, is under arrest and sentence of death. He tells his captors and the audience his story—a tale of marriage, birth, storm at sea, shipwreck and loss, as he and his younger son were separated from his wife, Aemilia, and the older twin. Shakespeare was to return again and again to these motifs. Loss and reunion (with or without storm and shipwreck) feature in all four of the 'late' plays. The final scene of reunion in *Pericles* is, once again, set in Ephesus.

# Twelfth Night

**If music be the food of love, play on,**
**Give me excess of it, that surfeiting,**
**The appetite may sicken and so die.**                    I.i.1-3

In no other play by Shakespeare do the opening lines so richly introduce the play's formal and thematic concerns. The image moves from rapture ('music', 'the food of love') to disillusion ('sicken and so die'). In addition the key words ('music', 'food', 'love', 'excess', 'surfeiting' and 'appetite') prepare the audience for the preoccupations and obsessions of most of the characters, (who are in different ways 'love sick'). The lines are spoken by Orsino, Duke of Illyria, a man almost paralysed by his passion for his neighbour, 'the fair Olivia'. But Olivia, in mourning for the recent death of her brother, has resolved to live like a nun for seven years and is indifferent to Orsino's passion. Although she has charged Malvolio, her puritanical, sober-suited steward, with maintaining a suitably sombre atmosphere in her household, Olivia is surrounded by a group of characters all, in different ways, caught up in a web of appetite and desire. The waiting-woman, Maria, has her eye on Olivia's uncle, Sir Toby Belch; his 'friend', Sir Andrew Aguecheek, fancies himself as a suitor to Olivia; and even Malvolio, in his 'self-love', cherishes an ambition to marry his mistress and become 'Count Malvolio'. Only Feste, the 'licensed fool' who divides his time between Olivia's household and Orsino's court, seems immune to love's appetite.

To fuel passions and further complications, Shakespeare introduces shipwrecked twins, separately cast up on the shores of Illyria. Viola, disguised as a young man, finds employment with Duke Orsino. 'I can sing / And speak to him in many kinds of music,' she says. The court is drenched in musical melancholy. When Feste is not singing songs of despised love, Viola and Orsino create their own lyrical duet:

For women are as roses whose fair flower,
Being once displayed, doth fall that very hour.

Orsino's image captures the brevity of life and love destroyed by time. Viola's chiming response -

> And so they are. Alas, that they are so,
> To die, even when they to perfection grow -

shows that she is completely in tune with Orsino; the audience, however, knowing that she is secretly in love with him, picks up the extra sadness in her tone. Orsino, assuming her to be a precocious youth, is happy to send her to Olivia as his messenger of love.

Though death haunts Olivia's household, the 'music' is less melancholy. Sir Toby enjoys singing and dancing, alongside drinking (and belching), but lacks any idealism about love. 'She's a beagle true bred, and one that adores me,' is his complacent comment on Maria; the romantic word 'adores' clashes comically with his unromantic image of dog-breeding. Sir Andrew Aguecheek's response, 'I was adored once too,' is wistful but also amusing, given the caricature-like features implicit in his name.

The character with the most significant name of all is the passionate but subtle Viola.[1] To appreciate fully the significance of her musical name, we need to imagine the experience of the original audience, who would have seen the play without knowing the text or the names of the characters. Viola's name is not actually heard until the ending of the play when the final scene of explanation culminates in the revelation of her true identity. 'Thrice welcome, drown'd Viola' says her twin brother, Sebastian, and the name rings out twice more in the next dozen lines, culminating in Viola's announcement, 'I am Viola'. Now, and only now, is Orsino's call for music finally answered, and Viola's claim that she can 'sing / And speak to him in many sorts of music,' fully realised.

The play does not end in musical concord, however. Malvolio (another significant name, suggesting both misery and malice) has shown himself the enemy to enjoyment and festivity. When he attempts to silence merriment in Olivia's house, Sir Toby retorts:

---

1. The viola da gamba was a member of the 'viol' family of musical instruments. In the 16th century, England was regarded as the centre of excellence for these instruments, but they eventually gave way to the modern 'violin' family.

**Dost thou think because thou art virtuous there shall be no
more cakes and ale?** II.iii.114-16

Malvolio's opposition to 'cakes' and 'ale' expresses in miniature the more
extreme Puritans' opposition to all forms of revelry, which constantly
threatened the existence of London's theatres throughout Queen
Elizabeth's reign. Having allowed Malvolio to be ridiculed and humiliated
by other characters in the play, Shakespeare gives him a memorable exit
line: 'I'll be revenged on the whole pack of you!' It is both ominous and
prophetic: some forty years later, after the beheading of King Charles I,
a puritanical government held power and all theatres in England were
closed until the Restoration.


# *Pericles*

**A terrible child-bed hast thou had, my dear,
No light, no fire. Th' unfriendly elements
Forgot thee utterly.** III.i.56-8

The setting is a storm at sea. Pericles has just been presented with
his newly born daughter and has been told that his wife, Thaisa, has died
in childbirth. With this moving image he prepares to abandon her to
the sea—the superstitious seamen believing that the storm will not abate
until the ship is cleared of its dead. So, with tender directness Pericles
lets his wife, 'scarcely coffin'd' go, imagining her body as it sinks into the
depths of the ocean, where

**The belching whale
And humming water must o'erwhelm thy corpse,
Lying with simple shells.** III.i.62-4

These are strange and beautiful lines, as sound and image move from the massiveness of the 'belching whale', through the mysteriously purposeful 'humming water' to the stillness of 'simple shells'. The journey of the body is vividly realised as it is seen and heard moving to its final rest.

Before abandoning his wife, Pericles has a moment to welcome his infant daughter, Marina. 'Thou hast as chiding a nativity,/ As fire, air, water, earth and heaven can make/ To herald thee from the womb'. Marina's 'chiding nativity' is followed by a life in which her struggle is not with the elements but with human wickedness. While Pericles criss-crosses the Mediterranean, she survives a murder attempt, kidnap by pirates and disposal to a brothel without losing her essential goodness and purity. 'If fires be hot, knives sharp, or waters deep/ Untied I still my virgin knot will keep,' she tells her brothel-keeper and in no time she has converted her would-be customers to 'divinity'. 'I'll do anything now that is virtuous, but I am out of the road of rutting forever,' says one.

With its focus on separation of parent and child, on loss, on longing and on humanity challenged by the elements but rising above them, *Pericles* seems at times to be the quintessence of Shakespeare's late plays. But much of the writing is clumsy and without the poetic flair of the storm scene or the raunchy, assured humour of the brothel scenes. The text of the play was not included in the Shakespeare First Folio, and though it is now accepted as a part of the canon, it is generally agreed that Shakespeare wrote the play in collaboration with George Wilkins, a somewhat pedestrian writer.

# *Cymbeline*

**On her left breast**
**A mole cinque-spotted, like the crimson drops**
**I' th' bottom of a cowslip.**                              II.iii.37-9

This must be Shakespeare's most intimate and original close-up, a poetically observed description of a mole on the breast of the play's sleeping heroine, Imogen. The speaker is Iachimo. Having tricked his way into Imogen's bedchamber, he is in the process of making notes on the furnishings when he discovers the 'flaw' on her half-naked body—a flaw which he will later use to convince her husband, Posthumus, that she has been unfaithful and which will result in Imogen setting out on the strangest of all Shakespearean journeys. When we first meet Iachimo he is a hard-talking, hard-drinking, cynical man of the world. We are quite unprepared for the vivid poetry of the bed-chamber scene—as illustrated in the above image. The words 'like the crimson drops i' th' bottom of a cowslip' would not have been out of place in *A Midsummer Night's Dream*, where many of the descriptions suggest the delicate observation of the fairy kingdom. For the duration of this scene at least, Iachimo is more like an evil fairy than an Italian courtier. And this is not the only fairy tale element in *Cymbeline*, a play which mixes history, tragedy and comedy in a range of styles.

Though Imogen's many predicaments through the play parallel those of a number of earlier heroines, including Cordelia, Desdemona, Viola and Juliet, she would seem to be modelled on a much more familiar, non- Shakespearean, character—Snow White. It is, surely, not accidental that her husband speaks of her seeming as 'chaste as unsunn'd snow'. Like Snow White, she has a wicked step-mother who dabbles in poisonous potions. Like Snow White, on leaving the court she is adopted and cared for by a small group of outcasts. In their cave she drinks a potion provided by her wicked step-mother and appears to die.

At this point the parallels with the Snow White story cease, but the plot remains in the realm of fairy tale. The cave dwellers are not dwarfs. In fact two of them are Imogen's older brothers, stolen in infancy from King Cymbeline by a wronged courtier. The young men are strangely attracted to Imogen, speaking of her (in her masculine disguise of 'Fidelio') as their brother. 'Are we not brothers?' asks one, to which Imogen, believing that they are low-born, replies, 'So man and man should be,/ But clay and clay differs in dignity'. These words have a powerful impact on the brothers. When they discover what they take to be Imogen/Fidele's dead body, they conduct a funeral service for her, honouring her with these lines:

**Fear no more the heat o' th' sun,**
**Nor the furious winter's rages,**

Thou thy worldly task has done,
Home art gone, and ta'en thy wages.
Golden lads and girls all must,
As chimney-sweepers, come to dust.          IV.ii.258-63


This image forms a part of Shakespeare's greatest dirge, which is, perhaps, best taken out of context since it speaks eloquently of death as a welcome end for those whose lives consist of suffering and servitude. Is it an intentional irony that the participants in the service are all of royal blood? What is more, the calm of the dirge is about to be shattered by Imogen's worst nightmare. She wakes up to find, lying beside her, the headless body of the play's comic villain, Cloten, whom she takes to be her dead husband. Could this be an intentional parody of *Romeo and Juliet*, where Juliet, waking from her potion, discovers the dead Romeo beside her? As it moves towards its comic resolution, *Cymbeline* again and again echoes with images and motifs from Shakespeare's earlier plays, in particular the tragedies.

# *The Winter's Tale*

And many a man there is (even at this present,
Now, while I speak this) holds his wife by th'arm,
That little thinks she has been sluiced in 's absence,
And his pond fished by his next neighbour—by
Sir Smile, his neighbour.          I.ii.192-6


Irrational jealousy dominates the first half of *The Winter's Tale*. Here Leontes, King of Sicily, reveals in a contorted monologue that he suspects his wife of having an affair with his boyhood friend, Polixenes, King of Bohemia. Convinced that they have been sexually intimate, Leontes indulges his fantasy, creating this crude image of his own humiliation. Hermione, Leontes' Queen, is seen as a fertile part of his property, his 'pond'; at the same time Polixenes is transformed into 'Sir Smile', a poaching neighbour. The crude language of innuendo ('sluiced', 'fished') and the tortuous syntax of enfolded parentheses effectively act out the thoughts of the paranoid Leontes as his mind loops and gouges into itself, elaborating, and almost enjoying, his role as victim. In the theatre Leontes' irrationality is further emphasised in the difference between seeing and interpretation. The audience see what Leontes sees—Polixenes treating Hermione with courtesy and a befitting graciousness. Only a mind caught in a nightmarish state of madness could make of his friend the grotesque, pantomime-like figure of Sir Smile.

Shakespeare had, of course, explored the theme of jealousy in earlier plays—comically in *The Merry Wives of Windsor* and tragically in *Othello*. In *The Winter's Tale* the tragic mode dominates the first half of the play as Leontes' irrational passion leads on to the destruction of his family—the deaths of Hermione and his young son Mamillius and the loss of his infant daughter Perdita. 'A sad tale's best for winter,' says the doomed little prince, unwittingly encapsulating the tragic mode and mood of the first half of the play. However, hints of a mythic transformation occur at the end of the third act.

The action moves from Sicily to a rustic Bohemia. This Bohemia has a coastline where Antigonus, the courtier charged with abandoning Leontes' supposedly bastard daughter, is shipwrecked before meeting the most unexpected of ends. 'Exit pursued by a bear,' reads the Folio stage-direction, a reminder that Shakespeare's Globe theatre was next to one of London's alternative entertainment venues, a Bear Pit. (Perhaps the original audience were thrilled by the entrance of a real beast.) Following Antigonus' exit, in a few deft lines the mood changes. Verse gives way to colloquial prose as a shepherd enters and discovers the abandoned Perdita. Then his son enters and gives a ramblingly comic account of both the raging storm and the dismemberment of Antigonus. The shepherd's comment on these happenings, though expressed in simple prose, has a poetic resonance:

**Thou met'st with things dying, I with things new-born.**

III.iii.113-4

There is a sense of balance in the structure of this image which stands pivotally at the centre of the play, as the death and destruction associated with the first three acts give way to the new life and regeneration which dominate acts IV and V.

At the start of Act IV Shakespeare completes the move from tragedy to romantic comedy with a jump of sixteen years and the bold, fresh voice of a new character, Autolycus. A 'rogue' in the guise of a country peddlar, Autolycus describes himself as 'a snapper-up of unconsidered trifles' as he charms both his victims and the audience. After the wintry events of the first half of the play, Autolycus ushers in the spring as he enters singing, 'When daffodils begin to peer'. The song continues:

> Why then comes in the sweet o' the year,
> **For the red blood reigns in the winter's pale.** IV.iii.4

There is an exciting pulse in 'the red blood reigns' as the 'pale' of winter is vanquished. ('Pale' could mean an enclosure as well as the drained colour of wintry bodies or landscape.) For Autolycus springtime brings chances for him to thieve 'the white sheet bleaching on the hedge' and to 'lie tumbling in the hay' with country girls whom he seduces with songs and ribbons. A sheep-shearing festival offers him the perfect opportunity and it is here that Shakespeare reintroduces the story of Leontes and Polixenes, now moved on a generation. Leontes' abandoned daughter Perdita (her name means 'lost'), adopted by the shepherd who found her, is about to be betrothed to Florizel, the (disguised) son of Polixenes. The betrothal takes place at the sheep-shearing feast, where Perdita becomes a personification of Spring. 'No shepherdess, but Flora/ Peering in April's front,' says Florizel as she proceeds to distribute flowers among the assembled guests, her language directly evoking the classical myth of Prosperpina (Persephone). But it is Perdita's own imagery which most richly expresses the transformation, when she celebrates the flowers of the new Spring world about her, beginning with

> **Daffodils,**
> **That come before the swallow dares, and take**
> **The winds of March with beauty.** IV.iv.118-20

This image parallels the courageous, perhaps foolhardy, optimism of the young lovers. It also stands as a breathtakingly accurate and dynamic expression of the loveliness of the simple, familiar daffodil. The verb 'take' used to have a range of meanings, incorporating not only a sense of 'capture' but also of 'delight', 'charm' and 'bewitch'—all of which senses, combined with its strong position at the end of the line, make this 'take' a word of particular power and richness.

The idyll of the Spring festival is about to be disrupted by Florizel's father, Polixines, who is present in disguise, and the young lovers are forced to flee from Bohemia, back to Sicily. What then happens should not be told; it should first be experienced in the theatre.

# The Tempest

**Be not afeard, the isle is full of noises,**
**Sounds, and sweet airs, that give delight and hurt not.**

III.ii.135-6

The speaker is Caliban—rather surprisingly, because Caliban is more usually thinking of rebellion or murderous revenge and tends to use language for cursing rather than calming. With this image he is soothing a couple of panic-stricken rogues, newly washed-up on shore, and is enjoying the sense of his own knowledge and appreciation of the island which they find so strange. In fact the 'sounds and sweet airs' are provided by Ariel, a spirit whom Caliban has never seen. The earthy monster Caliban and the delicate spirit Ariel represent, between them, the qualities of the island which is the setting of *The Tempest*. However, both characters are ruled by a third, Prospero, who is the human centre of the play.

Formerly Duke of Milan, Prospero was forcibly exiled from Italy and landed on the unknown island with nothing but his small daughter, Miranda, and his precious books of magic. That was twelve years ago. As the play begins, Miranda is fifteen and Prospero is set to find a husband for her and to deal with his old enemies. It just so happens that the men he is targeting are on a ship passing near to his island. The tempest of the title is conjured up by Ariel at Prospero's command and the shipwrecked survivors are landed diversely on the shore. Among them is young Prince Ferdinand who, assuming his father, Alonso King of Naples, to be drowned, is interrupted in his mourning by a song, coming from nowhere but apparently addressed to him:

> Full fathom five thy father lies,
> Of his bones are coral made:
> **Those are pearls that were his eyes:**
> **Nothing of him that doth fade,**
> **But doth suffer a sea-change**
> **Into something rich and strange.**                    I.ii.399-402

It is Ariel who sings this richly haunting, yet comforting, dirge as he lures Ferdinand towards the unsuspecting Miranda. Both are about to be transformed by love.

In fact Prospero's tempest offers a 'sea change', a chance of redemption, to several of the characters. The change of Alonso (who is not in fact dead) is prefigured in Ariel's image, as the King emerges from his symbolic drowning spiritually transformed. But he is the only one of the 'three men of sin' (those whom Prospero holds responsible for his exile) to be redeemed. The weak and greedy Sebastian (Alonso's brother) and the ruthlessly ambitious Antonio (Prospero's brother) remain cynical and unchanged.

In the final scene of the play all the shipwrecked, but unharmed, nobles are gathered together and Prospero reveals himself as the original Duke of Milan. Miranda is caught up in wonder:

> **Oh brave new world**
> **That has such people in it!**                    V.i.183-4

Gazing at the group of men, all dressed in courtly finery, Miranda is responding to her first glimpse of the civilized world, the world to which she is about to return. The word 'brave' could mean 'courageous' and 'fine' but could also mean 'brash' and 'showy' and her admiration demonstrates that appearances can be very deceptive. Given that the group of courtiers who have so excited her admiration include the play's unrepentant villains, it is no wonder that Prospero wryly qualifies his daughter's image with the words, ''Tis new to thee'.

The 'new world' which Miranda so admires is for her father the 'old world', the civilised world of Milan and Naples, a showy world of corrupt and shady politics. For the play's original audience, the term 'new world', was a familiar one, referring to the discoveries of the great European explorers, including Elizabethans such as Sir Walter Raleigh and Sir Francis Drake. There was much debate on the natures of the inhabitants of these newly discovered lands, natures uncorrupted by civilisation. Some, like the essayist Montaigne, argued that in the uncivilized 'new world' the inhabitants lived in a state of natural purity, as did the inhabitants of the mythical 'golden world' (see *As You Like It*). Others were more sceptical. *The Tempest* plays its part in the debate.

There is more than a hint of tiredness in Prospero's 'Tis new to thee'. Having arrived on the island as something of an idealist, ready to believe in the essential goodness of 'mankind', he has good reason to be disillusioned. After liberating the island from the tyrannical rule of the witch Sycorax, he set about educating her son Caliban, treating him with great kindness until he attempted to rape Miranda. Now, having used his magic to create the tempest which was to have engineered the repentance of his enemies, he has found that Sebastian and his own brother Antonio remain quite unmoved by guilt or any other redeeming human emotion. And Miranda is about to turn her back on her island past and, as Ferdinand's wife, immerse herself in the worlds of Milan and Naples.

However, all is not 'sea sorrow'. In addition to the happy transformations of some characters, Prospero benefits from changes in himself; he learns compassion, tolerance, even generosity. Ariel is set free. And even Caliban ends the play in positive and penitent mood, saying, 'I'll be wise hereafter,/ And seek for grace.' First, however, Prospero has to introduce Caliban to the assembled court:

**This thing of darkness I
Acknowledge mine.**                     V.i.275-6

It is a moment of profound insight. The resonance of the image suggests that Prospero has learned to accept 'darkness' as integral to his own and the human psyche. But it is a moment which also accentuates Prospero's disillusionment. As the play nears its ending he emerges as a tired old man, burdened by the loss of his kingdom, his daughter and his idealism. Following the masque which he presents to the young lovers, he compares the insubstantiality of art to the insubstantiality of life itself:

> **We are such stuff**
> **As dreams are made on; and our little life**
> **Is rounded in a sleep.**                                    IV.i.156-8

This is the concluding image to the great speech in which he describes how 'the cloud-capp'd towers, the gorgeous palaces/ The solemn temples, the great globe itself' will eventually 'dissolve' and 'Leave not a wrack behind'. Prospero the Magician: Shakespeare the Artist. Prospero usually refers to his magic as his 'Art' and there are clear parallels with Shakespeare's career as a playwright. The theatre for which he wrote— The Globe itself—was part of the cityscape so elegiacally remembered in this speech. The play itself can be seen as an exploration of the power and limitations of the art of the dramatist as much as the magician. Although Shakespeare did have a hand in a couple of further plays, *The Tempest* is generally acknowledged as his 'farewell to the stage'.

*The Tempest* has had an extraordinary after-life. Generation after generation of scholars have been drawn to its elusive mystery. No other play by Shakespeare has proved to be so prophetic on such a wide range of issues. Many no longer regard Prospero as essentially a well-intended father; for some he has emerged as a prophetic example of brutal, male, white coloniser. Caliban has been interpreted both as the dangerous energy of the 'primitive' Third World and as a forerunner of the Freudian 'id'. And Ariel, the 'tricksy spirit', has become synonymous with the technical advances of science, giving his name to products as varied as soap powder and missiles.

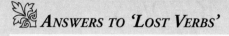
## Answers to 'Lost Verbs'

1. **(c)** quivers   The Nurse, *Romeo and Juliet*, II.iv.161-2
2. **(b)** fleet   Charles the Wrestler, *As You Like It*, I.i.116-9
3. **(b)** medicine   Iago, *Othello*, III.iii.330-3
4. **(a)** plague   Edgar, *King Lear*, V.iii.171-4
5. **(a)** danced   Beatrice, *Much Ado About Nothing*, III.i.334-5
6. **(b)** sluic'd   Leontes, *The Winter's Tale*, I.ii.192-6
7. **(c)** raught   Margaret, *Henry VI*, Part 3, I.iv.67-8
8. **(a)** repent   Aaron, *Titus Andronicus*, V.iii.189-90
9. **(b)** ascend   The Opening Chorus to Act 1, *Henry V*, 1-2
10. **(c)** paint   Hamlet, *Hamlet*, V.i.192-3

# TRAGEDIES

The First Folio (the original collection of Shakespeare's plays, published after his death, in 1623) listed eleven Tragedies (or twelve—there is a problem with *Troilus and Cressida*). For the purposes of this book the 'Tragedies' section of the First Folio has been subdivided: five are in 'Greek and Roman Histories' and one (*Cymbeline*) is in 'Tragi-Comedies'. That leaves five—*Romeo and Juliet* and the four often referred to as Shakespeare's 'great' tragedies.

In mediaeval times 'tragedy' meant the catastrophic downfall of a character. But gradually it took on a more specialised meaning, based on classical literature and theory, in particular the 4th century B.C. *Poetics* of Aristotle. The dramatic genre of Tragedy generally included the following elements: a central character who is 'great' but has a fault or weakness, and a downfall (culminating in death) which has awesome and wide-reaching impact. Bad luck, villains and Fate may also play their part. Sir Philip Sidney, an older contemporary of Shakespeare, criticised much Elizabethan drama and insisted, in his *Defence of Poetry*, that great tragedy required focus on a single line of action, a sombre tone, a constant location and a concentrated time-span. It is clear that Shakespeare was aware of these 'rules', but he tended to flout or bend them with extraordinary effectiveness.

The following essays take the five tragedies in order of their composition.

Romeo and Juliet  (1595-6)
Hamlet  (1600-1)
Othello  (1604)
King Lear  (1605)
Macbeth  (1606)

# Romeo and Juliet

**From forth the fatal loins of these two foes
A pair of star-cross'd lovers take their life.**

Prologue, Chorus, 5-6

These lines, with their regular beat and the marked alliteration, have a formal ring. They are in fact part of the ceremonial opening Chorus, written in sonnet form, which introduces this relatively early tragedy of young love. Romeo and Juliet are the archetype of doomed young lovers. The 'fatal loins' of their warring parents (the Montagues and the Capulets) is only one part of their doom; they are also 'star-cross'd'. This astrological image of Fate is constantly invoked during the course of the play. Romeo, on the verge of meeting and falling in love with Juliet, has a sense of destiny—'some consequence yet hanging in the stars'. Later, when in lonely desperation he decides to challenge this destiny, he shouts out: 'Then I defy you, stars!'.

Fate—or bad luck, or poor timing—results in a series of unnecessary deaths. The first is Mercutio, Romeo's mercurial friend, who recklessly courts death, is stabbed and exits cursing the feuding households with characteristic energy and humour: 'A plague a both your houses! They have made wormsmeat of me'. And he jokes sardonically that he is being transformed into a 'grave' man. Mercutio is one of several brilliantly individual characters who give a ballast of realism to what might otherwise be an ethereally romantic play. Another one is Juliet's foster-mother, the Nurse. The thirty or so lines[1] in which the Nurse answers a simple question as to Juliet's age form a breathtakingly sustained monologue which incorporates a whole family history as well as capturing her own personality.

---

1. The Nurse's monologue, I.ii.16-48, is now printed as verse in all modern editions. Both the original Quarto and the Folio text printed the speech in prose as did all further reprints and early editions of Shakespeare's text. Capell, the seventh editor of Shakespeare (following both Pope and Johnson),was the first to notice that in spite of her colloquial rambling the Nurse speaks in rhythmically perfect blank verse. Capell's edition was published in 1768.

But it is impossible to carve a quotation from the headlong syntax of this speech, so a separate image must serve:

**Now, afore God, I am so vex'd that every part about me quivers.**

II.iv.161-2

'Quivering with indignation' is a cliché but the Nurse's description of herself is hilariously fresh and precise. It comes as she is trying, not very successfully, to simmer down after having been publicly humiliated by the over-familiar jokes and innuendos of Romeo's friends. Her vexation is the more because, as Juliet's special messenger, she had been hoping to cut a dignified figure in front of the young noblemen. Of course drawing attention to 'every part' of her presumably ample anatomy merely serves to make her wounded dignity more ludicrous. And the dramatic build-up to the comically graphic word 'quivers' provides a fine example of bathos. The Nurse takes status very seriously. As an established member of the Capulet household she has revelled in her privileged relationship to the young heiress, Juliet. She acts as Juliet's surrogate mother, a source of encouragement, advice, comfort and, ultimately, betrayal.

In the end the young lovers are isolated; none of the responsible adults can protect them from their doom. Throughout their brief courtship they have seemed to be snatching moments of light from surrounding darkness. Death is seen as the almost inevitable partner of Love, a romantic idea which is lyrically developed throughout the play. Most powerfully, Death is personified as a lover, and this image is at the heart of Romeo's final speech. Hearing of Juliet's death, he has come to kiss her one last time. The tomb, a 'palace of dim night', seems to be transformed by Juliet: 'her beauty makes/ This vault a feasting presence, full of light'. Gazing at Juliet's body, Romeo imagines that Death is 'amorous' and that 'the lean, abhorred monster keeps/ Thee here to be his paramour'. Romeo is tormented by the idea:

**Death, that hath suck'd the honey of thy breath,**
**Hath had no power yet upon thy beauty.**          V.iii.92-3

The image of Death kissing Juliet is strongly theatrical (intensified by the traditional notion that a kiss might suck forth someone's soul). Although Juliet's beauty has triumphed, Romeo has accepted Death as his rival, and Death has defeated him. All he can do now is shake off 'the yoke of inauspicious stars' and die himself. There is a final twist but, as the Chorus concludes:

> never was a story of more woe
> Than this of Juliet and her Romeo.

## 🐚 Answers to 'Love and Lust'

1. **(a)** quicken   Orsino, *Twelfth Night*, I.i.1-3
2. **(a)** heaven   Cleopatra and Antony, *Antony and Cleopatra*, I.i.14-17
3. **(c)** holiday   The Host, *Merry Wives of Windsor*, III.ii.67-9
4. **(c)** peopled   Benedict, *Much Ado About Nothing*, II.iii.242-4
5. **(c)** warm   Katherina, *The Taming of the Shrew*, V.ii.147-51
6. **(c)** flower   Titania, *A Midsummer Night's Dream* , III.i.198-200
7. **(b)** wench   Hal, *Henry IV, Part 1*, I.ii.6-10
8. **(b)** beadle   Lear, *King Lear*, IV.vi.160-3
9. **(a)** thirsty   Claudio, *Measure for Measure*, I.ii.128-30
10. **(b)** spices   Timon, *Timon of Athens*, IV.iii.38-42

# Hamlet

O, what a noble mind is here o'erthrown!
The courtier's, soldier's, scholar's, eye, tongue, sword,
Th' expectancy° and rose of the fair state,          *hope*
The glass of fashion and the mould of form,
Th' observ'd of all observers, quite, quite down!

                                   III.i.150

This image gives Ophelia's impression of Hamlet and the Danish court before his 'madness'. She remembers him as an ideal renaissance prince, demonstrating the attributes of a courtier, soldier and scholar, admired and imitated by all as he prepared himself for kingship. However, when the play begins Hamlet's image of himself and of his world has been shattered. In a short space of time he has faced bereavement (the death of his father), 'incest' (the marriage of his mother to his uncle) and usurpation (his uncle Claudius being crowned as the new King of Denmark). 'Hyperion to a satyr' says Hamlet, reflecting on the difference between his 'sun-god' father and the goat-man who has replaced him. Ophelia's language, in its courtly prettiness ('o'erthrown', 'rose of the fair state', 'glass of fashion') reveals her limitations and her inability to understand and support the changed Hamlet who has recently returned to Denmark.

As 'the glass of fashion and the mould of form', the 'sane' young Hamlet both reflected and helped shape the niceties of courtly decorum. Following the revelation that his father had been murdered by his uncle, the transformed, 'mad' Hamlet of the play takes on the role of a very different kind of mirror ('glass')—showing the horrors which lurk beneath the surfaces of the seemingly untroubled courtly life. The 'purpose of playing', he tells the actors who are about to play 'The Murder of Gonzago' before the court, is

to hold as 'twere the mirror up to nature: to show virtue her
own feature, scorn her own image, and the very age and body of
the time his form and pressure.         III.ii.21-4

With these words, Hamlet eloquently expresses the generally held Renaissance idea that drama should reflect real life. But he is also preparing traps for his uncle and his mother. In the play-within-the play which follows, both Claudius and Gertrude find disturbing images of themselves. Claudius is so powerfully moved that he rushes off and attempts to pray. But Hamlet, despite being given an opportunity to dispatch him, chooses to let his uncle live while he pursues the game of mirrors with his mother, confronting her in her bed-chamber with the words: 'You go not till I set you up a glass/ Where you may see the inmost part of you'. A series of vivid images follows, contrasting his father with his uncle and culminating in a savage denunciation of Gertrude's new 'love' relationship:

> **Nay, but to live**
> **In the rank sweat of an enseamed bed,**
> **Stew'd in corruption, honeying and making love**
> **Over the nasty sty!**                                 IV.iv.91-4

Hamlet almost enjoys the scenario he has created as he pictures Claudius and Gertrude as a pair of pigs wallowing in their sweaty love nest ('enseamed' would suggest both 'greasy' and 'semen-stained'). Such is his passion that the Ghost of his dead father intervenes to remind him that Claudius, not Gertrude, should be the object of his rage. But when Gertrude, who does not see the Ghost, suggests that he is mad, Hamlet attacks her for trying to avoid the truth:

> **Lay not that flattering unction° to your soul,**        *ointment*
> **That not your trespass but my madness speaks;**
> **It will but skim and film the ulcerous place,**
> **Whiles rank corruption, mining all within,**
> **Infects unseen.**                                      III.iv.145-9

Hamlet's image is brutal: good flesh is eaten away by the infection of an ulcer, which can undermine invisibly because it is hidden by the 'film' of surface skin established by a 'flattering' ointment. It is a precise and menacing symbol of corruption, political as well as moral.

However, Hamlet's disillusion with life extends beyond the bedroom and the court. His tragedy, as every subsequent generation has discovered, is that of any idealist who moves through innocence into experience. He gives an eloquent account of his depression to his former friends, Rozencrantz and Guildenstern, who have been sent to spy on him. The former beauties of earth and sky (that 'majestical roof fretted with golden fire') now seem to him a 'sterile promontory' and a 'foul and pestilent congregation of vapours'. Above all there is a loss of belief in mankind:

> **What a piece of work is a man, how noble in reason, how infinite in faculties, in form and moving, how express and admirable, in action how like an angel, in apprehension how like a god! the beauty of the world, the paragon of animals; and yet to me what is this quintessence of dust?** II.ii.303-8

In this image Hamlet gives majestic expression to the renaissance vision of human potential before dashing it to nothing—a 'quintessence of dust'. However, he is not an aloof, detached cynic: his agony is that he sees himself as part of the problem as, once again, he challenges himself with a question: 'What should such fellows as I do, crawling between earth and heaven?' Drawing on earlier, mediaeval cosmography, Hamlet pictures himself uncomfortably stranded between the separate worlds of beasts and angels, pulled down by his animal instincts yet tormented by spiritual intimations.[1]

The realisation that human life is finally defined by death is most strikingly expressed in the almost surreal graveyard scene. Hamlet has identified a disinterred skull as that of Yorick, the long-dead court Jester. In an iconic tableau he addresses the skull face to face, as it were: 'Alas, poor Yorick'. But Hamlet is not interested in mere lament. Physical revulsion ('my gorge rises at it') moves to grotesque wit ('Quite chapfall'n'—metaphorically 'chapfall'n' would refer to the incongruity of

---

1. A generation later the poet, George Herbert, expresses a similar anguish, referring to himself as 'a crumb of dust stretched out from heaven to hell'.

a jester being 'down in the mouth'; literally the skull is without its cheeks or jaw, chapfallen).

And then comes a sneering suggestion. Still addressing the skull, Hamlet says:

> **Now get you to my Lady's chamber, and**
> **tell her, let her paint° an inch thick, to this**　　　*make-up*
> **favour° she must come; make her laugh at**　　*facial appearance*
> **that.**　　　　　　　　　　　　　　　　　　　V.i.192-3

'Painting' was a rich topic for satirists but this jibe of Hamlet's is particularly grim—even grimmer when it is revealed that the grave being dug is for the rejected Ophelia.

Such is Hamlet (the man)'s hold over our imaginations that it is now easy to forget that *Hamlet* (the play) would have been seen by the Elizabethans as belonging (somewhat uneasily) to the popular genre of the 'Revenge Play'. In the play's final scene, Hamlet does take on the role given to him at the start of the play by the Ghost and acts as a Revenger, killing the 'incestuous, murd'rous, damned Dane', his usurping uncle Claudius. Throughout the play, Hamlet's instinct to act (whether as a revenger or as a suicide) is repeatedly frustrated by what he calls 'thinking too precisely on th' event'. And no play written before or since has so effectively mirrored the rhythms of human thinking. The following image, taken from Hamlet's most famous soliloquy, 'To be or not to be', well illustrates a mind turning in on itself as it explores the ways in which conscious thought inhibits action:

> **Thus conscience does make cowards of us all,**
> **And thus the native hue of resolution**
> **Is sicklied o'er with the pale cast of thought,**
> **And enterprises of great pitch and moment**
> **With this regard their currents turn awry,**
> **And lose the name of action.**　　　　　　　III.i.82-7

# *Othello*

**Not poppy, nor mandragora,**
**Nor all the drowsy syrups of the world**
**Shall ever medicine thee to that sweet sleep**
**Which thou ow'st° yesterday.**                    *owned/had*
                                                    III.iii.330-3


These lines, both supremely beautiful and supremely vicious, are spoken by Iago as he frames Othello's entrance. He has, moments earlier, convinced Othello that his wife, the noble, young and virtuous Desdemona, is unfaithful. As Iago lists the opiates ('poppy', 'mandragora' and all the 'drowsy syrups') he seems to be relishing them and the 'sweet sleep' that they would normally engender. But what he is actually relishing is the fact that, thanks to his villainy, Othello will never sleep sweetly again. This private, almost sensual, moment may be the closest the audience ever get to Iago. They have been used to being directly addressed by him, as he has boastingly explained his stratagems; here, however, they are almost eavesdropping as he gloats over his victim. Iago is not usually lyrical—quite the contrary. He is a bluff soldier, Othello's 'ensign', and has the reputation of being honest—a straight talker. Often his language is vigorously crude. 'An old black ram is tupping your white ewe,' is what he calls out to Desdemona's father, alerting him to her elopement with Othello.

By contrast Othello's normal speech is rhetorical and musical. His character has been formed from strange adventures in strange landscapes and his language draws on alien, exotic references. He won Desdemona by telling her of 'antres vast and deserts idle' and when he learns that she has mislaid the handkerchief he gave her, he warns that it was no ordinary kerchief but one woven, from the thread of hallowed silkworms, by a two hundred year-old sibyl, before being dyed in a liquid prepared from the hearts of maidens! But beneath his romantic, heroic exterior, Othello has racial and social insecurities which make him vulnerable. Iago drips in the poison of Jealousy ('the green-eyed monster which doth mock/ The meat it feeds on') and the source of all Othello's happiness is destroyed. In one of the play's most powerful images Othello expresses his inner torment and sense of loss:

> But there, where I have garner'd up my heart,
> Where either I must live or bear no life;
> The fountain from the which my current runs
> Or else dries up: to be discarded thence!
> Or keep it as a cistern for foul toads
> To knot and gender in!          IV.ii.57-62

He is trying to grasp the agonising change in his love for Desdemona. Formerly it was like a pure fount of water, the very well-spring of his life; now he sees it as stagnant, a breeding ground for disgusting and poisonous toads. Once infected by jealousy, Othello's language begins to take on something of Iago's crudeness, and becomes full of animal and diabolic images.

In the play's final scenes, however—as Othello moves towards the execution of Desdemona—his language regains dignity and the poetry of the earlier scenes. 'It is the cause, it is the cause, my soul;/ Let me not name it to you, you chaste stars,' he says, elevating the act of murder to the status of a religious rite. Then, contemplating his sleeping wife, he seems to be imprinting her beauty on his mind as he resolves

> Yet I'll not shed her blood,
> Nor scar that whiter skin of hers than snow,
> And smooth as monumental alabaster.          V.ii.3-5

The whiteness emphasises the purity which he so valued in her but it also suggests the coldness of death. The unusual word order makes this a sensual, almost caressing, image which simultaneously preserves Desdemona forever, in effigy.

Othello is Shakespeare's most naïve hero and Iago his most complex villain and their relationship has puzzled commentators. Why does Iago destroy the 'noble Moor'? He himself gives several reasons, reasons so glib and improbable that audiences are generally unconvinced by them. 'Motiveless malignity,' Coleridge wrote, implying that Othello was a totally innocent victim. But later critics have been less generous to Othello—suggesting that his tendency to speak boastfully and bombastically indicates a lack of self awareness as well as the huge gulf between his world and that of his wife. Though it is difficult to see the exotic Othello as an 'Everyman' figure, it is tempting to see Iago as a descendent of the Vice of the Morality Plays—a dramatic manifestation of Othello's inner weakness. Developing this idea in practice, in a 1955 production at The Old Vic, Richard Burton and John Neville alternated roles in order to bring out the interdependence and balance of the two characters. They showed that seeing Iago and Othello as alter-egos can be both psychologically and dramatically illuminating.

# *King Lear*

**I have no way, and therefore want no eyes;**
**I stumbled when I saw.**                                   IV.i.18-19

These words are spoken by the blinded Earl of Gloucester, as he stumbles towards attempted suicide and death. We are reminded of Gloucester's 'way', his personal journey through life, at key moments throughout the play. In the opening lines when he introduces his bastard son Edmund, he is smug and insensitive: 'There was good sport at his making,' he tells Kent. We are never allowed to forget Gloucester's lecherous, adulterous past and it is Edmund who engineers his blinding (arguably the cruellest staged scene in all drama). Once blinded, like Sophocles's Oedipus, he begins to 'see' with visionary power.

**As flies to wanton boys are we to th' gods,**
**They kill us for their sport**                              IV.i.36-7

he declares. This despairing image of a malign universe where human cruelty mirrors a sadistic divine cruelty is expressed in stark and simple language. Later Gloucester's 'good' son, Edgar, will contradict this idea, telling the dying Edmund that their father's suffering can be seen as evidence of a hard, but essentially moral, universe:

> **The gods are just, and of our pleasant vices**
> **Make instruments to plague us:**
> **The dark and vicious place where thee he got**
> **Cost him his eyes.** V.iii.171-4

Which of these two images of 'the gods' has greater authenticity? *King Lear* provides questions but no answers.

Gloucester's metaphorical journey through life, forms a sub-plot, parallel to King Lear's. Both old men begin the play complacent and gullible, easily deceived by glib flattery. Both trust their flattering 'bad' children and, after terrible suffering, achieve reconciliations with the 'good', truth-telling children whom they initially rejected. As Gloucester comes to see only in blindness, Lear achieves wisdom only in madness. Driven out into the storm by his wicked daughters, Goneril and Regan, Lear begins to realise how a life of power and privilege has let him ignore the sufferings of his kingdom's poor. Before entering a hovel to take refuge from the storm, he prays and, in an image of great power, pictures the plight of his kingdom's dispossessed:

> **Poor naked wretches, wheresoe'er you are,**
> **That bide the pelting of this pitiless storm,**
> **How shall your houseless heads and unfed sides,**
> **Your loop'd and window'd raggedness, defend you**
> **From seasons such as these?** III.iv.28-32

There follows one of the strangest encounters in all literature as from the hovel emerges a physical manifestation of his prayer. It is the fugitive Edgar, playing the role of 'Poor Tom', a Bedlam beggar—'houseless', 'naked' and 'unfed'.[1] An extraordinary dialogue ensues between the King (on the verge of madness), Edgar (impersonating a mad beggar) and the Fool. By the end of the scene, Lear has entered the kingdom of the insane.

It has been suggested that *King Lear* is Shakespeare's most probing exploration of the question, 'What is Man?'. Gloucester's two sons provide important parts of the answer. Edgar, the Bedlam beggar, as 'unaccommodated man'—vulnerable humanity deprived of all the comforts of civilization—is offset by Edmund, the self-seeking opportunist who, until the play's closing moments, is devoid of all compassion. Born out of wedlock, Edmund feels himself free from the constraints of 'custom': civilization, tradition and human ties. He is prepared to use his intelligence and his charm to maim, murder and seduce as he manipulates his way towards absolute power. (Commentators have found in the rise of Edmund, the 'new man', a prefigurement of the emergence of the terrible dictators of the twentieth century: Hitler, Stalin, Pol Pot, Mao....).

Edmund declares 'Nature' to be his 'goddess' and is contemptuous of 'custom'. But the most penetrating dissection of the abuses of 'civilised' convention is made in the extraordinary scene (IV.vi) where, following his failed suicide, Gloucester encounters Lear. Here the 'mad' king projects onto Gloucester's blind eyes a succession of searing images which reveal the world as it is to those who are victims of authority. Ironically, it is Gloucester's adultery which initially seems to trigger Lear's hallucinations. He senses a vicious sexuality lurking beneath the veneer of civilised society and condemns all women: 'But to the girdle do the gods inherit/ The rest is all the fiend's'.

Anticipating the Freudian theory of repression, Lear sees the urge to punish as sexually driven, as he challenges an imagined officer whipping a condemned prostitute:

---

1. The great Russian film director, Kozintsev, kept a journal while making his film of *King Lear*. In it he argued that the conventions and limitations of the stage, which made it necessary to represent 'naked wretches' by a single image of poverty, could be transcended by the means available to the cinema. In his film, first Edgar and then Lear take refuge in a hovel which is crammed full of the rejects of society—rejects representing those disregarded by the powerful, whether in the mythic age where *King Lear* is set, or in Shakespeare's England, or in post-revolutionary Russia—or today.

**Thou rascal beadle, hold thy bloody hand!**
**Why dost thou lash that whore? Strip thy own back,**
**Thou hotly lusts to use her in that kind**
**For which thou whip'st her.**                     IV.vi.160-3


He then denounces the corruptions of wealth and power in another succinctly penetrating image:


Through tattered clothes great vices do appear;
Robes and furr'd gowns hide all.


Seen through their rags the small sins of the poor seem like 'great vices' whereas the wrong-doings of the privileged classes can be concealed by their expensive 'robes and furred gowns'. As the scene concludes, Lear's prophetic frenzy subsides into tenderness; he recognises Gloucester and comforts him in a speech of resigned stoicism:

**Thou must be patient; we came crying hither.**
**Thou know'st, the first time that we smell the air**
**We wawl and cry.**                     IV.vi.178-80


This image is simple, stripped of all rhetoric. Two old men, on the edge of being, pause to accept the essential cruelty of human existence. Then both are once more caught up in the play's relentless action. (In Samuel Beckett's *Waiting for Godot* the lines, 'Astride of a grave and a difficult birth. Down in the hole, lingeringly, the grave-digger puts on the forceps' would seem to be inspired by this tableau. It is generally agreed that *King Lear*, and this scene in particular, had a great influence on Beckett.)

The play's final scenes deal, though very differently, with the deaths of Edmund, Gloucester, Lear and his three daughters. Gloucester dies off-stage. According to Edgar, who accompanies him to his end, his heart 'burst smilingly'— happy in the knowledge that Edgar has cared for him and has saved him from despair.

The deaths of Lear and Cordelia are at the centre of the play's final harrowing moments. Having gone through the agony and bliss of reconciliation with his wronged daughter, Cordelia, Lear's final entry on stage follows this direction: 'Enter Lear with Cordelia dead in his arms'. As with poses of the Virgin with the dead Christ, this 'pieta' of parent with dead and totally innocent child is painful to behold but the audience, like the surviving characters standing round, are forced to be witnesses. Addressing the dead Cordelia, Lear challenges us all:

**Why should a dog, a horse, a rat, have life,**
**And thou no breath at all?**                              V.iii.307-8

Samuel Johnson, writing in the 18th century, expressed his despairing response, one which many will share: 'The death of Cordelia baffles the strong, indignant claim of Justice'. Contemporary audiences agreed and for almost 200 years *King Lear* was shown on stage only in Nahum Tate's adaptation, which substituted a happy ending. Shakespeare himself seems

to have felt a need to soften Lear's pain. In the Folio text (now thought to be his revision of the earlier text printed in Quarto format), these are Lear's final words:

**Do you see this? Look on her! Look her lips,**
**Look there, look there!**                                V.iii.311-12

The intensity of these short lines, with the repeated emphasis on 'look', 'look', 'look' suggests that, imagining that Cordelia still breathes, Lear's heart, too, bursts smilingly. What is the significance of this final image? Is it a vision or a false epiphany? The critics are divided.

## Answers to 'Epiphanies'

1. **(b)** blood    Macbeth, *Macbeth*, V.i.39-40
2. **(b)** darkness    Prospero, *The Tempest*, V.i.275-6
3. **(c)** naked    Cardinal Wolsey, *Henry VIII*, III.ii.455-7
4. **(c)** beauty    Troilus, *Troilus and Cressida*, V.ii.138
5. **(a)** sleep    Duke Vincentio, *Measure for Measure*, III.i.31-3
6. **(c)** lips    Lear, *King Lear*, V, iii.311-12
7. **(c)** dust    Hamlet, *Hamlet*, II.ii.303-8
8. **(b)** tears    Macbeth, *Macbeth*, I.vii.21-5
9. **(b)** raggedness    Lear, *King Lear*, III.iv.28-32
10. **(c)** idiot    Macbeth, *Macbeth*, V.v.24-8

---

# Macbeth

**Light thickens and the crow**
**Makes wing to th' rooky wood.**                    III.ii.50-51

This image, as sharply condensed as a Japanese haiku, sets the scene for the murder of Banquo, the second of Macbeth's victims. In the evocative phrase, 'light thickens', Shakespeare makes descending nightfall smotheringly tangible, before he focuses on the solitary figure of a crow moving towards the wood. The image well illustrates the poetic intensity of the play—as William Empson's famous analysis (in his *Seven Types of Ambiguity*) cogently demonstrates. Empson suggests that at a subliminal level both Macbeth and the audience sense that the crow is a loner, moving ominously towards the habitation of the more social rooks, whose nests in the wood are about to be plundered. Whether or not Shakespeare intentionally made this distinction between crow and rook, the image becomes even more sinister as the speaker, Macbeth, goes on to picture 'night's black agents' rousing themselves to hunt their prey. His own black agents are already set to hack down Banquo and his young son.

As in many great poems, each part helps to illuminate the whole. No other play by Shakespeare is as richly patterned as *Macbeth*. Against the blackness of the night there is a continuous preoccupation with images of blood. Some of these are visual images: the 'bloody' sergeant who describes the battle in which Macbeth kills and decapitates a rebel enemy; Macbeth's hands following the murder of King Duncan; the 'blood boltered' ghost of Banquo which disrupts the feast that Macbeth has pretended to host in his honour—and many others. But the verbal imagery of blood is even more potent. In particular it is King Duncan's blood, the 'filthy witness' which marks their first murder, which keeps returning to haunt the imaginations of both the usurper and his wife. 'A little water clears us of this deed', Lady Macbeth says brusquely as she returns from the scene of the murder with blood-stained hands. But in her absence Macbeth has, in an elaborate hyperbole, imagined Duncan's blood turning the green of all the world's oceans to red. Following his murder of Banquo, Macbeth develops this image, seeing himself as a doomed man, wading through a sea of blood:

**I am in blood**
**Stepp'd in so far that, should I wade no more,**
**Returning were as tedious as go o'er.** III.v.135-7

He is on the brink of becoming a tyrant, submitting to the almost inevitable logic of escalating destruction. And, like many modern tyrants, he sets up a secret service to ensure that he can deal speedily and brutally with any potential political dissent. As we see in the scene where the murderers 'surprise' Macduff's castle, innocent women and children are not to be spared from Macbeth's paranoia. While Scotland 'bleeds' under his regime, he becomes indifferent to the ensuing killings.

At the end of the play, Macbeth and his wife are dismissed by the new King Malcolm as, 'this dead butcher and his fiend-like queen'. In the popular imagination, Lady Macbeth is indeed 'fiend-like', almost inhuman. Fearing that her husband might be 'too full o' th' milk of human kindness' to commit the murder which will make him king, she renounces her feminine nature in order to become the sharp spur to his ambition. She then shames the faltering Macbeth by proclaiming her own masculine resolve: in one of the play's most terrible images she tells him how she would have been prepared to 'dash the brains out' of her own suckling infant ('the babe that milks me') rather than give way to pity and remorse. The image seems to point ahead to the slaughter, later in the play, of Macduff's innocent babes. In fact Lady Macbeth is guilty of neither atrocity; it is in the brutality of her language and apparent immunity to feeling that she seems to be the personification of Evil. But although she manages the killing of Duncan with calm practicality, she cannot adjust to being 'in blood'. In her final 'sleep-walking' scene we discover that the horror has merely been repressed; ironically it is she who is now haunted by the blood.

> **Yet who would have thought the old man to have had so much blood in him?** V.i.39-40

she asks as she attempts to wash Duncan's imagined blood from her hands. The stark, monosyllabic question suggests her horror even more effectively than her more obviously poetic, self-pitying exclamation ('All the perfumes of Arabia will not sweeten this little hand').

Two of the play's most complex images chart the enormity of Macbeth's own fall from grace. Before murdering Duncan, he was able to imagine the consequences of his actions against a vast Blake-like panorama of good and evil, where Duncan's virtues would 'plead like angels, trumpet tongu'd/ Against the deep damnation of his taking off':

> **And pity, like a naked new-born babe,**
> **Striding the blast, or heaven's cherubin, hors'd**
> **Upon the sightless couriers of the air,**
> **Shall blow the horrid deed in every eye,**
> **That tears shall drown the wind.** I.vii.21-5

In this double simile, Macbeth's imagination leaps from the relatively simple image of 'Pity' as 'a naked new born babe' to a vision of the heavens in turmoil as the 'babe' becomes an apocalyptic angel, riding on the winds and causing universal lamentation by revealing to all the horror of his 'deed'.

But by the conclusion of the play, Macbeth has become so hardened to horror that when he is told of the death of his wife his response is a weary dismissal of the value of life itself. In the soliloquy starting 'Tomorrow, and tomorrow, and tomorrow,' he constructs a chain of negative images, each one collapsing into insignificance:

> **Life's but a walking shadow, a poor player,**
> **That struts and frets his hour upon the stage,**
> **And then is heard no more. It is a tale**
> **Told by an idiot, full of sound and fury,**
> **Signifying nothing.**                                   V.v.24-8

The empty crescendo of 'sound and fury' drops finally to the even bleaker emptiness of 'nothing'. Though these words might be seen to anticipate the 20th century 'theatre of the absurd', where the drama centres on the meaninglessness of existence, within the context of Shakespeare's play Macbeth's soliloquy gives a terrible image of personal emptiness and loss.

*Macbeth* can be seen as a moral and psychological drama, focusing on a couple whose ambition leads to their destruction. But Shakespeare starts his play with the entry of three Witches, who seem to be crucial to the tragedy. The 'Weird Sisters' (their name comes from the Anglo-Saxon word for Destiny) target Macbeth in particular and he trusts them until the last minutes of his life—too late to avoid the fate they have brought him. The upright Banquo, warning Macbeth against these 'instruments of darkness', expresses what would have been the orthodox view of witches in Shakespeare's time. Thousands of people were put to death for 'serving the devil' through their practice of witchcraft. Whatever his personal beliefs, Shakespeare saw the theatrical potential of the three supernatural beings who, in the Holinshed chronicle that was his source, confront Macbeth. What is more, King James, a Scot reputedly descended from the virtuous Banquo, had a firm belief in witchcraft and had written a book on Demonology in which he 'proved' that witches really did have Satanic powers. *Macbeth*, 'the Scottish play', performed for James by the company of players now officially called 'The King's Men' must have seemed like a special compliment to their new patron.

## ANSWERS TO 'ABSTRACTIONS'

1. **(a)**  mercy  Portia, *The Merchant of Venice*, IV.i.184-6
2. **(h)**  imagination  Theseus, *A Midsummer Night's Dream*, V.i.7-8
3. **(c)**  fortune  Brutus, *Julius Caesar*, IV.iii.218-21
4. **(e)**  conscience  Hamlet, *Hamlet* ,III.i.82-7
5. **(f)**  grief  Constance, *King John*, III.iv.93-6
6. **(i)**  virginity  Parolles, *All's Well That Ends Well*, I.i.141-3
7. **(g)**  time  Troilus, *Troilus and Cressida*, IV.iv.42-8
8. **(b)**  corruption  Hamlet, *Hamlet*, III.iv.145-9
9. **(j)**  perturbation  Hal, *Henry IV*, Part 2, IV.v.23-5
10. **(d)**  mind  Ophelia, *Hamlet, III.i.150*

# GREEK AND ROMAN HISTORIES

These plays are all listed simply as 'Tragedies' in the original collection of Shakespeare's plays (the First Folio, 1623). All except *Titus Andronicus* share a single major source, the *Parallel Lives* written around 100 AD by the Roman historian Plutarch. These paired biographies, focusing on the psychological and political aspects of famous characters, were published in 1579 in an English translation by Sir Thomas North, called *Lives of the Noble Grecians and Romans*. North's Plutarch seems to have been devoured by Shakespeare. But he used the source creatively, sometimes following the original very closely but also selecting, combining and inventing in the interests of making a good play.

Both Holinshed's *Chronicles* (see ENGLISH HISTORIES) and North's *Lives of the Noble Grecians and Romans* were printed by Richard Field, a Stratford contemporary of Shakespeare, who also printed his two long narrative poems, *Venus and Adonis* and *The Rape of Lucrece*.

The essays which follow take the plays in order of their composition.

# Titus Andronicus

**If one good deed in all my life I did,**
**I do repent it from my very soul.**                    V.iii.189-90

These last defiant words are spoken by Aaron, the Moor, Shakespeare's first study in absolute villainy. He has just received his sentence: to be buried in earth and starved to death. When, mid-way through the play, the Andronicus family make their exit in search of 'Revenge's cave', their gruesome little tableau (Titus, holding the head of one of his sons in his single hand, his brother Marcus carrying a second son's head and his daughter, the ravished Lavinia, tongueless and handless, carrying Titus's amputated hand in her mouth) is Aaron's masterpiece; his cunning lies behind this host of mutilations.

*Titus Andronicus* centres on the struggle between the 'good' Titus Andronicus, the upholder of Roman values and customs, and the 'evil' opposition—the weak emperor Saturninus, his wife Tamora Queen of the Goths and her paramour Aaron, the blackest of them all. And yet when Aaron's wicked deeds are placed against the actions of his victim, Titus, they begin to pale a little. It is Titus who at the start of the play sets in process the cycle of revenge by presiding over the ritual sacrifice of Alarbus, Tamora's 'proudest' son. It is Titus who ends the cycle of savagery by feigning madness, killing Tamora's remaining two sons (Lavinia's rapists) and then feeding them in a pie to their mother before killing her too. And it is Titus, the 'good Andronicus', who, in upholding his and Rome's code of honour, kills two of his own children—Mutius for challenging his authority and Lavinia for the shame that she has suffered.

These last mentioned killings throw into sharp relief one of Aaron's final actions. This is the bargain which he makes to save the life of his son, the 'beauteous blossom', born to his mistress, Tamora. The infant's life is preserved in exchange for a 'show' of 'wondrous things', which turns out to be Aaron's catalogue of his evil deeds against the Andronicus family. Although the nurse, shortly before Aaron stabs her, speaks of the babe as 'a devil', and Aaron imagines him growing up as an image of himself, audiences are likely to see the saving of the baby (which is present on stage) as a redemptive deed—a deed which might return to trouble its perpetrator's black soul when he is boasting of his wickedness in Hell!

Aaron, who relishes the idea of living and burning 'in everlasting fire, descends dramatically from Satan—and, like the Vice in morality drama, he is not without charm, his direct addresses to the audience coming as something of a relief from Titus's wooden worthiness. Aaron's 'brood' is not just his bastard child but a succession of more subtly drawn villains in later plays—Iago, Edmund and Antonio. His main adversary, Titus, is an early study of rigid, intemperate old age moving into madness and as such anticipates King Lear.

*Titus Andronicus* is one of Shakespeare's earliest plays, more memorable for its deeds than for the quality of its language, and any plot summary will make it sound more like a comedy of terrors than a Senecan tragedy. However in recent years a number of film and stage directors have found that the play speaks eloquently to today's audiences—audiences whose television screens regularly reveal to them images of factions caught up in cycles of savage revenge.

# *Julius Caesar*

**He doth bestride the narrow world
Like a Colossus, and we petty men
Walk under his huge legs, and peep about
To find ourselves dishonourable graves.**                    I.ii.135-8

The man described is Julius Caesar, recently returned to Rome as a war-hero; in a matter of hours he will be dead. The speaker is Cassius, ring-leader of the conspirators. In these lines he creates an image of Caesar as a giant among men, comparing him to the huge statue of Apollo which was said to have stood astride the harbour of Rhodes, a legendary wonder. Cassius fears Caesar's god-like aspirations (while he speaks there are shouts off-stage as Caesar is cheered by the Roman crowd), but as the image develops it becomes almost comical, with little men who 'peep about', dwarfed by the 'huge legs' of the Colossus. Cassius is contemptuous of these little men—'petty' is the word he spits out—but what fuels his resentment is the fact that he is one of them. As he tries to persuade Brutus to join a group of disaffected republicans plotting to assassinate Caesar, he pictures their alternative—lives of abject obedience, leading only to 'dishonourable graves'.

In fact Cassius's description of Caesar is sneering rather than admiring and Shakespeare himself tends to emphasise Caesar's weaknesses rather than his strengths. Although Caesar claims to be 'constant as the northern star', he is easily swayed by flattery and his impressive-sounding statement of valour, 'Cowards die many times before their deaths', has an empty ring of boastfulness. This Colossus is no wonder of the world—but his death, on the steps of the Capitol, is world-shattering.

In the immediate aftermath of Caesar's assassination, the conspirators—the 'petty men'—are in control, but Caesar's most loyal supporter, Mark Antony, though at first seemingly compliant, soon emerges as the conspirators' main opponent. In a private moment of grief he addresses the corpse of his friend with the words: 'O pardon me, thou bleeding piece of earth,/ That I am meek and gentle with these butchers', showing his genuine feeling. Briefly, he is all heart, agonised at the gruesome spectacle of the corpse and the blood-stained hands of the assassins. Probably the audience need this opportunity to regret the brutality of Caesar's death, but when Mark Antony enters the public forum, we see that he is, above all, a politician. Though repeatedly referring to Brutus and his fellow conspirators as 'honourable men', the rhetorical cunning of his 'Friends, Romans, countrymen' speech succeeds in turning the fickle Roman crowd against the 'butchers'.

We, however, remain sympathetically caught up in their cause. Cassius, fuelled by passionate pride and intelligence as well as by envy, comes across as more roundedly human than Brutus, who is the only man of 'honour' among the conspirators. Acting always in the interests of the Roman republic, Brutus sees the death of Caesar as a necessary sacrifice and himself as an instrument of destiny. These are his words just before the final battle, at Philippi:

**There is a tide in the affairs of men,**
**Which taken at the flood, leads on to fortune;**
**Omitted, all the voyage of their life**
**Is bound in shallows and in miseries.** IV.iii.218-21


This is typical of Brutus' language. He speaks with conviction, in general rather than personal terms, and seems to be expressing an inevitable truth. The image here is simple, vivid and eloquently developed. The surging beat of the first two lines, in which Brutus gives his philosophy of confident courage, breaks, like the tide, to contrast the alternative life of weak indecision, 'bound in shallows and in miseries'. The irony is that, for all his conviction, Brutus keeps making the wrong decisions. It is Mark Antony who takes the tide 'at the flood' and finds that it does indeed lead on to fortune. Ultimately a more mature and magnificent Antony will face his own Shakespearean tragedy.

# *Antony and Cleopatra*


Cleo. **If it be love indeed, tell me how much.**
Ant. **There's beggary in the love that can be reckon'd.**
Cleo. **I'll set a bourn° how far to be belov'd.** *limit*
Ant. **Then must thou needs find out new heaven, new earth.**
I.i.14-17


This is the audience's first image of Antony and Cleopatra. Their opening dialogue takes the form of a short poem[1]—a teasing, tender, speculation on the limits and limitlessness of love. The balanced verse establishes a moment of grace and harmony. Grace and harmony, however, are short-lived. Antony's 'new heaven, new earth' (with its echo of The Book of Revelations and its implications of a love which will transcend

---

1. In *Romeo and Juliet* the lovers' first words together take the form of a carefully-wrought sonnet.

death) is shattered by a third 'new', as a messenger enters announcing, 'News...from Rome'. From this moment until their deaths, the lovers will be caught up in the Roman world, with its political marriages and alliances and its wars. Only in their dying will the pair begin to re-create the 'new heaven, new earth' of this exchange.

*Antony and Cleopatra* is the most filmic of Shakespeare's plays. As time and action move forward towards the suicides of the two protagonists, there is a succession of flashbacks which remind the audience of Antony's 'Roman' heroism, Cleopatra's 'Eastern' magic, and the richness of their union. The most striking and extended of these, which celebrates the lovers' original meeting on the Egyptian River Cydnus, comes precisely when Antony is strengthening his Roman bonds through an arranged marriage with Octavius Caesar's sister. The ironic timing is underlined by the fact that the speaker is the habitually cynical Enobarbus.

> **The barge she sat in, like a burnish'd throne,**
> **Burnt on the water. The poop was beaten gold,**
> **Purple the sails, and so perfumed that**
> **The winds were love-sick with them.**            II.ii.191-4

These lines introduce a famous set-piece which is a poetic reworking of a passage from Plutarch. It is interesting to note what Shakespeare has added. Although the 'barge, the 'poop of gold' and the 'purple' of the sails are all in Plutarch, Shakespeare has added the simile 'like a burnish'd throne', the metaphor 'burnt on the water' and the notion of the 'love-sick' winds. The encounter takes place on water but Shakespeare's additions produce an image composed of fire and air. And 'fire' and 'air', considered to be the higher of the four elements, remain important motifs throughout the speech.

Most of Shakespeare's audience would have accepted the Aristotelian notion that all matter was created from a mixture of earth, water, air and fire and that, whereas the lower elements were subject to mutability and decay, the higher elements were more permanent. Shakespeare's plays abound with incidental references to these ideas, but in no other play are the elements as central to theme and action as they are here. When discord breaks out between Antony and Caesar there is much debate concerning military tactics: should Antony and Cleopatra's forces fight Caesar's by land or by sea? It soon becomes apparent that Caesar and the Roman empire have mastery of both these lower elements ('I would they'ld fight i' th' fire or i' th' air,' Antony exclaims whimsically) and, let down by the Egyptian navy, Antony and Cleopatra face inevitable defeat. However, from this moment, the nadir of their political and military alliance, an extraordinary transfiguration begins as they approach their deaths.

Both lovers look on death as a form of sexual release: dying becomes orgasmic as each of them relishes the approaching end. The name of Antony's faithful servant, Eros (in Greek mythology the god of sexual love), was supplied by Plutarch and Shakespeare makes full use of its significance as Antony, wrongly believing Cleopatra to be dead, calls on Eros to despatch him.[2] The faithful Eros, however, fails in his final duty, killing himself rather than his master, so Antony is left to fall clumsily on his own sword. This botched attempt at suicide means that he does eventually die in Cleopatra's arms and she is there to howl out her great lament, beginning 'The crown o' th' earth doth melt' and culminating in the image of a moon constantly revisiting a desolate earth:

> **Young boys and girls**
> **Are level now with men; the odds is gone,**
> **And there is nothing left remarkable**
> **Beneath the visiting moon.**                IV.xv.65-8

---

2. In two short scenes Antony addresses Eros by name more than a dozen times, almost conjuring with the word as he anticipates an eternal existence with Cleopatra in Elysium:

> *Eros!—I come, my queen!—Eros!—Stay for me!*
> *Where souls do couch on flowers, we'll hand in hand,*
> *And with our sprightly port make the ghosts gaze.*
> *Dido and her Aeneas shall want troups*
> *And all the haunt be ours. Eros, Eros!*

It is a strange, intensely yearning flight of fancy, the defeated soldier imagining a hereafter where he and his beloved are the envy of other ghosts as they usurp the legendary Dido and Aeneas. (In Dante's *Inferno*, both Dido and Cleopatra are condemned to the second level of Hell where, as a punishment for earthly lust, they are eternally tormented by a ceaseless battery of violent storms.)

Cleopatra's elegy is, of course, highly subjective: the Antony she mourns as a military hero—cut off at the height of his power—has died ignominiously, discredited and defeated, a betrayer of honourable Roman values. However, having re-invented Antony, Cleopatra then prepares to join him, eventually acting out her own death in grand style.

Throughout the final scenes of the play, the language repeatedly defines death in terms of darkness and rest. 'Unarm, Eros, the long day's task is done,/ And we must sleep' is Antony's response to defeat. And this is echoed by Iras, Cleopatra's handmaiden, who is about to join her in a formal suicide: 'Finish, good lady, the bright day is done,/ And we are for the dark'. But Cleopatra intends to go in a blaze of glory. 'I am again for Cydnus/ To meet Mark Antony,' she says as she starts her theatrical exit:

> **Give me my robe, put on my crown, I have**
> **Immortal longings in me.** V.ii.280-1

'Husband, I come,' she continues, her death momentarily becoming a marriage ceremony. And then with the words 'I am fire and air,' she provides us with a last reminder of her association with those 'higher elements'.[3]

Surprisingly, perhaps, the death scene ends in a very different image, a gentle, maternal one:

> **Peace, peace!**
> **Dost thou not see my baby at my breast,**
> **That sucks the nurse asleep?** V.ii.308-10

---

3. It is only at her end that Cleopatra associates herself with the higher elements. Earlier in the play a succession of images connects her with 'earth' and 'water', the 'mud' of the Nile. First she tells us that Antony would refer to her as 'my serpent of old Nile'. Then, in the carousing scene on Pompey's barge, the drunken Lepidus maintains that 'your serpent of Egypt is bred now of your mud by the operation of your sun. So is your crocodile'. Finally, when Anthony is asked 'What manner of thing is your crocodile', his reply comically and ironically presages Cleopatra's end: 'It is shap'd, sir, like itself, and it is as broad as it hath breadth. It is just so high as it is, and it moves with its own organs. It lives by that which nourisheth it, and the elements once out of it, it transmigrates'.

Of course it is not a baby that is sucking her to sleep but an asp injecting her with poison. The rustic 'Clown', who provides the asps hidden in a basket of figs, has an extraordinary dialogue with Cleopatra, full of humour and sexual innuendo but also comfort, leaving her with a sort of blessing: 'I wish you joy o' th' worm'. Then, after her death it is the normally cold and unsentimental Octavius Caesar who provides the final image of Cleopatra:

> **She looks like sleep,**
> **As she would catch another Antony**
> **In her strong toil° of grace.**                   *net or snare*
>                                                            V.ii.346-8

This is a generous and beautiful tribute, seeming to establish Cleopatra, statue-like, for an eternity of grace.

Taken together these final images illustrate the complexity of Shakespeare's Cleopatra. In the words of Enobarbus: 'Age cannot wither her, nor custom stale/ Her infinite variety'.

### 🦉 ANSWERS TO 'SCAPES'

1. **(i)** bank   Oberon, A Midsummer Night's Dream, II.i.249-52
2. **(e)** heaven   Lorenzo, The Merchant of Venice, V.i.58-62
3. **(f)** land   Bishop of Carlisle, Richard II, IV.i.142-4
4. **(g)** town   Antipholus of Syracuse, The Comedy of Errors, I.ii.97-102
5. **(a)** water   Enobarbus, Antony and Cleopatra, II.ii.191-4
6. **(b)** isle   Caliban, The Tempest, III.ii.135-6
7. **(h)** blood   Macbeth, Macbeth, III.v.135-7
8. **(j)** world   Cassius, Julius Caesar, I.ii.135-8
9. **(d)** court   Richard, Richard II, III.ii.160-3
10. **(c)** bed   Hamlet, Hamlet, III.iv.91-4.

# Coriolanus

I saw him run after a gilded butterfly, and when he caught it, he
let it go again, and after it again, and over and over he comes,
and up again; catch'd it again: or whether his fall enrag'd him,
or how 'twas, he did so set his teeth and tear it. O, I warrant,
how he mammock'd° it!                                          *tore*

I.iii.60-65

This image comes from a scene which stands out from the rest of
*Coriolanus*. In a play that is notably masculine in its content, characters
and style, here is a scene given over to women in a very domestic setting.
It starts with a stage-direction for Volumnia and Virgilia, mother and
wife of Coriolanus, to 'set them down on two low stools, and sew'.
In contrast to the blank verse which dominates the play, the dialogue
here is mostly in a casual prose which is continued as Valeria, a visiting
friend, contributes this description of Coriolanus's young son at play. Her
repeated 'and', 'again' and then 'over and over' give a relaxed informality
to Valeria's anecdote, but set against this is the nature of the action being
described—a child tearing a butterfly to pieces. And instead of deploring
such viciousness, Volumnia, the ultimate Roman matriarch, comments
approvingly, 'one on's father's moods': she sees her grandson developing a
creditable likeness to his warrior father.

There is no trace of this scene in Plutarch's *Lives*, and it would seem
that Shakespeare has created the exchange to provide his audience with
an insight into both his hero and the society which has helped mould
him. As the action of the play unfolds, we learn that in the war-hero,
Coriolanus, there is much of the pampered child. In combat he is
completely without pity or fear; at home, faced with the need to show tact
and diplomacy, he is soon without control, raging intemperately when
crossed or challenged. He is no match for the Tribunes of the People, who
manipulate his moods in order to undo him. Banished and vengeful, he
joins forces with the Volsci, an enemy tribe, and prepares to 'mammock'
Rome and all its inhabitants.

The tragedy comes to a climax in a scene which once more features the women and the young boy; they have been sent to persuade Coriolanus to forego his revenge and spare the city. In a rare moment of tenderness, Coriolanus greets his wife: 'O, a kiss/ Long as my exile, sweet as my revenge!' Though this is passionate and lyrical, the fact that the sweetness of the kiss is measured in terms of revenge, gives an indication of Coriolanus's unbending resolve. He calls Virgilia his 'gentle silence'. However it is not her 'silence' but his mother's stern criticism which eventually persuades this Roman to sacrifice his sense of personal honour and to save Rome—but not himself.

# *Timon of Athens*

### This is it
**That makes the wappen'd° widow wed again;**     *sexually worn out*
**She, whom the spittle house and ulcerous sores**
**Would cast the gorge at, this embalms and spices**
**To th'April day again.**                 IV.iii.38-42

These lines (about 'gold') spoken by Timon, might be loosely paraphrased as follows:

> Gold makes remarriage possible, even for a widow so sexually worn-out that her looks (but for her wealth) would make the ulcer-ridden inhabitants of hospitals for the incurably diseased vomit uncontrollably. However, being wealthy, the gold (which should more properly be used to prepare her corpse for burial) works its alchemy on her so that her elderly body is preserved and perfumed to enable her to experience a second youthful wedding day.

At the start of the play we see Timon surrounded by sycophantic flatterers who revel in his lavish entertaining and his foolish, unselective generosity. When he discovers that his fortune has run out and that his 'friends' have deserted him, he becomes a misanthrope, retires to a cave and rails (again unselectively) against all mankind. In the scene from which the above lines are taken, Timon, while digging for roots outside his cave, discovers gold, ('yellow, glittering, precious gold') which he sees as a symbol of all that is worst in human nature and human society. It is a commodity which will make 'black, white; foul, fair; wrong, right; base, noble; old, young; coward, valiant'... This theme is developed graphically in the image of the 'wappen'd widow', an image which well illustrates both Timon's disgust in human sexuality and his new found delight in indulging in vitriolic, quasi-poetic invective.

Following his discovery, Timon returns to his giving vein, heaping gold and curses on all who visit him. The giving of gold to Alcibiades, a banished general, brings about the downfall of Athens, the city of Timon's birth.

*Timon of Athens* seems to be an unfinished play and there is evidence to suggest that Heminge and Condell, Shakespeare's first editors, did not initially intend to include it in the First Folio. Shakespeare apparently discovered the story of Timon while reading the section of Plutarch's *Lives* which inspired *Antony and Cleopatra*. It has been suggested that he abandoned writing *Timon* on realising that in *King Lear* he had already treated the theme of ingratitude with far greater subtlety.

## ANSWERS TO 'DO IT YOURSELF'

1. **King**   Richard, *Richard II*, III.ii.54-5
2. **lovers**   Chorus, *Romeo and Juliet*, Prologue, 5-6
3. **world**   Henry V, *Henry V*, IV.iii.57-9
4. **mirror**   Hamlet, *Hamlet*, III.ii.21-4
5. **dust**   Guiderius, *Cymbeline*, IV.ii.258-63
6. **sun**   Richard, *Richard III*, I.i.24-7
7. **baby**   Cleopatra, *Antony and Cleopatra*, V.ii.308-10
8. **heads**   Michael Williams, *Henry V*, IV.i.134-8
9. **eyes**   Gloucester, *King Lear*, IV.i.18-19
10. **cargo**   French Lord and Soldiers, *All's Well that Ends Well*, IV.i.65-6

# ENGLISH HISTORIES

Eight of these ten plays cover consecutive events, with a sense of cause and effect, so it seems a good idea to present them chronologically—not in the order in which they were written.

In *Richard II, Henry IV Parts 1 and 2* and *Henry V,* Shakespeare deals with abdication, usurpation and leading a country to war. These four plays share a theme (what makes a good king?) but Shakespeare, writing as a mature dramatist, gives each an individual style and tone. The three *Henry VI* plays and *Richard III* focus on the civil conflict (the Wars of the Roses) which followed the original usurpation and which is finally resolved in the accession of the Tudor King Henry VII. These four plays are remarkably similar, sharing both the strengths and the weaknesses of Shakespeare's early writing. The language and characterisation tend to be unsubtle but Shakespeare is already a genius at creating dramatic scenes. *Henry VIII* shows the triumph of the 'Tudor myth' (the idea that the Tudor dynasty had restored peace and unity to a kingdom ruined by almost 100 years of civil conflict)[1]. Despite its subject matter, it shares several of the theatrical qualities of Shakespeare's other late plays. *King John* belongs to a much earlier period of English history, but here again Shakespeare's focus is on the legitimacy of a king's rule and his effectiveness.

Shakespeare took most of his material from the 1587 edition of Holinshed's *Chronicles of England, Scotland and Ireland,* though he used other 16th century histories as well. He built up whole scenes and characters from the slightest hint and was happy to alter facts if this made a good dramatic point. The generally accepted dating of the English history plays is as follows:

| | |
|---|---|
| King John (1594) | Henry VI, Part 1 (1589) |
| Richard II (1595) | Henry VI, Part 2 (1590) |
| Henry IV, Part 1 (1596-7) | Henry VI, Part 3 (1591) |
| Henry IV, Part 2 (1598) | Richard III (1592) |
| Henry V (1599) | Henry VIII (1612-3) |

---

1. See 'Usurpation, The Wars of the Roses and the emergence of the Tudor line' on p.129

# King John

**Grief fills the room up of my absent child,**
**Lies in his bed, walks up and down with me,**
**Puts on his pretty looks, repeats his words,**
**Remembers me of all his gracious parts.** III.iv.93-6

These lines are spoken by Constance, mother to young Arthur, who, as the rightful heir to the English throne has been abducted by the usurper, King John. In all her other speeches Constance indulges in exaggerating her emotions, and just before she speaks these words she has been told that she seems as fond of grief as she is of her lost child. This accusation triggers a simple but profound reflection on the relationship between grief and loss. For just a moment, real feeling bursts into a play dominated by rather formal rhetoric. Constance's image of grief as a substitute for her lost son, reminding her of all his most treasured features, seems to be based on genuine experience.

Shakespeare chose to make the fate of young Arthur a central feature of the last two acts of the play. King John, believing that his hold on the English throne will be secure only when Arthur is dead, places the child in the care of one Hubert, who agrees to blind and murder him. However, the child's 'words', 'pretty looks' and 'gracious parts' awaken mercy in Hubert's cruel heart. He abandons the murder but sends word to King John to say that Arthur is dead and need no longer be feared. Arthur, in trying to escape, falls from the city's wall and dies. The English nobility are appalled at the news of Arthur's death and revolt against John's rule. Linking John's downfall directly to Arthur's death was a form of poetic licence, typical of Shakespeare's treatment of historical events. The real King John reigned on for thirteen years after the death of his young nephew.

A few editors and critics have sensed that Constance's meditation on grief is so authentic that it must have been based on Shakespeare's own experience. They have suggested that in writing these lines he was drawing on his own feelings after the death of his son, Hamnet, who died in 1596. Most, however, reject this as sentimental and argue that most of the text of *King John* is so laboured in style that it could not have been written at the same time as the eloquent *Richard II*, *Romeo and Juliet* and *A Midsummer Night's Dream*. Only Constance's lament and the vivid language in the scenes of King John's death (inwardly burning from poison and desperately begging 'cold comfort') indicate Shakespeare's future development.

# *Richard II*

**Not all the water in the rough rude sea**
**Can wash the balm off from an anointed King.**         III.ii.54-5

When he speaks these words, King Richard has just landed in Wales, following a tempestuous crossing of the Irish Sea. Having survived the 'rough rude sea', he is momentarily confident that, as the anointed King of England, he need not fear his rival, Bolingbroke, whom he dismisses as a 'thief', a robber baron. Given to indulging in hyperbole he supports his case by arguing that for every soldier 'press'd' by Bolingbroke, he, Richard, has 'a glorious angel' in his 'heavenly pay'. Such, he believes, is the potency of 'the balm' with which he was anointed when crowned as king.

Richard's confidence is short lived. Two messengers enter. The first tells of the defection of 'twenty thousand' Welshmen; the second describes in detail how throughout the whole of England young and old have joined the uprising and how his favourites have been executed. These 'tidings of calamity', provoke a poetic meditation on the precarious mortality of kings, culminating in one of Shakespeare's greatest and most complex images:

**For within the hollow crown**
**That rounds the mortal temples of a King**
**Keeps death his court, and there the antic sits,**
**Scoffing his state and grinning at his pomp.**         III.ii.160-3

The dying Gaunt had warned Richard that 'A thousand flatterers sit within thy crown', and now—hearing that his principal flatterers are dead—Richard imagines his crown as a space containing a King and his court. In a reversal of traditional order, this rival King is an 'antic'—a grotesque fool or jester. He mocks and grins, sneering at the apparatus of temporary earthly power. Shakespeare only used the word 'grinning' on two other occasions. Both grinners are dead, (the most haunting being Yorick, the Jester, whose skull prompts Hamlet's reflections on mortality)[1]. Here, in Richard's image, the grinner is King Death himself.

The 'antic' death is not the only powerful skull image in the play. Richard is soon to abdicate, and with his fall and the rise of Bolingbroke (crowned as Henry IV), comes one of the play's most memorable prophecies—a vision of the mayhem which will follow as a result of Bolingbroke's usurpation. The speaker is the Bishop of Carlisle:

**Disorder, horror, fear, and mutiny**
**Shall here inhabit, and this land be call'd**
**The field of Golgotha and dead men's skulls.**          IV.i.142-4

Golgotha was the Hebrew name for the hill on which Christ was crucified; it means 'place of skulls'. Shakespeare's audience would have known that this was no empty prophecy. The 'disorder, horror, fear and mutiny' to which Carlisle refers had been chronicled by Elizabethan historians, had been the subject of Shakespeare's early history plays and would be a feature of the *Henry IV* plays which follow *Richard II*. Carlisle is immediately arrested on a charge of treason, but the image of 'the field of Golgotha' remains to haunt Henry until his own death.

The reference to Golgotha is one of a number of biblical references in the play. Richard himself is quick to draw connections between his own deposition and Christ's passion. Was not Christ—God's original deputy on earth—tried and executed by earthly powers? But the analogy is audacious, characteristic of Richard's rhetorical daring. In the opening scenes of the play Shakespeare has shown him to be an incorrigible egoist,

---

1. The other grinner is Sir Walter Blunt, dead on the Shrewsbury battlefield in *Henry IV, Part 1*.

insensitive to the responsibilities of kingship and to the sufferings of others. In contrast Bolingbroke emerges as a strong, efficient leader of men.

Shakespeare's *Richard II* was first printed in quarto in 1597. In this version the actual scene of Richard's deposition is omitted. Clearly the censors felt that Queen Elizabeth would not approve of a play text which contained a scene showing the overthrow of an anointed monarch. Others were aware of the potential power of such a scene. In February 1601 Elizabeth was threatened by an insurrection led by her sometime favourite, the Earl of Essex. Friends of the Earl, in an attempt to stir up popular support, paid members of Shakespeare's company to put on a performance of *Richard II* which included the deposition scene. The insurrection failed. The actors were arrested but later released; Essex and some of his supporters were executed. It is reported that Queen Elizabeth, when reflecting on the incident, said: 'I am Richard II'.

# Henry IV, Part 1

**What a devil hast thou to do with the time of day? Unless hours were cups of sack, and minutes capons, and clocks the tongues of bawds, and dials the signs of leaping-houses°,** *brothels* **and the blessed sun himself a fair hot wench in flame-color'd taffata°.** *fabric often worn by prostitutes*
I.ii.6-10

With this light-hearted image, which parallels the measurement of time with a range of sensual pleasures, Falstaff, the greatest of all Shakespeare's comic creations, is introduced to the audience and the world. The speaker is Hal—Prince Henry—soon to become Henry V. Falstaff has been a surrogate father to Hal, introducing him to a world of perpetual adolescence—a world of irresponsible eating, drinking, whoring and—as the quotation eloquently demonstrates—a world of verbal play. The succession of 'and's' in the image emphasises the irresponsibility of

Falstaff's life-style, which seems here to be immune to cause and effect. In the previous scene the audience have been introduced to Hal's real father, King Henry IV (the Bolingbroke of *Richard II*). He is a man 'wan with care', ridden with guilt as the usurper of the throne, and now struggling with a kingdom on the brink of civil war. His cares are compounded by the knowledge that he is dying and that Hal, his heir, appears to be an egotistical young pleasure-seeker unfit for the responsibilities of kingship. But although Hal is about to become involved in one last escapade with Falstaff—a highway robbery at Gadshill—he is well aware of the responsibilities that lie ahead of him. He tells the audience, in an aside at the end of this scene, that his time of 'playing holidays' is about to end with a 'reformation' that will astound the world.

Much of the action in *Henry IV, Parts 1* and *2* charts Hal's reformation. The developing rift between himself and Falstaff becomes apparent when, in preparation for Hal's approaching interview with the King, the two entertain the occupants of the Boar's Head Tavern to a 'father and son' role-play. First Falstaff pretends to be the King and playfully advises Hal to strengthen his bond with that 'goodly portly man', the man of 'virtue', Falstaff. But when they exchange roles, and Hal begins to play his father, the tone changes:

**There is a devil haunts thee in the likeness of an old fat man**

II.iv.447-8

he says before launching into a vitriolic attack on Falstaff as a 'misleader of youth'. The language which follows is brutal. In striking contrast to the gaiety of the opening quotation, Hal elaborates on the appetites of the 'old fat man' and their consequences. In a crescendo of images he stresses Falstaff's physical grossness (referring to him as 'that huge bombard of sack' and 'that stuff'd cloak-bag of guts'), his crudely animal nature ('that bolting hutch of beastliness', 'that roasted Manningtree ox with the pudding in his belly') and his diseases ('that swoll'n parcel of dropsies'). The idea of Falstaff as a devil is further developed as Hal calls him 'that reverent Vice, that grey iniquity, that vanity in years'. The terms 'Vice', 'iniquity' and 'vanity' were all names for devil figures in mediaeval morality drama. Most morality plays had a character named or referred to as 'the

Vice', a composite of the seven deadly sins, who both entertained the audience and led the central figure ('Mankind' or 'Youth' or 'Everyman') astray. Clearly this is how King Henry sees Falstaff, a disastrous influence on his wayward son, but at this point in the role-play it becomes apparent that Hal is starting to speak and think not as his father but as himself, the future King of England.

Falstaff, who has been cast in the role-play as Hal, initially pretends to defend the 'old fat man' in Hal's voice. Then—perhaps sensing that when Hal does become King he will reject his Boar's Head companions—he, too, abandons the role-play. 'Banish' the others (Peto, Bardolph, Poins), he tells Hal, but don't banish me:

**Banish plump Jack, and banish all the world.**      II.iv.479-80

The term 'plump Jack' is endearingly jolly—in marked contrast to Hal's brutally insulting descriptions—and Falstaff's 'banish all the world' suggests that he sees himself not as the Vice, but as a mentor who has introduced Hal to a world of merry good-living of a kind which most princes could never experience. However, Hal's response is chillingly prophetic: 'I do, I will'.

Hal is about to undergo a reconciliation with his father and to immerse himself in a world of combat and valour (and real politics) appropriate for a Prince. The action of the play will move to the Battle of Shrewsbury, where Hal will be set against the young Henry Percy, known as 'Hotspur'. Shakespeare deliberately altered history by dropping this character down a generation, so that he could act as a dramatic rival and contrast to Hal. Though champion of the rebel forces, the charismatic Hotspur, a 'Mars in swathling clothes', is seen by Henry IV as an ideal son. It will be up to Hal to prove his father wrong.

# Henry IV, Part 2

**O polished perturbation, golden care!**
**That keep'st the ports of slumber open wide**
**To many a watchful night.**                          IV.v.23-5

These lines are spoken by Hal as he sits beside his dying father, his hard-won crown (the 'polished perturbation') beside him on the pillow. The Prince can see that the crown is a 'troublesome bedfellow', but has now accepted it as his destined right and responsibility. He is ready to listen to his father's guilty confidences on the 'by-paths and indirect crookt ways' which led to his acquiring the crown—not through 'divine right' but through an act of usurpation. He will also (as Henry V) profit from his father's experience. (The politically astute advice to 'busy giddy minds/ With foreign quarrels' has modern resonances.)

The second part of the *Henry IV* chronicle continues the subject matter of the previous play, but is very different in tone. It is altogether more subtle and is dominated by the King's melancholy, of which his wasting sickness seems to be a manifestation.

As King Henry seems to decay from within, Falstaff is gradually overtaken by age and his own excesses, but he continues, in this play, to be defiantly funny. As he says, 'I am not only witty in myself, but the cause that wit is in other men'. An example of such wit is provided by Hal as he spies on Falstaff fondling his whore, Doll Tearsheet:

**Saturn and Venus this year in conjunction.**            II.iv.263

Saturn, the planet of old age, represents Falstaff; Venus, the planet of Love, stands ironically for Doll Tearsheet. Henry and his companion provide a sneering commentary: 'Is it not strange that desire should so many years outlive performance?' But this merely throws into relief the humour and unexpected tenderness of the 'conjunction' they are witnessing. Doll refers to Falstaff as her 'whoreson little tidy Bartholomew boar-pig' and

Falstaff achieves an unusual level of honesty as he admits, 'I am old, I am old'.

Old age and the passing of time dominate a later section of the play when, recruiting soldiers, Falstaff visits Justice Shallow, an old acquaintance with jurisdiction over an obscurely rural part of Gloucestershire. (Shakespeare's deft, exquisitely atmospheric, depiction of country life in the Gloucestershire scenes is one of the glories of this play). Falstaff's arrival triggers in Shallow a stream of recollections of their long-vanished 'madcap' student days.

### We have heard the chimes at midnight, Master Shallow.

III.ii.214-5

Falstaff's twelve-syllabled reply seems to chime with Shallow's recollections as, momentarily, the two old men engage in reverie, recalling long dead acquaintances. But Falstaff soon distances himself from the pervading mood of nostalgia. 'How subject we old men are to this vice of lying,' he says to the audience, when Shallow departs, and he proceeds to tell them of his plan to help himself to a share of Shallow's wealth.

Believing that Falstaff will hold high office when Hal becomes King, Shallow is generous with his time and money. With news of the old King's death he joins Falstaff in a dash to London. But following Hal's coronation both are to be disappointed. Falstaff's eager and confident greeting gets a simple but chilling answer: 'I know thee not, old man, fall to thy prayers.' These are Henry V's words as he crushingly dismisses his old companion. It is one of Shakespeare's great dramatic scenes, leaving us impossibly torn in our sympathies. At one level it is a great betrayal of friendship. But we know that Falstaff, despite his vitality, is no fit companion for a king.

# Henry V

**But if the cause be not good, the King himself hath a heavy
reckoning to make, when all those legs and arms, and heads,
chopp'd off in a battle, shall join together at the latter day and
cry all, "We died at such a place".**                    IV.i.134-8

It is the night before the battle of Agincourt. The speaker is
Michael Williams, a common soldier who, fearing his imminent death,
contemplates the Last Judgement ('the latter day'). The simplicity of the
prose accentuates the power of this image—a vision of the mutilated
war dead reassembling their bodies and facing the architect of their
destruction: the King. The lines echo down the ages as a terrible warning
to any Christian leader who commits his or her troops to fight in an unjust
war. Unknown to Williams, the disguised King Henry is moving among
his troops and listens to his rumination. 'If the cause be not good…?'.
The audience will remember the second scene of the play in which the
Archbishop of Canterbury attempts to justify Henry's invasion of France
in a dense and convoluted argument, linking French and English history
to Salique law. 'May I with right and conscience make this claim?' Henry
had asked—impatient with the prolixity of the Archbishop's case. 'The
sin upon my head', his spiritual adviser had replied. But now, with the
odds of battle seemingly against him, Henry is forced to reconsider
'the cause'. 'Upon the King…' he says, echoing Williams's words, as he
soliloquizes first on the cares and responsibility of kingship and then on
the uncertainty of his claim—not just to France, but also to the English
throne.

But the Henry who addresses his troops in the scene which follows,
shows no signs of inner turmoil or guilt. He builds from the day's date,
the Feast of St Crispian (October 25), picturing its future significance:

**And Crispin Crispian shall ne'er go by,
From this day to the ending of the world,
But we in it shall be remembered.**                    IV.iii.57-9

With their soaring iambic beat Henry's lines build a triumphant vision, promising the soldiers their own chance of immortality. The rhetoric is all-inclusive as he offers to share his nobility with those who fight beside him: 'He today that sheds his blood with me/ Shall be my brother'. What a transformation, as time and memory in this world are foregrounded and the walking judgmental dead of Michael Williams' nightmare become instead, 'We few, we happy few, we band of brothers!'

In the scenes which follow, anxiety over the justness of the cause gives way to jubilation as the French are vanquished. 'God fought for us,' Henry reminds his loyal Welsh officer, Fluellen, who has already initiated the mythologizing of his leader, comparing him to Alexander the Great and interpreting even his most dubious of actions, the killing of all French prisoners, as a deed of honourable revenge.

*Henry V* remains Shakespeare's most probing analysis of the ethics of war. It is also distinctive as his most probing exploration of the nature of the Elizabethan stage.

**O for a Muse of fire, that would ascend**
**The brightest heaven of invention!**                    Prologue, 1-2

The play starts with these declamatory lines, the Chorus calling for an inspiration that would offer the audience an appropriately realistic image of kings and battles. However, in the great tradition of rhetoric, this is a feigned apology and as the Chorus continues it calls on the audience to assist in the imaginative process by working to make up for the absent reality. When the Chorus says

**Think, when we talk of horses, that you see them**
**Printing their proud hoofs i'th' receiving earth**

                                        Prologue, 36-7

the words instantly create the required heroic image of horses and hooves in the mind of any spectator prepared to 'imagine'. Given the shared endeavour of playwright and audience, the 'rules' of realistic drama (the Unities of Time and Place) can be ignored as the action quickly moves from the war preparations in England (where 'They sell the pasture now to buy the horse') to the confrontations in France.

On the night before the climactic Battle of Agincourt, it is the conjuring of the Chorus that gives the words of Michael Williams their authenticity. We are asked to picture the plight of 'the poor condemned English' as, camped within earshot of the enemy, they wait for the light of dawn. The visual inadequacies of a stage become irrelevant as the Chorus creates the night-time atmosphere through an image which enacts the very sounds it is describing:

> **Steed threatens steed, in high and boastful neighs**
> **Piercing the night's dull ear; and from the tents**
> **The armourers, accomplishing the knights,**
> **With busy hammers closing rivets up,**
> **Give dreadful note of preparation.**
>
> Act IV, Chorus, 10-14

The Chorus's yearning for 'a muse of fire' was to be realised with the coming of the cinema and there have been a number of attempts to film the play. Two of the more successful have taken very different views of *Henry V*'s central 'message'. Laurence Olivier's film, made during World War II, captured Britain's mood of purposeful patriotism and—with a few deft textual omissions—celebrated Henry as an ideal leader fighting for an heroic cause. Kenneth Branagh's film, made in the aftermath of Britain's defence of the Falklands, reflected an altogether more sceptical and troubled response to war. Shakespeare allows for both interpretations. In Nicholas Hytner's 2003 production at London's National Theatre, it was the war in Iraq which seemed most relevant.

## ANSWERS TO 'PLAUSIBLE MISPRINTS'

1. **brave** for 'grave'   Miranda, *The Tempest*, V.i.183-4
2. **shadows** for 'sadshows'   Theseus, *A Midusmmer Night's Dream*, V.i.211
3. **harsh** for 'hash',   Don Adriano de Armado, *Love's Labour's Lost*, V.ii.930-1
4. **haunts** for 'hunts'   Hal, *Henry IV, Part 1*, II.iv.447-8
5. **chastity** for 'charity'   Isabella, *Measure for Measure*, II.iv.185
6. **Saturn** for Satan   Hal, *Henry IV, Part 2*, II.iv.263
7. **reigns** for 'reins'   Autolycus, *The Winter's Tale*, IV.iii.4
8. **chimes** for 'crimes'   Falstaff, *Henry IV, Part 2*, III.ii.214-5
9. **Banish** for 'Bash'   Falstaff, *Henry IV, Part 1*, II.iv.479-80
10. **string** for 'spring'   Ulysses, *Troilus and Cressida*, I.iii.109-10

---

122

# Henry VI, Part 1

**Civil dissension is a viperous worm**
**That gnaws the bowels of the commonwealth.**   III.i.72-3

The speaker is the young King Henry, lamenting the fact that his two mighty uncles, Gloucester (the Protector) and Winchester (the Cardinal) cannot be at peace together. Henry voices here the theme that is at the heart of all the plays which Shakespeare subsequently wrote on the subject of pre-Tudor history. The phrase 'civil dissension' is abstract and aloof-sounding but what follows in the quotation is very forceful and direct. The 'worm' at the centre of the image is 'viperous'—a poisonous snake, which recalls the original evil of the Biblical serpent. But it is also a disgusting maggot in the gut, the verb 'gnaws' having a particularly visceral nastiness.

This play shows how rivalry between the Yorkists and Lancastrians erupted into the Wars of the Roses and the loss of England's territories in France. The English hero, Talbot ('Terror of the French') is matched by

Joan 'La Pucelle' (Joan of Arc). Although Talbot fights with exemplary heroism, he ends up as a corpse on the stage, dismissed by Joan as 'stinking and fly-blown'. In fact there is a succession of brave English lords who die on stage, most of them betrayed in some way by the 'civil dissension' which has spread throughout the ranks of the nobility.

# Henry VI, Part 2

**I charge and command that, of the city's cost, the pissing conduit run nothing but claret wine this first year of our reign.** IV.vi.2-4

This is Jack Cade speaking. He leads a group of rebellious commoners who take advantage of the disorder that prevails when the nobility are fighting each other. As Cade's uprising approaches London, Shakespeare highlights its brutal anarchy, but there is also plenty of humour. (Is the Butcher's excited 'The first thing we do, let's kill all the lawyers!' frightening or funny?) In the Jack Cade scenes verse turns to prose and the earthy language and characters give a solid base as well as a contrast to the warring nobility with their high-flown, declamatory style.

Elsewhere in the play the feud between Gloucester and Winchester, powerful uncles to the weak Henry VI, climaxes in two extraordinarily vivid death-scenes. Gruesome deaths, like comic episodes and characters, were a sure-fire ingredient of popular Elizabethan drama and Shakespeare shows in this play that he can do both. No wonder that his contemporary playwright, Robert Greene, was stung into taunting that young Shakespeare was 'in his own conceit, the only Shake-scene in the country'.

# Henry VI, Part 3

**Come, make him stand upon this molehill here
That raught° at mountains with outstretched arm.**           *grasped*

I.iv.67-8

The power of this image springs from the nature of the Elizabethan stage and Shakespeare's use of it, as much as from the words. The speaker is Henry's queen, Margaret, and the 'him' refers to Richard of York, whose steady rise through *Part 2* is about to be terminated. In the first scene of this play York had deliberately elevated himself, literally mounting the throne and challenging the King. Now Queen Margaret subjects York to her revenge. Shakespeare's imagination gives it a subtle resonance. The Elizabethan stage, without scenery, was basically a neutral area for action; props or stage furniture were used sparingly, but with deliberate, often symbolic, effect. In this play a small dais, placed centrally at the back of the stage, would have served for both the State (a raised platform with throne, signifying royal authority) and the molehill. So when the Queen orders York to be placed on 'this molehill' and has a crown mockingly placed upon his head, she is demonstrating the consequences of his ambition: he aspired to the mountain but ends up with a molehill.

But the molehill / throne idea does not end here. Later in the play poor Henry humbly sits himself on 'this molehill' when his Queen and other Lords want him out of the way as they indulge in another bloodthirsty battle. As he reflects on the random hazards of civil war and his own inadequacy as a king, Shakespeare's stage-directions set up a striking group image:

> Enter a Son that hath killed his father, at one door.... Enter a Father that hath killed his son, at another door.

As the bereaved Son and Father separately lament their loss, the central figure of the King acknowledges his failure and we see him at the apex of the triangle, seeming to preside over the savage consequences of civil war.

It makes a profoundly ironic and powerful tableau and is a good emblem of Shakespeare's achievement in this trilogy of plays.

# Richard III

**Why, I, in this weak, piping time of peace,**
**Have no delight to pass away the time,**
**Unless to spy my shadow in the sun,**
**And descant on mine own deformity.**                     I.i.24-7

This image forms a part of Shakespeare's virtuoso opening to the play, a soliloquy by Richard of Gloucester, later to become the monstrous King Richard III of historical myth. Richard's resentment is triggered by the period of peace which has been established since the civil battles of Henry VI's reign. Now the Yorkists, under the rule of Edward IV, Richard's oldest brother, are firmly in power. But ambitious Richard, who flourished as a bold and ruthless soldier, scorns 'this weak, piping time of peace'. Throughout the soliloquy there is a sustained musical metaphor: Richard imagines himself giving an ironic 'descant' to the melodies of peacetime, a descant which, through savage alliteration, is paired with his 'deformity'. Richard's hunch-back shape inspires another sustained metaphor, a visual one. Earlier in the soliloquy he has described himself as not made 'to court an amorous looking-glass' and here he pictures a self-mocking alternative—'to spy my shadow in the sun'. The sun, adopted as a Yorkist heraldic emblem, provides the sneering pun with which Richard opened the soliloquy and the play: 'Now is the winter of our discontent/ Made glorious summer by this son of York'. At the end of the next scene (having successfully wooed the widow of the prince whom he has murdered!) Richard will twist the image again in a moment of wry self-congratulation: 'Shine out, fair sun, till I have bought a glass/ That I may see my shadow as I pass'.

Richard blames his wickedness on his deformity. 'Therefore', he says, 'since I cannot prove a lover… I am determined to prove myself a villain'.

The Elizabethan 'determined' could be passive as well as active, the idea being that destiny, in the form of deformity, had made Richard's villainy inevitable. The irony in Richard's theory is that he can and does 'prove a lover', not least in making himself attractive to the theatre audience. His witty, sardonic personality ensures that we enjoy following his fortunes, through a remorseless succession of murders, right up to the climax at Bosworth. On the eve of the battle, Richard is visited in turn by the ghosts of eleven of his victims (including the two 'princes in the tower'), each one cursing him to 'Despair and die!'. However when Richard is finally hacked down, after the last despairing cry of 'My kingdom for a horse!', we surely, if perversely, wish that someone had provided a trusty steed to whisk him away from the battlefield. But of course Richmond, the dull but virtuous adversary, has to win; he will be crowned as Henry VII and the houses of York and Lancaster will be united under the single Tudor rose.

# Henry VIII

**Had I but serv'd my God with half the zeal
I serv'd my king, He would not in mine age
Have left me naked to mine enemies.**                    III.ii.445-7

On hearing from his enemies that Henry VIII has deprived him of his office and his lands, Cardinal Wolsey delivers this memorable epitaph on himself. The sentiment is moving—but, in a play subtitled 'All is True', how true are Wolsey's words? According to the subversive chattering of his many enemies, a major part of Wolsey's 'zeal' has been for his own ends rather than the King's. It is rumoured that he has spent money lavishly to further his own career and that he has been ruthless in his destruction of anyone who stands in the way of his ambition. His first entrance is appropriately symbolic: Enter 'CARDINAL WOLSEY the purse born before him.' 'The Purse' contains 'the Great Seal'—the outward sign of Wolsey's office as chancellor. It soon becomes clear that Wolsey controls the purse strings of the nation and that he spends lavishly for both the King's glory and his own advancement. Shortly before his fall, we—with King Henry—learn that he has sent great sums of money to Rome in an attempt to obtain for himself 'the popedom'.

For the first three acts of the play, whether on or off the stage, Wolsey dominates the action, manipulating the lives of all around him. The Duke of Norfolk, in conversation with the Duke of Buckingham, compares him to a great spider that, lacking 'ancestry', creates his web out of his inner being. Almost immediately Buckingham is trapped in the web, tried and executed for high treason, a charge orchestrated against him by the Cardinal. The next to fall is Katherine, Henry's first wife. According to the gossip of his enemies, Wolsey is behind the divorce proceedings, planning that Henry, once separated, should marry the French King's sister. This strategic marriage contributes to Wolsey's eventual downfall, King Henry finding the alternative allure of Anne Boleyn irresistible. 'All my glories in that one woman I have lost forever,' says the Cardinal on discovering that, while he was planning the French alliance, the King had secretly married Anne.

Wolsey is a sufficiently complex and interesting character to make him a proper subject for a tragedy. But with his death at the end of the third act, the play seems to lose its dramatic centre. In acts four and five he is almost forgotten as the action centres on the saintly death of Queen Katherine, the rise of Cranmer as Henry's new favourite and the birth of Queen Elizabeth. Critics have argued that *King Henry VIII* should be regarded as a collaboration between Shakespeare and another—probably John Fletcher—and that the disunity results from a lack of clear purpose. Others have attempted to justify the shift in action by suggesting that the play combines history with the spirit of the 'romances' written in the same period—moving from imminent tragedy into a mood of reconciliation. And as in these other late plays there is considerable interest in pageantry. *Henry VIII* abounds in scenes of visual splendour, showing as much as telling the story of the events which lead to the birth of Elizabeth and the emergence of a protestant England. And it was this concern with realistic show which was to lead, very dramatically, to the destruction of the Globe Theatre and the ending of the greatest episode in the history of the English stage.

Though Shakespeare's life as a whole is sparsely documented, there are a number of vivid accounts of the ending of the Globe. It happened at a performance of *Henry VIII* presented on June 29, 1613. In the scene in which Wolsey's dinner party is gate-crashed by a group of masquers led by the pleasure-loving King, the stage-direction announcing the arrival of the royal party reads: 'Drum and trumpets; chambers discharg'd'. Sir Henry Wooton, a famous ambassador, present at the final performance, described what happened in a letter to a friend:

> Now, King Henry making masque at the Cardinal Wolsey's house, and certain chambers being shot off at this entry, some of the paper or other stuff wherewith one of them was stopped did light on thatch, where being thought at first but an idle smoke, and their eyes more attentive on the show, it kindled inwardly, and ran round like a train, consuming within less than an hour the whole house to the very grounds.

Fortunately for the audience there was no loss of life. Fortunately for Shakespeare and the other shareholders in the King's Men their stock of costumes was hardly damaged. Fortunately for posterity, the company's stock of plays also survived, enabling two of Shakespeare's fellow actor/shareholders to publish, some years after Shakespeare's death, the Shakespeare First Folio. Had the fire consumed the company's theatrical manuscripts, twenty of Shakespeare's plays (those not printed during his lifetime and including *Macbeth* and *The Tempest*) would have been lost forever in the fire.

# Usurpation, the Wars of the Roses and the emergence of the Tudor line

The background to Shakespeare's two historical tetralogies is very complicated. What follows is intended to provide the reader with an outline of the problems of succession which ensued following the usurpation and murder of King Richard II—a period of uncertainty which ended with the emergence of the Tudor line.

King Edward III died in 1377, having fathered seven sons. Each son was given a dukedom—the first dukedoms in English history. The descendents of four of these dukes were, directly or indirectly, caught up in power struggles which were to divide England until the coronation of Henry VII in 1485.

After Edward III's death it was a grandson, Richard II, who succeeded him. Richard's inadequacies eventually alienated most of his family and his subjects, leading to usurpation by his cousin, Henry Bolingbroke—son of John of Gaunt, the first Duke of Lancaster. Under Bolingbroke (crowned as Henry IV) and his eldest son Hal (crowned as Henry V) England experienced a period of relative peace. However Henry V's son, crowned Henry VI in infancy, was never strong enough to become a convincing ruler. He had no heir, but even during his lifetime his rule was challenged by the Duke of York, directly descended from Edward III's fourth son.

The Wars of the Roses were fought between the houses of Lancaster and York. Following Henry VI's forced abdication in 1461, England was ruled by two Yorkist kings, Edward IV and Richard III. Then, after the overthrow and death of Richard III, Henry Tudor was crowned as Henry VII, bringing to an end the rivalries between Lancaster and York. (Though traces of the rivalry remain in cricket matches between Lancashire and Yorkshire, whose emblems are the red and white roses.)

Henry Tudor's claim to the throne was in some ways more tenuous than those of his predecessors. His great-grandfather had been an illegitimate son of John of Gaunt's mistress, Katharine Swynford. Though shortly before his death, John of Gaunt had married Katharine, under a law passed by Henry IV the off-spring of this liaison were banned from succession. By marrying Elizabeth, King Edward IV's daughter, the emergence of the Tudor Line brought together the houses of Lancaster and York and brought to an end the long period of civil war in England. Henry Tudor's son, Henry VIII, was the father of Elizabeth I, whose mother Anne Boleyn was the most famous of Henry VIII's six wives.

# What do we mean by a Shakespearean image?

Traditionally the image has been seen as an essential element of poetic language. An image might take the form of a direct, vivid description ('Light thickens and the crow/ Makes wing to the rooky wood') or a striking comparison, in the form of either a simile ('Pity, like a naked new born babe') or a metaphor ('Life's but a walking shadow'). In literary criticism the term imagery has been extended to cover not only mental pictures but also any use of language which appeals directly to the senses, and not just similes and metaphors but a host of other poetic devices, including rhythm, onomatopoeia and assonance. Central to all these aspects of 'the image' is the transformation of abstract ideas into concrete, vivid, sensory experience.

In Shakespearean drama images are often used to establish setting and atmosphere without resource to props, backdrops or lighting ('Look how the floor of heaven/Is thick inlaid with patens of bright gold'). And staging is an important non-verbal aspect of all of his images. Sometimes, as in the framing of Hamlet's encounter with Yorick, the tableau which Shakespeare creates is as memorable as the language: an actor, possibly dressed in black, making a direct address to a skull in a graveyard.

Several commentators have seen Shakespeare's use of images as the key to his plays, noting how meaning' is often conveyed through an accumulation of images which illustrate the abstract ideas at the heart of each play (light versus darkness in *Romeo and Juliet*, disease and corruption in *Hamlet*, etc.) This book builds on this tradition by relating individual images to plot, character and theme.

# Shakespeare's texts

It would seem that Shakespeare, though he took care to see that his poems were carefully printed, was indifferent to the preservation of the texts of his plays. During his life-time seventeen of his plays were printed as single editions (in Quarto format.) Some of these editions were intended to replace pirated versions of the plays (now called Bad Quartos). Others may have been printed to raise money for his company. In 1623, some years after Shakespeare's death, thanks to the labours of two of his fellow actors, Heminge and Condell, the Shakespeare First Folio was printed. This publication included all the plays discussed in this book, with the exception of *Pericles*.

The terms 'Quarto' and 'Folio' refer to book size. Elizabethan and Jacobean printers printed all their books from a standard size of paper. Each sheet in a quarto was folded twice to form four leaves, or eight pages. The much larger folio format was constructed from sheets folded only once, forming two leaves, or four pages.

In keeping with editorial tradition, the text in this book is eclectic, drawing on both Folio and Quartos. The line numbering follows *The Riverside Shakespeare*.

# Postscript

This book had its genesis at a re-union party hosted by a recently re-married friend where we met a number of old acquaintances whom we hadn't seen for over thirty years. We came away with two strong impressions. The first was of Time as a wicked cartoonist who had transformed most of the guests into parodies of their younger selves. Gone was the flush of youth, the brightness of the eye, the lustre of the hair—where hair remained. In their place were double-chins, expanding bellies, deepening wrinkles—and a general sense of well-to-do greyness. The second impression was of the Glittering Prizes which, for many, seemed a compensation for lost youth. There were people with status, titles, dutiful offspring, valuable houses... And, of course, our hostess had a second husband who, though not himself decorative, had on retirement become something of an art collector. During the course of the evening, he introduced us to some of the jewels of his collection. All, he assured us, had been excellent investments—the glitter of his potential profit seeming to shine more brightly in his eyes than the beauty of the images themselves.

As we drove home we converted our envy into thinking of the riches we had amassed through years of reading and teaching literature and we began to discuss the differences in 'value' between visual and literary images. Why should a Turner water colour be worth a million or more pounds, while Wordsworth's 'Lines Composed Upon Westminster Bridge' can be 'owned' and enjoyed by any educated reader? Why is a Van Gogh 'Sunflower' more valuable than William Blake's? The next day we started to take stock of 'our collection', making a list of favourite short poems. Then we moved onto Shakespeare. What would one pay to be the sole owner of a single line like 'Thou art as wise as thou art beautiful'? When we started to collect together one hundred of our favourite images, the idea of this book was born—and the arguments began. By deciding to include at least one image from every play, and no more than six from any single work, our choices became more restricted. For weeks we read and re-read the plays, surprised, despite the wrangling, at the high correlation in our choices. Initially we had intended to introduce the images in a simple quiz form—'who said?' and 'in what play?'. We soon realised that a quiz like this would become tedious and the book's current format, based on categories and word-games, emerged.

Our next problem centred on the title. 'Discovering Shakespeare' seemed too bland. 'Brush up your Shakespeare' had an earlier claimant. Eventually we settled on 'Shakespeare's 100 Greatest Dramatic Images'. The title is, of course, provocative, so we are linking the book to a website in order to open the concept of 'the greatest' to discussion. If you are irritated by our selection, or by any part of it, or if you sense that we have overlooked some images of great power, log onto **www.shakespearesgreatestimages.co.uk**. Here you will find a selection of favourite images chosen by some notable figures from the worlds of literature and the theatre and you will be able to take issue with our choices and add suggestions of your own.

# Join us in Shakespeare's Greatest Images

The book's website **www.shakespearesgreatestimages.co.uk** invites readers to post their own favourite image.

The site features contributions from well-known actors, directors, poets and authors including:

* *Actors and directors:* Sam West, Sarah Badel, Dame Judi Dench, Patrick Garland

* *Poets:* Andrew Motion, Brian Patten, Vicki Feaver, Maggie Sawkins, Hugh Dunkerley

* *Authors:* A.S. Byatt, Alison MacLeod, Bethan Roberts, Brian Martin, Linda Cookson

Write to **info@shakespearesgreatestimages.co.uk** and contribute a favourite image to our 'Other Voices' section, ideally with a sentence or two explaining your choice and a few words about yourself.

Would you like to comment on our 'Top Ten'? If so, please let us know your favourite and your least favourite image from our chosen ten.

.

*The
Divorced
Woman's
Guide
to Meeting
New Men*

# The
# Divorced
# Woman's
# Guide
# to Meeting
# New Men

## ERIC WEBER

*William Morrow and Company, Inc.*
*New York    1984*

Copyright © 1984 by Eric Weber

All rights reserved. No part of this book may be reproduced
or utilized in any form or by any means, electronic or mechanical,
including photocopying, recording or by any information storage
and retrieval system, without permission in writing from the
Publisher. Inquiries should be addressed to William Morrow and
Company, Inc., 105 Madison Avenue, New York, N.Y. 10016.

Library of Congress Cataloging in Publication Data

Weber, Eric, 1942–
   The Divorced woman's guide to meeting new men.

   1. Dating (Social customs)   2. Divorced women—
Psychology.   3. Men—Psychology.   I. Title.
HQ801.W58   1983        646,77        83-742
ISBN 0-688-01841-6

Printed in the United States of America

First Edition

1 2 3 4 5 6 7 8 9 10

BOOK DESIGN BY PATTY LOWY

## Contents

# Introduction

This is a practical book.

It shows you how to meet men—not so much by inspiring you, but by providing you with well over one hundred tangible, practical, *executable* techniques for bringing more men into your life.

You will discover, I think, that nearly all of these techniques have a simple, modest quality about them, that they seem more like baby steps than giant steps. There is a reason for that. It's easy for me to tell you to glide over to a man at a discotheque and ask him to dance. It's much less easy for you to walk all the way across the dance floor and go ahead and do it. I think far too many how-to books follow a tried-and-tired formula that ultimately proves of little help: Pump up the reader with hollow confidence through an inspiring pep talk, then ask her to scale the mountain.

The only problem is, scaling mountains is hard work. A quarter of the way up, you can find yourself running out of energy, courage, and confidence. And, unfortunately, the kind of "how to" book I've just described rarely shows you how to climb higher, or even how to let yourself back down gracefully and comfortably, without feeling an overwhelming sense of defeat.

No, my strategy isn't to stoke you up with a lot of hype so that you go rushing through the front doorway to tackle the first passing man and wrestle him to the ground, only to leave you embarrassed and unsure about what to do next. Instead, I'll show you places to go where men are likely to outnumber women two or three or even ten to one, how to draw these men into conversation with a light, casual, subtle approach, how to employ your friends, your family, even your children to aid and abet your social life, how to keep going when you're feeling miserable about your chances and yourself, how to make the most of when you're up and having a good-looking day, and basically how to people your life with such a multitude of men that sooner or later one or three or even a dozen begin to take a real shine to you.

Be aware of this. Any divorced or separated or widowed woman can dance with, date, become engaged to, and marry men a second or third or fifth or even twentieth time. All she needs is the right program. And I think the one contained herein is *it*. It's easy to understand, easy to follow, easy to execute, and rarely asks you to try something that is not now, or may never be, an act that you feel comfortable with. My experience has been that although courage is a trait we all thrill to in books and movies, the truth is, it's found in short supply among real people. I don't mean that as a criticism. Millions of kind, smart, attractive, charming, entertaining, and accomplished men and women are about as courageous as deer, myself—much more often than I'd like—being one of them.

And so instead of pretending that it's the easiest thing

in the world to call up a strange man to ask him over to your place for dinner (if you can do that, so much the better), I'll show you alternate ways to get him into your living room— ways that don't make you giddy with fear or terrified of rejection, but which can be every bit as effective as a more frontal approach.

In short, the aim of this book is to show you how to meet men without asking you to try feats that may feel dangerously beyond your present strengths and talents. I think that we'll all have a lot more fun and success if we work with you as you really are, rather than pretend that with a little bit of nurturing all women can be as forward as Scarlett O'Hara. What is depicted in a novel rarely works as smoothly as when it's tried in real life. But I'm confident that what I suggest in this book will work like Gangbusters in real life. So let's begin.

# The Divorced Woman's Guide to Meeting New Men

# CHAPTER 1

## First
## a Word About
## Men

Every Sunday morning at 10:00 A.M. I play in a touch football game. There are about a dozen of us, give or take a fellow or two. We are architects, policemen, dentists, doctors, brokers, lawyers, businessmen, and a writer. A few of the guys are single, a few of them divorced.

Our ages range from about twenty-five to forty-five. And although we have our share of bald spots, paunches, wrinkles, and sags, by and large we are not an unattractive group. If you walked into a dinner party and saw us sitting around the table, you'd probably think, *H'mm, not bad. There are two or three men here I could get interested in.*

I've got news for you. Two or three of the men in my touch football game, and possibly a whole lot more, could get interested in you, too.

Oh, I know what some of you are thinking. *No, no, not*

*in me they couldn't. I'm too chubby, too old, too tall, too short, too quiet, too dependent, too depressed, too chatty.* I've heard 'em all, every excuse in the book.

But you know something? Men don't really care if you're far from perfect. You see, men like women. Men need women. Men want women, women just like you.

I'll let you in on a little secret. Men aren't all they're cracked up to be. They're strong, but only sometimes. They're brave, but only rarely. They're loners who really need somebody. They never cry, except when they do.

The point is, for every James Bond, for every man who's got it knocked, there are nine or ninety-nine who are frail, self-effacing, lonely, and longing for companionship. Women, I know, make the same mistake men do. They take one look at the opposite sex, focus in on an ideal, someone who is perfectly attractive, self-sufficient, sought after, and thus highly choosy, and come to the conclusion that all others of that gender are equally blessed except for a few pathetic stragglers no one wants anyway.

You, of course, know that for every Catherine Deneuve there are dozens of Rhodas, Brendas, and spinsterish Aunt Matildas. Understand that the great body of men is equally unsure of itself in love. Men come in all different shapes and sizes, and almost all of them are looking for acceptance and warmth, for someone to love them. When a man heads out for a party or dance, his mind-set is probably a lot closer to *I hope somebody likes me* than it is to *I'm going after the best-looking dame in the joint.*

I tell you all this because I want you to know how much power you have over men, how important it is that you like us, how blessed and secure it makes us feel.

If you've been viewing the opposite sex as nothing but a bunch of lecherous, loveless cads who couldn't care less if you like them or not, because there are hundreds more just like you, you've been misreading us, the vast majority of us, anyway. For beneath our swaggering, *macho* exterior we're often as confused and as lonely, as hungry for companionship as you are. I think if you know that, perhaps you'll feel a little more confident and daring the next time you find yourself among a group of men.

Consider what happens when a lone woman, even a perfectly ordinary woman, even a woman accompanied by another man, enters a pub that for the past several hours has been occupied only by men. A wave of electricity passes through the assemblage. The men sit up straight, pat their hair, smile at the woman. Just by entering the room she has brought a touch of glamour, of romance, of possibility to the night.

Without her, the bar was dark, spiritless. In an instant she has transformed it into a veritable *boîte de nuit*, a night spot, simply because she is there and she is a woman.

Women tell me the same thing happens when a man takes a cooking course or shows up at a beauty parlor. His mere presence excites and enlivens the women who are about.

Well, you have as much power among men as that one man has among women. Remember that the next time you're wondering about your chances of ever finding a new man. Men are attracted to the female sex as strongly as to individual members of it.

Helen Reddy's song "I Am Woman, I Can Do Anything" may be a bit of an overstatement, but not much.

# Going Public

My first advice to you is simple: Go public. It's easy after a divorce to get into the habit of staying home watching sitcoms, knitting, or reading every night. But it's also disastrous for your social life. Even if you don't meet men right away, getting back into the world and *mingling* will vastly improve your chances.

I'm not saying you should rush right out to a singles bar (unless, of course, you're in the mood). Just take a few easy steps at first. If you like reading, take your book to the library, park, or beach. If you exercise at home, why not take an exercise class? Any hobby you enjoy at home can be done in public. Join a chess club, a church choir, a rock-gardening society.

Once out of the house, you'll meet men in the unlikeliest places, as Sandy, a twenty-seven-year-old divorced woman in Worcester, Massachusetts, discovered. "I really dislike tennis, jogging, and most other sports," Sandy says. "And once Ted and I split, all the couples who'd been our friends drifted away. I guess they felt uneasy asking only me out—as if they were taking sides." Finally, just to escape home on lonely weekends, Sandy volunteered to work for a charity that helps senior citizens.

"I really wasn't planning on meeting anyone," Sandy relates. "I thought all the men I'd meet would be at least seventy and have to be spoon-fed! But one Saturday I had to take Mrs. Muro grocery shopping and when we pulled into the driveway coming back I saw this man trimming Mrs. Muro's hedge. After carrying Mrs. Muro's groceries inside, I came back to my car and the man was near the garage, trimming the hedge just a few steps from me. He was about my age, and he was no Adonis. But he had his shirt off, and his muscles, damp with a slight perspiration from the heat, glistened in that sexy way men look when they're a little disheveled. I said something trivial like 'Hot day, huh?' and he stopped to talk a while. He told me his name was Burl and he owned a Venetian blind company. I thought he was attracted to me (as I was to him), but neither of us could find the right words, so I left.

"But the next Saturday, when I came to help Mrs. Muro, there was Burl mowing her lawn. And the Saturday after that, I took Mrs. Muro to the doctor's, and he took down her storm windows. As the weeks passed, Burl and I got friendlier and more relaxed with each other. And I knew he was kind and compassionate, or he wouldn't be helping a helpless older woman. The fourth Saturday Burl finally asked me to go sailing with him on a nearby lake. I've discovered outdoor sports *can* be fun with someone you like . . . and Burl's every bit as gentle as I imagined."

Sandy would never have met a man she liked, though, if she hadn't first left home. And neither will you. I know you may not feel quite ready to face the world, but the sooner you do it, the better. As Dr. Allan Fromme says in *The Ability to Love*, "People become easily addicted to the relief of not having to bother about others, yet the private world they've chosen will become ever narrower and more inward." Dr. James J. Lynch cites statistics in his book *The Broken Heart* proving that *illness* is as much as 76 percent more likely to strike among sad people who hang out alone than women surrounded by lovers and friends!

So plan right now to spend *this* evening or weekend in public. No excuses. If you have kids and no baby-sitter, take the whole family bowling, or to a movie. If you're broke, plan a picnic in the park. (If it's snowing, go *sledding.*) Realize that any excuse that pops into your head ("I'm too tired . . . I've got a cold . . . I'm too busy with work . . .") is just that—an excuse.

In *I'm O.K., You're O.K.*, Dr. Thomas A. Harris describes a psychological game you may tend to play when you feel rejected, depressed, or otherwise "not O.K." The game is called "Why Don't You? Yes, but," and it's played most often by the woman who fears to break old patterns and change.

The game, played recently by a Philadelphia divorcée named Marla and her well-meaning friend, goes something like this:

MARLA:   Now that I'm divorced, I'm so bored. I just hang around the house with nothing to do.

FRIEND:   Why don't you just get outside and have some fun?

MARLA:   Yes, but I've got children and I don't know what to do with them. I can't afford the rates baby-sitters charge these days and I feel *guilty* leaving them alone.

FRIEND:   Kids love the beach. Why don't you take them swimming?

MARLA: Yes, but my swimming suit's so old and faded everyone would think I'm wearing a rag.

FRIEND: You could buy a new one.

MARLA: Yes, but I haven't got the cash.

FRIEND: O.K., you've got a great new tennis racquet—maybe you should play tennis instead.

MARLA: Yes, but my backhand's so rusty I'm afraid everyone would laugh at me.

FRIEND: Then why don't you take tennis lessons?

MARLA: Yes, but the tennis court's two miles from here, and my car's on the blink.

FRIEND: If you really wanted to go, you could walk.

MARLA: Yes, but that's easy for you to say, you always seem so energetic. I'm just exhausted and depressed all the time.

FRIEND: No wonder you're depressed. All you do is sit around and watch soap operas about other people's problems.

MARLA: Yes, but I have to have *something* to do. That's all there is to do when you're bored and depressed like me.

I'm sure you get the idea. No matter what solution her friend suggests, the person who's "it" finds a reason why it will fail. Eventually, the friend gives up in exasperation and Marla "proves" all along she was right: Her case is hopeless.

The point is, you can find a zillion excuses *not* to go public and only one reason why you should: It's a good first step, and you'll feel better.

Trust me. It works.

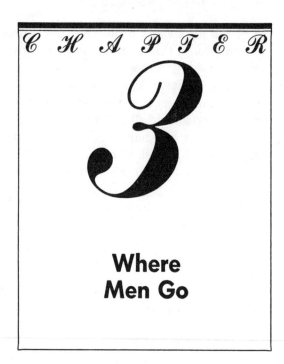

# Where
# Men Go

Okay, now that you've decided to "go public," where can you actually go? Well, there are thousands of places obviously, everywhere from the movies to a Christian Science reading room. At any of them—except perhaps at a women's consciousness-raising seminar—it is entirely possible to meet a man.

Yet I want it to be more than possible. I want it to be *probable.* Therefore, I'm going to suggest some places where men dramatically outnumber women *and* where the atmosphere is light and friendly, or festive and conducive to easy mixing ... places where men are likely to talk to you just because you are there and you are a woman. Prize fights are heavily attended by men, yet I find the atmosphere there harsh and boisterous. The men are too caught up in what is going on in the ring, and the actual event is the kind that unleashes a man's aggression. If I, as a man, find an evening at a boxing match a touch scary, I fear you, as a woman, might find it even more off-putting.

There are, however, numerous places where men gather in large numbers and where the pervading feeling is pleasant and harmonious. The same man who leaps to his feet at a prize fight screaming, "Kill 'em!" may be an absolute pussycat at a Cub Scout jamboree.

So, then, where *do* you go where you'll find lots of men in a friendly, outgoing mood? What I've done is asked myself, *Where do I go? Where do my male friends go? What kinds of things do we do that are pretty much "male" things?*

First on my list is the high school track. Four or five times a week, I go there after work to jog. Men outnumber women about ten to one. And to those of you who would say, "Yes, but the men want to concentrate on their running, and I'll just be annoying them if I try to start up a conversation," I respond, *"Nonsense."* I see women begin talking with men all the time at the track, and men begin chatting with women, as easily as one asking the other, "How many laps have you done?" or declaring, "I wish it wasn't so humid."

I have one separated neighbor who has three dating relationships that have arisen out of meeting men while jogging. "And if I don't happen to meet anyone on a particular day," she says, "at least I'm getting fit, not fat."

Her favorite time of day to go to the track is around six to six-thirty in the early evening. It is cooler, she finds, and thus a more pleasant time to run. "And by six o'clock, most everyone is finished with work. That alone puts people in an upbeat frame of mind." Of course, if you're an early bird, by all means go running in the morning. Almost as many people run before work as after.

What to do if you're not a runner? *Walk* around the track. I've seen hundreds of people who get their exercise this way.

And while I'm on the subject of track, you also might consider going to a horse race. Horse racing is an event that is heavily attended by men, and there is no easier atmosphere in which to begin a conversation than when you and a man are jumping up and down, cheering on your pick. I think you'll also find it perfectly comfortable to ask your neighbors' advice about certain horses or jockeys.

If the prospect of going to the track alone frightens you, then go with a friend. Even with the added bit of competition, there will still be a couple of thousand extra men to go around.

Bowling is also an activity in which men often vastly outnumber women. And there is a strong possibility that there will be a man or a group of men bowling in the alley on either side of you. This, too, is a good activity to pursue with another woman friend.

Where else do men gather in large numbers? In men's clothing stores, at sports car races, at softball games in the park. They attend outdoor concerts in greater numbers than women, do a lot more hiking and fishing and camping and bicycling than women.

Recently, I bicycled through Napa Valley and encountered about ten male bicyclists for every woman on a two-wheeler. And the nice thing about bicyclists is that they usually wave at one another and/or stop to chat and compare routes. Bicycling is a particularly convivial way to meet.

A higher proportion of men than women take lifeguard training courses, fly model airplanes, coach children's soccer teams, browse through hardware stores, go to boat and automobile shows, attend wine tastings and courses on oenology, and get deeply involved with photography. Courses on the latter are unusually fertile grounds for meeting men.

Also, tennis matches and golf tournaments all draw many more male than female spectators. And unlike boxing matches, these events usually are subdued and peaceful. Picture how easily you could whisper to the man standing next to you in the gallery at the U.S. Open, "Do you think Nicklaus is going to hit a wood or an iron?"

These are some of the places and events I've been attracted to over the years. And while there, I've often thought, *How nice it would be if only there were more women around.* I find it much more fun if the stranger bowling in the alley next to me is a woman rather than a man. It adds just that much more spice and festivity to the evening.

And don't tell me, "Yes, but only if the woman is young and pretty." I'm talking about *all* women. Women seem to me generally less guarded and more accepting than men; women add counterpoint, are unique in the kind of environments where men prevail.

At martial-arts classes, which are about 95 percent male; at a racquetball/fitness center, where men usually make up about 80 percent of the clientele; and at stereo stores and backgammon nights at hotels, where one rarely even sees a woman, your mere presence will be noted and enjoyed. Men like having women around, particularly in places where there are hardly any. With all that's been written over the years about the ritual of men gathering in all-male clubs and pubs, the truth is most men find such places dull. I understand that even lodges such as the Elks now admit women. Perhaps it's under the guise of bowing to the times. But if you ask me, secretly those Elks are thrilled.

# CHAPTER

## 4

## Conversational Icebreakers

The next step after getting out of the house and going someplace where you're likely to meet men is learning how to strike up a conversation with them.

Let's say you're at a party (one of the best places to meet new men). The room's full of attractive, single men, and there's one tall, blond, Swedish-looking one standing nearby. He looks at you. You look at him. Should you speak to him? Of course. Most people at parties *like* to talk, and since the man has gone to all the trouble of coming, it's probably because he wants to meet people (including you). So remember, by speaking to him, you're not being sexually aggressive, just friendly and *polite*.

What to say? Generally, it's best to keep icebreakers simple. Zingers like "Hi, did you know Anne Boleyn had three breasts?" will undoubtedly get his attention, but it's hard to parlay that line into any long-term conversation.

24

"What do you think of the oil crisis?" is too planned and dull. (Do you really *care*?) "Haven't I seen you somewhere before?" sounds made up and should be avoided—unless you really do know him from somewhere. Even "Hi, what do you do?" or "What's your name?" can make him feel obligated to talk to you, so it's best to keep your openers offhand and casual. That way, if he feels awkward or wants to scoot on back to his girlfriend, he can move on without either of you feeling embarrassed.

An example? One Portland divorcée, Norma, tells me that at parties she makes frequent trips to the hors d'oeuvres table and when there's an intriguing man nearby she remarks simply, "Here, try one of these canapes, they're good." As Norma says, "If he's interested, he can say, 'Oh, really? The shrimp puffs are good, too.' If he's just waiting for his wife to return from the powder room, he can say 'Thanks,' then drift away, and neither of you will feel uncomfortable or rejected."

So stick with the casual, uncluttered remark. "What's that you're drinking?" "Where did you get that tan?" "Do you have a light?" "Doesn't it feel *warm* in here to you?" Simple, natural openers can be parlayed into long, intimate conversations, or dropped in two minutes if the man turns out to be a clod who wants to tell you about his stuffed-owl collection. Then you can open your next conversation with, "Wow, that guy I just met was the most incredible bore." (Take care with this opener, though: The second man will invariably be the bore's *brother.*)

On days you're feeling especially confident, you might risk a more personal opener. Some examples:

- "You look happy."
- "You remind me of my brother."
- "What a nice smile!"
- "Well, what do you think of the party so far?"
- "Where do you know Bill [the host] from?"

At parties, it's not too difficult once you've screwed up your courage to strike up a conversation, because most people there are just waiting for a chance to talk. But what about in bars? Some men in bars, after all, are trying to *forget* women, and if you finally manage to speak to that cute fellow sipping Scotch and soda, he may just sit on his stool and sulk. Again, simple openers work best. "Pardon me, do you have a match?" has probably launched more friendly chats—and love affairs—than any other line. If you know you could just never, *ever* bring yourself to speak first to a man in a bar, that's O.K., too. After one or two drinks, most men are usually forward enough for both of you. So choose a friendly, cozy little bar (nothing sleazy) where a crowd of regulars often gather—the kind of place where after a visit or two the bartender knows your name and favorite drink. Then sit alone casually flipping through a magazine (a *book* looks too serious) and avoid getting absorbed in a story (you'll look as if you'd detest being interrupted). If you look relaxed and approachable, eventually some man will sidle over to say hi. If he's nice, invite him to sit down.

What about icebreakers on the street, or in supermarkets, bookstores, or department stores? (All, by the way, are great places to meet *male* shoppers; I've never heard of a woman asking another woman home to dinner after they've compared the price of cat food, but one *couple* I know did meet that way.) In such places, unlike parties and bars, the direct approach works best. You have no time for introductions. One woman says that whenever she catches a man eyeing her, she immediately pipes up, "Have we met somewhere before?" (That line works well on the street, oddly enough.) If you yourself are reluctant to employ such a frontal approach, remember, you can always chitchat about the weather. Ask the man next to you in the department store if he thinks *this* necktie would please Uncle Harry. Or tell him he's about your brother's size and would he please mind trying on this pair of gloves.

In the supermarket, every aisle produces its own ice-breakers:

- "Have you tried this floor wax?"
- "Don't you think that T-bone steak looks a little brown?"
- "My puppy won't eat dog food. What brand does *your* dog like?"
- "Do you know where I can find the mayonnaise?"
- "Would you like to *split* a carton of eggs? I can't use a whole dozen."
- "Don't you have trouble finding vegetable cans small enough for *one*?"

Or here's a repertoire of sample comments for airports or depots:

- "I've got a three-hour wait between trains. Do you know anything I should see while I wait?"
- "Pardon me, do you know where I can check my luggage?"
- "Do you have change for a dollar?"
- "Is there a decent place to eat in the airport?" (One divorcée told me she asked a man in an airport coffee shop if he'd split a chef's salad with her because it was too big for one. They wound up chatting for hours between planes, and they date whenever either happens to be visiting the other's city.)
- "Have you seen a coffee machine anywhere around here?"
- "Excuse me, but do you know where the TWA ticket booth is?"

People in airports, railway depots, and bus stations are constantly confused, lost, or late, so it's perfectly acceptable to ask for help. Still, if even the most innocent conversation opener sounds too direct for you, why not try the silent icebreaker? Meg, a shy but sociable divorcée in Houston, tells how:

"Whenever I travel, I always carry one more package or piece of luggage than I can gracefully manage," Meg explains. "I mean, I don't try to look clumsy—just overburdened. Then, when I spot an attractive man who seems to have time on his hands (that's important—a man rushing to catch a plane won't even glance in your direction), I just juggle my bundles precariously in front of him. Or if I have a heavy suitcase, I just sigh sweetly and let it drop with a *plunk*. A generous man will almost always offer to help. An added advantage of this tactic is it weeds out the losers: Who wants a man so thoughtless he ignores a woman in trouble?"

One final word about icebreakers: I've seen books and articles advising you to play dumb. To get a man's attention, they suggest going into your fluffheaded female routine. (In a bookstore, for example: "You're planning to read the whole *Gulag Archipelago*? Silly me, I can't even read an entire *Mad* magazine.") I'd avoid that. If you open a conversation with a moronic remark, such as "Is that Picasso painting from his blue or his rose period, I never can tell?" or "You look like a man who *thinks* for a living," you're likely to attract only another moron. Worse, the man may look at you as if you're an idiot, and you'll be left standing there feeling hurt and angry with yourself.

Nor should you attempt being the wittiest conversationalist he ever met. Joan Rivers–style comments ("My last husband thought I was a potato . . . when we went to bed, he put a bag over my head!") sound fine on the Carson show but showoffy—even tiresome—at the bus stop. So just relax, be yourself, and keep your openers simple, sincere, and friendly. Believe me, men like and respond to friendly people. Don't you?

# CHAPTER

## 5

# Keeping a Conversation Going

Okay, you've employed one of the icebreakers from the preceding chapter, and, miracle of miracles, it's actually worked. You've broken the ice with a man, not exactly Warren Beatty, it's true, but a pleasant, presentable fellow nonetheless. There you sit, side by side on the sofa, sipping margaritas, asking him questions, listening to his answers. Suddenly there's an awkward pause. Silence. Panic sets in. However can you keep him talking?

Relax. The art of conversation sounds complicated and formidable when you think about it in the abstract, but in fact it's quite simple. You needn't be as witty or adroit with words as Orson Welles on *The Tonight Show*. What you see on talk shows aren't really conversations at all—they're well-timed, carefully prepared monologues. Watch Joan Rivers. She doesn't talk *to* Johnny Carson, she talks *at* him.

Listen closely and you'll see she's simply running through a sit-down comedy routine. In real life, the good conversationalist doesn't hog the limelight. She cares little for her own glib anecdotes. Instead, she brings out the shy man—and lets *him* talk.

How?

One way is to ask questions. If the man you're with is a natural talker, any open-ended query will work. The classic line "Tell me about yourself" can keep an egocentric man rambling for hours. If you fret that when the lights are low and you're suddenly called upon to talk your nerve will fail you and you'll only be able to sit stupidly biting your lip, think up a dozen or so questions to ask before the evening begins. One woman named Nancy is so painfully shy that her mind goes blank the minute any reasonably attractive man approaches her. To compensate, she writes emergency questions inside a matchbook. If caught in a conversational stalemate, she whips out her matches, lights a cigarette, and continues her conversation. "I realize this is an extreme step," Nancy admits, "and, good heavens, a man once borrowed my matches and saw my questions all neatly printed inside! But just knowing I have a repertoire of comments to use in a pinch bolsters my confidence. I usually don't have to resort to them. By the time I reach what I call my 'matchbook stage,' the man and I are both so bored Barbara Walters couldn't save us." What to ask? Your queries needn't be earth-shattering. Ask him about himself. Elicit his opinions. Typical, all-occasion comments might include:

- "Where are you from?"
- "Do you come to this park [museum, stadium, etc.] often?"
- "I'm looking for a health club to join. Do you know of any good ones for single people?"
- "So what's new with you?"
- "All the movies I've seen the past two months have

been real drags. Have you seen any good ones you'd recommend?" (If he mentions *On Golden Pond,* which you saw and hated, pretend that you haven't seen it.) Next question: "Oh, really? What did you like about it?"

- "I'm looking for some exciting new books to read. Have you read any lately you think I'd like?"
- "I'm giving a party next weekend, and I'm lost about entertaining everyone. What do you think I should do about party games [or a caterer, refreshments, etc.]?" Once he gives you several clever suggestions, reply, "Those are marvelous ideas. Say, why don't *you* come to the party, too?"
- "Have you heard how bad this snowstorm tonight is supposed to be?" (If he says three feet of snow are expected, reply, "Oh, my, I hope I can get home all right *alone.*")
- "Did you hear how the Celtics-Knicks basketball game came out?" (Any sports event will do.)
- "My car has this little ping-ping-plat in the engine every time I turn a corner. Do you think that sounds serious?" (Maybe he'll offer to look under the hood for you.)
- "I'm planning to buy a used car [or stereo, air conditioner, whatever] this weekend, and I don't know the first thing about it. Could you tell me what to look for?" (He may decide to come along to help.)
- "I want to buy a coat for my brother, and I love your taste in clothes. Where would you suggest I shop?"

Any topic he knows oodles—and you know nothing—about can keep you chatting for several minutes, if not hours. When he mentions a fact you didn't know, respond, "I didn't know that. What other intriguing ideas are you thinking?" Or during a lull, look at him intently and say, "Fascinating. Please tell me more," or "You're quite remarkable. Do you know that?" A good listener can keep a man talking for hours, and when the evening's over, he'll swear you're the best conversationalist he ever met.

Whatever you do, pay attention. Look interested in what he says. Some women feel so shy or self-conscious when talking to a man that they stare at the floor, fiddle with their fingers, or look blankly at the wall—all of which can unnerve the most gregarious guy.

Be careful, too, before revealing all your strongest opinions. One woman I know still recalls with horror the time she blithely aired her views on suicide and how she thought any woman who killed herself probably had a rotten home life and a thoughtless husband or surely he'd know she was depressed, only to have the man look at her sorrowfully and reply, "My wife shot herself last month." Yes, but how likely is that to happen? Likelier than you think. Inevitably when you comment, 'Look at that awful woman. Don't you think she could have used just a *ton* less makeup?" the man you're addressing will be her husband—or her son. If in the midst of a chat about politics, you remark, "Don't you think Reagan just *stinks*?" more likely than not your listener will be head of your local "Re-elect Reagan" committee. So best keep comments (especially about politics, religion, and other hot topics) neutral, at least until you get to know the person a little better. "How *about* that Ronald Reagan?" is a noncommittal opening gambit. (He won't know if you think Reagan's a blessing or a curse.)

At times, of course, a spirited argument can spice up an otherwise dull evening. While some men deplore being contradicted, others love hearty debates (it shows you have spunk). I know one married couple who met each other in a local debate on tax breaks for homeowners (she was for, he was against). So if you honestly disagree with a man's statement, I see nothing wrong with telling him so. Politely point out that he may be right, but there could be another viewpoint. Disagreeing with a man can give you a clue to his relationships with women. If he accepts your opinion thoughtfully, he's probably considerate and willing to compromise.

Which brings us to another question about conversation: Is there any topic you *shouldn't* discuss? Well, yes. When you were married, chances are you built up many "married" conversation topics that, while they're not awful, aren't the best subjects to chat about with a single man at a party or bar. Topics best left for coffee klatches include:

- "Cute" things your kids said or did.
- Whether Cheer really makes clothes cleaner.
- The obscenely high prices of milk and fuel oil.
- Johnny's problems in sixth grade.
- How tough it is today to find a decent pot roast.
- All other domestic and child-related topics, unless he, too, has kids and wants to chitchat about the PTA.

Now that you're a single woman, you need to think in single terms. Learn to talk about vacations, parties, wind surfing, skiing, art galleries, Beethoven—and, most of all, *him* (the man you've just met, not your ex-husband). One divorced woman I know commits the ultimate *faux pas*: Whenever a handsome male is near, she launches into a diatribe against her ex. If the man she's just met will tolerate it, Emily will talk for hours about how Fred deserted her with one can of fruit cocktail in the cupboard, kidnaped the kids, and still hasn't paid a nickel of alimony. Usually, Emily's victim soon excuses himself to get another martini and never returns. I'm sure you know that talking constantly about your problems makes you sound tedious and self-pitying. It's easy to fall into that trap if your world seems to be tumbling about your shoulders, you're having trouble finding a job, and the electric company's threatening to turn off your lights. Still, no matter how bleak the world looks, resist the temptation to fall into the poor-little-me routine.

At the same time, avoid being overly jolly. One divorcée, to hide the pain and insecurity that haunt her day and night, has fallen into the Hilarity Habit. No matter what a man says to her, Adelaide emits a horse laugh as loud and as feminine as a fire alarm. I've seen Adelaide compulsively chortle over comments about heart attacks, ice storms, war wounds, and grilled-cheese sandwiches. No matter how insecure the man she's conversing with may be, he's bound to realize in a few minutes that he couldn't be *that* witty, and Adelaide's not even listening. So, while it's lovely to be easily amused, keep your smiles calm and your laughs soft and musical.

I hope all these caveats haven't totally unnerved you. Conversation, as I said before, really is baby simple. It's easy to avoid all pitfalls: Just listen. Listen to what the man says, ask for his opinions, look bright and perky, smile occasionally, get him talking about himself. In a pinch, echo the man's viewpoints. If he's just told you he thinks John McEnroe's the best tennis player who ever lived, repeat his opinion: "So you really think McEnroe's great?" If he fails to pick up the ball and expand on his original idea, prompt him by asking *why* he feels that way.

The most commonly used word in conversation is "I." Bores talk about themselves consistently. A poor conversationalist, after babbling for half an hour about her life, pauses, gasps for breath, and says, "Now tell me about your vacation. . . . Oh, by the way, did I tell you I just got back from Tahiti?" Work until your most commonly used word is not *I* but *you*. It's astonishing how that one simple change in pronouns can energize all your conversations.

If all of the above sounds like too much to practice and keep in mind, calm yourself with the thought that the hardest part is breaking the ice. Once most conversations get going, they keep going. People like to talk. It's why most of us are standing around the punch bowl in the first place— we want to *talk* to someone.

## CHAPTER

# 6

# Compliment
a Man

If you'd like to meet a man but can't think of anything to say to him, you might want to try complimenting him. What will he think? (He'll think you're nice.) Men often compliment a woman the minute they meet. It's not out of the ordinary for a guy to say, "What beautiful eyes!" or "Oh, so *you're* the brilliant new researcher over in marketing that everyone is talking about."

But would you say the same to him?

Let me tell you something about myself that I suspect is true of most men. I somehow feel it's my job to compliment women on a regular, ongoing basis, not to be seductive or manipulative, but because it's expected of me . . . because it's polite. I only wish women complimented me as frequently as I compliment them.

*Well, Weber,* you're probably thinking, *maybe there's just not that much about you to compliment.*

You're probably right. On the other hand, I've discussed my feelings with dozens of other men and found that they, too, are rarely complimented. My analysis is that parents just don't program their daughters to compliment boys the way they do their sons to compliment girls. What a shame!

I remember the all-too-few compliments women have paid me as clearly as if I'd heard them yesterday. The ones I recall with particular relish were comments about the way I looked. Twenty years ago I sat on the steps of the Englewood, New Jersey Public Library taking a study break with a friend named Ellen, a promising young sculptress.

"One day I'd like to sculpt you," she said. "You have the most perfectly shaped head I've ever seen." I luxuriated in the afterglow of her comment for months. She hadn't said I was manly or clever or forceful or any of those other things that women tend to say when they praise a man. She'd complimented me on the way I looked—and I loved it!

My response, of course, was to find her more interesting and attractive than I had only moments before. She'd made me feel great . . . and consequently I wanted to spend more time with her.

The point is, it's important to compliment men. It tells them you're secure enough to notice good qualities in others—and confident enough to let your admiration show. And most important of all, it makes a man feel wonderful when you let him in on some of the nice thoughts you are having about him. It helps to establish a tone of warmth, of positiveness, at the very beginning of your relationship.

How else can you compliment a man besides to remark on his looks? As with the conversational icebreakers we discussed earlier, it's best to keep comments simple and sincere. A man's clothes are always a good, neutral subject. No matter how shy you feel, it's remarkably easy to say, "Hey, I like your windbreaker [or cuff links or tie]." Paid such a simple, unadorned compliment, no man could possibly think you forward.

More intimate, personal, and risky are comments about him. Examples:

- "What sparkling eyes you have!"
- "You have a wonderful laugh."
- "Where did you get that cute dimple?"
- "That cleft in your chin makes you look a lot like Kirk Douglas. Has anyone ever told you that?"
- "With those handsome, broad shoulders, I'll bet you played football."
- "Mmmmmm. You smell good."

Personal comments are probably likeliest to catch a man's attention, but, unfortunately, also most likely to flop. So do be careful. When a man sneezed at a party, one woman blurted out, "Oh, what a cute sneeze . . . you sound just like my cat." The man was not flattered. Another woman said to a stranger who'd just asked her to dance, "For a beginner, you dance divinely." The man gave her a withering glare and replied, "I teach classes at the Arthur Murray studio." Another fellow who stands about five-foot-three and worries that he's too short was less than pleased when told he was "as cute as a button." So think before you speak, and try to picture the man's reaction. A comment like "I adore those little tufts of hair on your wrist" might alienate one man but turn another on.

In the right situation, you can also compliment a man on his skills or expertise. A few examples:

- "What a marvelous backhand. Are you a tennis pro?"
- "A hole in one! That's incredible. Can you teach me to do that?"

- "Pardon me, but I couldn't help overhearing your views on Ronald Reagan. Your ideas are better than anything I've read in Kirkpatrick's column."
- "I was watching you swim across the pool. You've got a great breaststroke."
- "You're the best mechanic I've ever had!" (This remark can be tailored, of course, to any profession. Examples: "I've never had a stylist cut my hair as well as you do," or "I'll bet you're the best electrician in the state!")
- "Oh, how did you fix that dishwasher so fast? You must be a mechanical genius!"
- "So *you're* the intelligent new executive I've heard so much about." (He's bound to wonder what you've heard and who told you.)

Anyway, you get the point. Everybody does something well. Look for a man's strong points and compliment him on them. Believe me, he'll be pleased and flattered, not put off.

One final word about compliments: Just as important as complimenting a man is learning to *accept* his compliments graciously. When a man says you're sexy or remarks that you have a terrific figure, don't giggle and bury your face in your hands. The *worst* you can do is roll your eyes, laugh, and look at a girlfriend (he may not realize you're embarrassed and assume you're laughing at him). A simple "Thank you" will do. Or you can do what one gracious woman I know does: You can respond with a subtle compliment of your own. Let me explain. I don't mean that when a man says he likes your hair you should blurt out, "Oh, I like your hair, too." We're talking here about *subtle*. When told you're cute, you might reply, for example, "That's sweet of you to say so." Or if he says he's amazed at how much work you put in on that report you just gave, you could respond, "How thoughtful of you to notice."

It helps, too, when you compliment a man to remember

how flustered, shy, or embarrassed sudden, unexpected flattery may make you feel. So if you tell a man you like his tie and he happens to let out a brutish guffaw, look arrogant, or mumble into his collar, realize it's not because you've offended him. It's just that you've thrown him off balance and he feels insecure. That's when a smile can reassure him and get your relationship rolling. But, then, a smile actually works wonders *anytime*—as we shall now see.

CHAPTER 7

# Smile

Perhaps you think you're among the least assertive women in the whole world. Maybe some of the ideas in this book seem totally inappropriate to you because you're just not the kind of person who can walk up to a man you don't know from Adam and say, "I like your tie"—not today, not ten years from now, not *ever*. Well, you know something? You're not alone, not by a long shot. For although it seems as if women are pursuing men everywhere these days with a heretofore unexpressed aggressiveness, the truth is that *most* of the divorced, separated, and widowed women I interviewed confessed that they had never "made the first move" with a man (that is, addressed him before he addressed them), and many of them feel that they'll never be able to do so. *It just isn't me,* they say. Well, neither you nor they need despair. For in this section we're going to discuss

40

a facet of body language that can have an astonishingly magnetic effect on getting men to approach you—the smile. *The smile??!!! That's the oldest idea around.* Perhaps it is. Maybe that's why it's fallen into disuse. But just ask yourself: When was the last time you smiled at a stranger on a bus, a train, an elevator, sitting next to you at a play, even on the street? To smile at a man is one of the simplest, mildest, noncontroversial, low-risk overtures a woman can make toward a man. It takes no rehearsal, no cleverness, no creativity, no money, and very little courage. And yet if you were to do it, let's say, but once a week, you might soon have more good men in your life than right now seems even remotely possible. For to a man, a smile from a woman is literally like a flower on a spring day, colorful, inviting, promising, warm. It is an overture, yes, but a mild one, polite, measured; an opening gambit, perhaps, but one tempered with restraint. If he takes you up on it and starts a conversation, the chances are good that he will assume you are amiable, a lady not opposed to meeting him, but not necessarily someone who is going to run off and hop in the sack with him (although if that's your intention, then fine). And if he doesn't respond except perhaps to smile back, then you can assume that he has accepted your smile for what it is on its most basic level, a hello, a gesture of friendliness. And the two of you can go back to reading your newspapers.

I realize, of course, that if you're not now in the habit of smiling at men you don't know that it can seem as awesome as actually walking up and addressing one. Yet it can be accomplished as easily as drawing back the corners of your mouth; and if it doesn't succeed, it will disappear as noiselessly and as quickly as a yawn. On the other hand, if it works, it can totally change your life, as it did for Peggy, a forty-year-old New Yorker who has been divorced for seven years.

"It was a bright Saturday in June—the first, to be exact, and I remember the date because June 1 was the day

of my first date with my ex-husband fifteen years before,"
Peggy relates. "I was feeling down and rotten, riding home
on the Madison Avenue bus after my exercise class wearing
a dirty old leotard and a dirty old raincoat. I was sitting in
the back of the bus contemplating my only-adequate job and
the fact that I had no jolly summer plans. My children's
plans: sleep-away camp. My plans: rattling around our
empty apartment watching the dust fly in. Others would be
laughing gaily on the tennis court. Not me. I don't play tennis. Some would be laughing joyously at beaches. Not me—I
had no car and knew no one with a beach house. My pros-
pects were bleak—not just for the summer, for my whole
life! Through this not-so-minor depression, I noticed a man
in the front of the bus burdened with two large shopping
bags from Bloomingdale's. He was a reasonably attractive
redhead, about forty, and because of his raincoat I took him
to be a reporter or espionage agent. *I smiled.* Not because I
intended to approach him—I felt too icky and morose for
that—but out of enjoyment of my own reverie of misery. *He
smiled at me.* My God, I thought, I'm irresistible. He picked
up his shopping bags and sat next to me and started chatting. Now it happens that I can be under a black cloud and
ready to slash my wrists or hang myself in the closet, but if
a man seems interested in me, I rise to the occasion. He told
me that he was a former New Yorker who lived in London.
He was here on business for two weeks and had shopped in
Bloomie's at the request of two friends and his children.
Children! (No matter.) A wife! (Another matter.) He told
me I was unusually friendly and attractive and would I
mind if he walked along with me on my Saturday errands. I
didn't mind. I was pleased. He walked with me to the cleaners and the hardware store, and I was pleased to see a look of
admiration on his face whenever I spoke or moved. That
low, low sense of self-esteem was rising rapidly. I told him I
was divorced and happy to be; he said he was separated.
Ah-ha—perfect. When we got to my apartment door, he

asked if he could come up, and I said no, but that I was in the phone book.

"He called the next morning and asked if I would accompany him to the airport. He was going to Cleveland on business for two days. How romantic, I thought. In short, it turned out he didn't know how to drive a car and always had drivers take him everywhere. I was slightly aghast at such ineptness, but I decided it was quaint and charming and old-fashioned, and I wouldn't really mind being chauffeured everywhere myself. He called me at my office from a private airplane, and when he returned in two days we started seeing each other every night—lovely dinners, taxis, compliments. My depression cleared up entirely. During the two weeks we went out, I learned that although he was married, he always had affairs in the European tradition, and we planned that I would spend my two- or three-week vacation in London while his wife was in Spain with their two boys. I would go with him to Geneva and Paris for occasional business trips.

"My friends were horrified that he was married and asked what good this would do me. 'All the good in the world,' I said. 'I want to go to Europe with a man who's an insider and can speak languages. I don't want to go on a tour.' So off I went, was met at the London airport, checked into my hotel (Dukes, a charming hotel in Green Park), and had a whirlwind romance with candlelit dinners, theaters, trips to Paris, Geneva, and a week in the Alps.

"John, it turned out upon close inspection, was not so wonderful. He is cautious, biased, conservative, and even stingy—but I did travel in Europe as an insider (he spoke many languages), met his wife and ninety-year-old mother, and polished my drawing-room skills. Our on-and-off three-year affair never materialized into a substantial relationship, but no matter. Though he wasn't the man of my dreams, he was a nifty substitute."

And all because Peggy smiled at the man, even though

she was having a hopeless, helpless, whatever-will-become-of-me kind of day. Can you do the same? If you have a nice, warm smile, you can. And if you do, I think you'll be amazed at the number and the quality of the men you'll soon begin to meet.

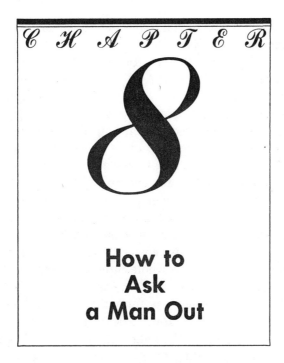

# How to
# Ask
# a Man Out

Suppose you've noticed a man you really like and you've tried every tactic I've suggested. You've broken the ice with a simple, casual remark, smiled at him, told him you like everything from his tie to his tush, and *zilch*, nothing. It could be you're wasting precious time on the wrong man (maybe he has seven secret girlfriends or maybe he's gay). But if you think this man really is made for you and you'd be perfect for one another, why don't you ask him out?

No matter what your Aunt Gertrude told you, it's perfectly acceptable today for a woman to take the initiative and ask for the first date. Chances are, of course, you'd feel less than comfortable—oh, all right, *terrified*—about phoning a man and inviting him to dinner. If you can do that without batting an eyelash, you probably wouldn't be read-

45

ing this book because you'd already have more men in your life than you could handle.

Still, I maintain even the shyest, most unassertive woman can ask a man out. And you can do it, too, if you follow a few simple rules. I'm not suggesting you invite a man to a dance or dinner (though if you can manage that, all well and good). The secret to taking the fear out of invitations is to make the time and place as casual and informal as possible. It's always easier to ask a man to go out with you during *daylight* hours, for example. (Somehow, after sunset, dates begin to get serious.) A Sunday afternoon barbecue in your backyard with his and your kids, a visit to the zoo, or an afternoon at a local ball park are all innocent dates to suggest. It's also easier to ask him for a relatively *brief* date, rather than a whole Sunday afternoon. The classic old standby, of course, is the traditional cup of coffee.

Here's how Stacey, a forty-three-year-old mother of three from Des Moines, Iowa, asked the apple of her eye for a fifteen-minute date. "I thought it was the end of the world after my divorce," Stacey recalls. "Thanks to eating my way compulsively right through the divorce, I was twenty pounds overweight. I was sure a man would date an armadillo before he'd ask me. But there was this friendly butcher at the supermarket I always go to. He was always really nice. He'd save me a special round steak to one side, or he'd always make a point of suggesting the best buys that week. We'd talked a lot whenever I bought meat, so I knew his name was Arthur and he'd lost his wife six years before in one of those multiple-car pileups that tragically occur some foggy nights. Arthur had steel-blue eyes, the kind that make you feel all weak and schoolgirl gushy when you look into them. That man could have sold me giraffe meat for filet mignon, and I never could have looked him in the eye to complain. But no matter how much I tried to make him see I was interested and available, Art wouldn't ask me out.

"So I decided to do the unheard-of and ask *him*. I was

as jittery as a boy asking for his first date, and like a young boy, I planned everything. I would ask him to go to dinner with me, then suggest a movie afterward, then a drink, and let it go from there. On the Big Day, I got all dressed up, put on my most alluring makeup, and marched into the meat department. When Art cheerily asked me what I wanted today, all that would come out of my mouth was, 'I'll take a pot roast.' My nerve failed me completely, and all I got was a four-and-a-half-pound roast!

"I nursed my wounds and nerves for a few days over this close encounter of the dumb kind before I hit on a solution. If you don't want to feel like a loser, I told myself, don't make asking him out such a big deal. Not far from the supermarket where Art worked, a new doughnut shop had just opened. The next time I bought meat, I asked Art if he'd tried their doughnuts yet. When he said no, I said, 'They're great. Since I'm recommending them, I'll treat. When's your break?'

" 'In about twenty minutes,' he said.

" 'Good. I have to go by the cleaners. Why don't I meet you at the doughnut shop?' I said. I walked out of that supermarket in euphoria. Art and I had a couple of doughnuts (thank God, they really *were* good), and Art went back to work. About four days later, I asked him again to have coffee with me. The second time was easier, for both of us, I think, because we'd already done it once. I was trying to build several short dates up into one longer one: I thought that after we'd been together a few times, Art might ask me out for a real evening. It worked. We grew more relaxed with each other and on our third coffee date he asked me to go bowling with him that night. I went, we had a good time, and now we're dating regularly."

*That's fine for her,* you may think, *but my nerve would fail me every time. I'd end up with a whole freezer full of roasts and still fail to pop the question.* If so, then don't ask a man for a date at all. Ask for a favor. That's what Eloise, a thirty-six-year-old who works as a pharmacist's assistant in Minneapolis, did.

"After my divorce, I was fed up with all men," Eloise recalls. "I swore men were the ruination of women, and they all brought us pain, suffering, and then a terrible loneliness. Fortunately for me, I was so penniless I had to take a job, and I found a position as an assistant to a pharmacist named Julius, and from my first day there, I knew my ideas about men were silly and irrational. Julius convinced me of that just by looking at me with his kind, gentle brown eyes. Silly? Absolutely. But then so was my previous cynicism. I guess I'm a creature of extremes.

"Anyway, as the days went by, I learned that Julius was separated from his wife and he was sure they'd soon be divorced. I tried to get him to ask me out, but he wouldn't. Maybe his separation was too painful. Finally, after two months of fruitless flirting, I decided if anybody was going to make a date, it would have to be *me*.

"Now, Julius was—and is—quite conservative. I thought he might be shocked, even offended, if I invited him to dinner and a play. I realized what I needed to ask him out was a damned good reason. Finally, it came to me. I like old movies, especially the musicals, the sort they don't make anymore. And some of these movies are rereleased every year, but they don't run in first-run theaters. They usually show up at little theaters in rundown neighborhoods. About five months after I'd started working for Julius, *The Sound of Music* was being shown in a small theater in a sleazy section of town. At work Friday, I asked Julius if he was busy Saturday night. He wasn't, so I said, '*The Sound of Music* is playing this weekend only, here in town. I want to go see it, but all my friends have seen it and don't want to go again. Just my luck. It's playing in a part of town I can't go into alone. Would you go with me as sort of my bodyguard? If you will, I'll pay for our tickets and treat you to dinner afterward.'

"He was flattered, and as it turned out, *The Sound of Music* was one of his favorites. He'd seen it five times but said he'd love to see it again. My plan worked beautifully. Julius was pleased I'd asked him for protection, and when we went, we did so with a spirit of adventure, as if this were a feat of derring-do and we were entering a dangerous land. Actually, it wasn't all that dangerous. We parked in front of the theater on a well-lighted street. But the sense of danger did add a thrill to our evening. When I paid for dinner afterward, it tickled Julius to be treated by me, but at the same time his pride was satisfied because he was doing me a favor.

"The next Sunday, he asked me to go picnicking with him by Minnehaha Falls (that's the waterfall here in Minneapolis that Longfellow wrote about in his poem *Song of Hiawatha*). Anyway, it's a gorgeous park and we had a lovely time, and now we go out about twice a week. In a couple of months, Julius and his wife will be divorced, and though Julius doesn't *know* it yet, I'm going to marry him!"

Another way to ask out a man is to offer something in addition to yourself. For example, "My boss couldn't use his tickets to the hockey game. Are you free Thursday night?" An approach like this will probably keep you from feeling as exposed, as open to rejection, as a more direct request for his company. You're not asking him out because you've fallen desperately in love with him. It's simply that you lucked into a pair of tickets.

And don't think that the man you call will instantly deduce that you have a crush on him. I remember my wife—back when she was someone I had dated but two or three times—calling to invite me to a Harvard-Yale game because her father had an extra ticket. I didn't think, *Hah! What a ruse! She's in love with me!* I thought, *How nice. Her father has an extra ticket for the Harvard-Yale game.*

Needless to say, you don't have to *wait* until someone offers you tickets they can't use to ask a man out to the theater or a sports event. In this case, a minor fib is perfectly okay. If the relationship ever gets off the ground, he'll be charmed that you went to such great lengths to win him.

If you need something moved, I was about to advise you not to choose too heavy a moving job—a piano, for example—that might throw his whole back out of whack. But a female friend disagrees. "That would be *perfect*," she says. "Then you could feel guilty and act obligated to nurse him back to health. You could make him chicken soup, *massage* his back . . . oh, it would be just lovely." So when it comes to how heavy an object you choose, you're on your own.

A variation of this technique is asking a man to bail you out in an emergency. You might call him at five o'clock on Thursday and say breathlessly, "Gee, I'm sorry to bother you like this and tell me no if you can't, but my car won't start and Jimmy has a Little League championship game in fifteen minutes. . . . Could you *please* give us a lift to the ball park?" Then, as an afterthought, add, "We'll take you out for pizza afterward." Another example: "I hope I'm not interrupting anything, but I'm desperate. My furnace won't click on and it's going to be twenty below zero tonight. Could you please see if you can get it to work?" Make sure in this last case that the problem is something simple, like a blown fuse, not a major mechanical overhaul. If the poor guy can't locate the trouble, you can eventually suggest tentatively: "God, you don't suppose it's some simple thing like a *fuse*, do you?" After he's fixed your furnace, be enormously grateful and invite him to stay for an intimate hot toddy. Such spur-of-the-moment dates can be hard to get (the man may not be home or may legitimately have to visit his sister in the hospital that night). Whatever you do, don't take rejections of your last-minute pleas seriously. Assume he really is busy that night. Wait a couple of weeks. Then phone with some less urgent request, such as, "Jimmy just got a bike for his birthday and I can't even figure out which wheel goes where. Can you please help?"

I think you can see from these examples that I'm not suggesting you act like a moron who can't tie her shoes for herself. Few men want a helpless waif they'll have to baby through life. If you can fix your car generator with a hairpin, don't pretend you're a senseless fluffhead who has trouble turning on the windshield wipers. (Blatant lies somehow always show through.) But I'm sure when you think about it there are some things he knows that you don't, that he can do better or more easily than you can. Once you've found his strengths, use them to ask him for a date. By asking for something only *he* can do, you've satisfied the most *macho* of men. He'll be flattered you've noticed and he may not realize till months later that he's been asked out by a woman.

So much for social graces. You now know how to do everything from starting a conversation to asking a man out. No matter how socially skilled you become, however, there still may be a more critical stumbling block keeping you from meeting men—namely, you and your *attitudes*. I'm not going to tell you never to feel discouraged and always to act courageously. You will feel low and shy at times. But there are self-defeating attitudes you may have and not even realize you have them, attitudes that can be easily corrected once you know what they are. So let's turn now to how you *feel* about meeting men and how you can take a few short, simple steps to bring many more men into your life.

# Do You Really Want to Meet Men?

Here's a question I want you to consider seriously: Do you *really* want to meet men? You may reply, "What kind of stupid question is that? Why else would I have paid money for this book?" I know you *think* you want more men in your life, but what I'm asking is this: Do you *really* want to take the extra effort—go out of your way, if need be—to meet guys?

Let's say it's a drizzly Friday night and you're planning to stay home tonight and wash your hair, curl up under a cozy comforter, and watch *Gone with the Wind* on TV. You love Clark Gable as Rhett Butler, and you wouldn't miss this film for the world. Just as you step from the shower, your hair dripping wet, the phone rings. It's Chauncy, a man you met last weekend in an Irish pub; he wants you to go drinking with him. What do you do? If you say okay, quickly blow-dry your hair, and are ready to have fun in an hour, great. If you think of the gray drizzle outside and say, "Gee, Chauncy, I'd love to *another* time, but tonight I'm watching a movie," maybe you really don't want to meet men as much as you believe you do.

Or let's say you've stopped by the coffee shop on your way to work to pick up a cup of Sanka to go, and the debonair man in the three-piece suit standing in line behind you says, "Boy, I'd just love to call in sick today and go to the beach. Wouldn't you?" Do you say, "Me, too. I'll do it if you will"? Or do you just laugh off his comment with a "Yeah, too bad we can't. What a grind"?

Exactly how far are you willing to extend yourself to meet men? Quite often, maybe because you're insecure or hesitant, you may let the most trivial details stand in your way. I know when I was single, I'd call up a woman to ask her out for, say, Saturday night, and maybe she'd reply, "Sorry, Eric, but I'm busy Saturday. I'm free for lunch Tuesday, though." Then, partly because I felt a bit let down, I'd say, "Aw, no, Tuesday's out. I promised Joe I'd lunch with him Tuesday." And so it would go, and we'd never get together. Only later would I realize that my lunch date with Joe wasn't all that crucial and could easily have been changed to another day. Do you find yourself making lame excuses like "I can't go to the party tonight because I simply have to do laundry" or "I'd love to see that play, Johnny, but this is my bowling night"? If so, you may be sabotaging all your man-meeting efforts.

Be willing to put yourself out to meet men. Be ready to change plans, shift gears, and even improvise when opportunity knocks.

Kit, a thirty-one-year-old Seattle mother of two small boys, told me how she took extra pains to meet a man—but it paid off. "I car-pooled with four other people—one other woman and three men," Kit explains. "I was the silent one. You know, the one who's always sitting quietly in a corner

of the back seat and only opens her mouth once every fifth
Friday to say, 'My turn to drive next week. See you then.'
That was me. I was just incredibly shy.

"But there was this divorced man named Clete in the
car pool. I wanted to open up to Clete. He was no Robert De
Niro—in fact, he looked more like a crumpled Walter
Matthau—but he seemed so pleasant and considerate, just
the sort of man I needed most. Once, during the middle of
the week, someone in the front seat asked him what he was
doing that weekend. Clete made a wry face and said, 'I want
to watch the game Saturday, but I have to mow the lawn
Sunday morning, so I guess I'll fix the lawn mower. It's
busted. That'll take my whole Saturday. Wish I could borrow one for the weekend.' Before I knew what I was saying,
I piped up, 'You can borrow mine.' He gladly took me up on
my offer. The only trouble was, my ex had the lawn mower. I
always *hired* a man to cut my lawn!

"At work I sat and fretted for about two hours, wondering why I'd gotten myself into this pickle. And then I
thought, 'This is dumb. You can get a lawn mower somewhere.' So that evening after work, I went out and rented a
mower to loan Clete that weekend. He came by, picked it up,
and when he brought it back Sunday, I was ready with a
six-pack of beer in the fridge. I knew he'd be thirsty after
mowing his lawn that morning. And I knew since I'd loaned
him 'my' mower, he'd feel obligated to stop and talk awhile,
and we might hit it off. Well, he wound up staying for *three*
beers. He was sweet, considerate, and pleasant, and we had
so much fun talking that after polishing off the six-pack, we
went out to see *Reds* that night.

"Next weekend, Clete asked me to go with him to the
downtown waterfront. There are a bunch of old piers down
there with quaint shops, restaurants, an aquarium, sight-
seeing boats, and lots of places to watch the harbor. We had
lobster at one rustic little cafe, fed bread to the sea gulls,

and had a great time. Now we see each other every weekend, and my two boys think Clete's just wonderful."

Tammy, a thirty-six-year-old Miami, Florida, mother of three girls, went to even greater pains to get her first date with Ray. "Ray and I knew each other only enough to say hi," Tammy recalls. "He was actually a friend of a friend's husband. I'd see Ray around on occasion at a wedding reception or a Christmas party. I knew Ray had gotten divorced about the same time I did, and I hoped if I bided my time he'd notice me. But he didn't. Sigh. That's the story of my life. Then I found out he was starting to date several other women, and I suddenly realized I might lose any chance to know him if I didn't act soon.

"One Sunday afternoon I was at my friend's house when her husband had some friends of his over watching the Dolphins on TV. Ray was there. He's an avid Dolphin fan, and the Dolphins were locked in first place with the New England Patriots, who were scheduled to play here in Miami the next week. Ray was sitting cross-legged in an easy chair watching the waning moments of the game while the announcer talked about the exciting game next week with the Patriots, and Ray said, 'Jesus, I'd love to go to that game. But the tickets were sold out ten days ago.' It suddenly occurred to me, bright and clear, that if I could get tickets to that game—somehow—Ray would go with me!

"For two days after that, I phoned everybody I knew who might have tickets to the game and might be willing to part with them. But it was useless. Then I tried my uncle, who loves sports so much I swear he'd spend his last dime to watch a water polo contest at an old folks' home. Of course, Uncle George wouldn't let me have his tickets, but he said I could surely get some from a scalper if I didn't mind paying as much as seventy-five dollars a ticket. When he said seventy-five dollars, my heart sank to my shoes because I knew I had a little extra money in the bank but I was planning to use it to buy a new suit. Then I said to myself, 'Oh, what the hell.' And, knowing I was in danger of really blowing it with Ray, I called him Friday night and told him I already had two tickets to the Dolphin game that Sunday if he'd like to go with me. He couldn't believe his good fortune. I told him I had to run an errand in the city, and I'd meet him at one o'clock at the stadium just before the game. I wouldn't have gone to all that trouble for just any guy, but I knew Ray well enough I thought we'd be good together.

"Then I panicked. All Saturday I fretted that I'd never get the tickets, and I could picture Ray looking at me like I was ready for the loony bin. Sunday I was awake at dawn and by ten o'clock I was standing near the ticket window in front of the Dolphin stadium, waiting for the scalpers to ply their wares. What happened? Zero. Not a single scalper showed up. Time was getting dangerously close to kickoff, and I still had no tickets. I thought I'd die with anxiety. Once I felt on the point of tears. But I said to myself, 'That will be cute—you standing here alone, crying like an idiot.' So I pulled myself together and tried to think.

"Anyway, when I was just about to come apart at the seams, I overheard this bearded guy with glasses saying he'd just paid an arm and a leg to buy three tickets from a scalper, and though I'm usually too timid to talk to strangers, I was so desperate I ran over to him and asked him where the scalpers were. I told him I'd been waiting three hours and hadn't seen one. He answered, 'No wonder. Scalpers don't stand in front of a ticket booth. You've got to go to the parking lot where people come into the stadium.'

"I thanked him and practically sprinted to the parking lot. Almost right away I came up behind a man who was holding up two tickets and offering them for sixty dollars apiece. I didn't know whether I was supposed to haggle or not, but I just eagerly bought the tickets from him for that price; he'd probably never seen anybody so eager to be ripped off! Our seats weren't on the fifty-yard line, but they

weren't in the end zone, either. As I started back for the stadium, I met Ray. The game was fantastic. Miami won. And
to celebrate, Ray took me out to a chic little Polynesian restaurant for dinner. One date led to another, and Ray and I
have been married now for two years. When I told Ray what
I'd done to get those tickets, he laughed for an hour. But he
was enormously flattered. Now he teases me and says he
didn't stand a chance, that other women were ready to give
their eyeteeth for him, but I was willing to be scalped!"

What are you willing to do to meet men? Will you go to
a party alone on Saturday night, or stay home to read *Scru-
ples* for the fourth time? When a man calls three minutes after supper and suggests a spur-of-the-moment get-
together, will you leave the dirty dishes piled in the sink
and *go*? Or will you listen to archaic recordings from your
childhood ("Nice girls aren't easy ... play hard to get")
and tell him you have other plans?

I say any time you can make a date with a man, do it.
Worry about petty details like what to wear or when to re-
schedule your dental appointment later. Men are always
going out of their way to meet women, you know. A guy will
rent an expensive apartment, cancel business meetings,
send flowers, get tickets to concerts he detests, and go up to
his ears in hock to buy a Porsche—all just to catch a
woman's eye. Don't you think it's about time you invested
in extra effort, too?

# CHAPTER 10

## Inner Looks

About half a dozen years ago I wrote a book with the above title. It think its basic point is as valid now as it was then: We spend too much time, money, and thought trying to make ourselves *physically* attractive. We believe that if we can only become handsome or pretty enough, we'll never have to work at finding a lover again. Members of the opposite sex will be drawn to us in droves. We'll be able to sit back and take our pick, a new date for every night of the week.

*Inner Looks* then goes on to prescribe a different approach, one that stresses more of a reliance on "inner looks"—your warmth, your sexuality, your energy, your creativity—rather than just your figure and your face.

I guess what I find so damn depressing about relying totally on "outer looks" is that its success depends almost exclusively on others. You just sit there trying to look pretty. If on that particular night no one happens to be smitten by you, you don't meet anyone. The title of this book speaks of meeting new men. If that doesn't happen, I've let you down.

That's why I favor a much more active approach to improving your social and love life. I've interviewed far too many lonely women who somehow feel that it's not "ladylike" to make an effort, that it's not the way things are supposed to be.

Don't think I'm unsympathetic to such a mind-set. I've been a victim of it myself. Why isn't the phone ringing? I've often railed. Here I am, a reasonably well-known writer. Why aren't publishers calling me? Why isn't Hollywood beating a path to my door?

The answer, of course, is that there is a dumb, brute, primitive inertia to life. It tumbles on its merry course without giving us a tiny fraction of the thought we give ourselves. You walk into a cocktail party imagining that every man in the place is sizing you up, deciding whether or not to like you. The reality is that if one or two men even *noticed* you, you're doing better than average. Others simply aren't as aware of us as we are of ourselves. If we want them to get involved with us, we're simply going to have to help them; we're going to have to make it easy and fun and important for them to become *engaged* with us.

*Okay,* perhaps you're thinking, *you make a good point. To sit around and wait for men to approach me probably isn't the most effective way to improve my social life. But what exactly are these "inner looks" you're talking about? And how in the world do I get anybody to notice them?*

A few paragraphs back I mentioned your warmth, your sexuality, your energy, and your creativity. These are all very real character traits, but in many women they tend to be hidden, submerged.

Others have no trouble seeing your nose. But unless

you demonstrate it, they will not be able to tell you have a great singing voice, or the ability to make someone feel special and loved. And that is why it is so important to work at unlocking your inner looks, the part of you, I maintain, that can be vastly more attractive to men than simply your face and your figure.

## *Your Inner Sexuality*

I don't have to recite for you all the reasons why many women are embarrassed by their sexual feelings. No one wants to be thought of as easy, trampy, or cheap.

Yet I believe that to hide and suppress your sexuality is even more self-destructive than to flaunt it. When I was in high school it was widely held that any girl who slept with a boy before marriage would never get married. But when I looked around at my fifteen-year reunion, I couldn't help but notice that all the girls who were reputed to be promiscuous back in high school were or had been married, while many of those whose reputations were impeccable were still single, had a somewhat sere, asexual quality.

The message, I think, is simple. Men are more attracted to women with a healthy streak of sexuality in them than to women who regularly deny or resist their own sexuality. This isn't to say that you should attend your next cocktail party in a dress cut down to your belly button. Though they are loath to admit it, most men are probably as turned off by a woman who blatantly advertises her availability as they are by a woman who seems sexless. No, the trick is to strike a balance, to communicate somehow to a man that you can be a physical, sensuous, passionate woman without making him feel that you are about to pounce on him.

This is best accomplished not so much by *dressing* sexier, but by giving in more to your natural instincts to hug, to be hugged, to *talk* about sex, to *think* about sex.

We all walk around with our own built-in censor. In cartoons for children, it's often depicted as an angel perched on one's shoulder. We think of an off-color or suggestive remark, and our censor fixes us with disapproving eyes. In some of us the censor has gained more power than is good for us. We sit among a gathering of people who are drinking wine and dancing and carrying on, and we feel a prisoner of our own "good" behavior. To others we appear stiff and prudish. But inside we are actually yearning to join the fun.

Now, I realize it's much easier for me to *tell* you to unleash your inner sexuality than for you to go ahead and do it. A lifetime of "good" breeding and social training can't be overturned overnight. Nor would I want it to be. As I said earlier, this is a book of little challenges; it's neither fair nor realistic nor even desirable to ask you to try to be someone you're not. All that usually happens when we attempt to violate our basic character is that we wind up feeling confused, paralyzed.

How, then, do you actually go about unlocking some of your inner sexuality without making yourself crazy?

In little ways. You're chatting with a stranger at a mixer. He makes a slightly suggestive or off-color remark that you find funny, perhaps even sexy. Normally, your censor would instruct you to frown or remain expressionless. Tell your censor to get lost. Give in to your natural instinct to smile or chuckle. No big thing, really, but your reaction will make its point. You're not a prude. There's as much sexuality in you as in the next woman.

Or let's say the man sitting next to you at a dinner party compliments your dress. You feel a rush of warmth toward him, an impulse to touch his arm. Don't stand on ceremony; give in to your natural instinct to be affectionate.

Or maybe as you're talking to a man in your office you can't help but notice how tall he is, or what a marvelous head of hair he has. Words well up at the back of your throat. *I never realized how tall you are. What a great head of hair.* Well, don't let them stall there. Let him hear those words from you.

You're not propositioning the man, not by a long shot. What you are doing is communicating to him that deep inside you is a woman who, at least with part of her being, thinks about men and their bodies. Men like to know that. If they are drawn to you, you will be helping them to feel optimistic and intelligent about their attraction.

The beautiful woman across the room who looks as if she has just stepped out of the pages of *Vogue* may be throwing off vibrations that are icy and sexless. Beneath their surface attraction to her, men will also be picking up her message of coldness, not wanting to be touched, to be messed. If you, on the other hand, are sending out signals that tell a man you're the kind of woman who can really enjoy herself dancing and hugging and making love, your message will be taken in and remembered.

Men are attracted to women who like sex.

## *Your Inner Warmth*

Dozens of studies have shown that almost everyone thinks of himself or herself as warm, generous, and kind. Even some of the world's most notorious tyrants pictured themselves as sentimental softies, helpless boosters of the underdog.

What about you? Chances are you think of yourself as sweet, helpful, accepting, and approachable. But are you really? When you attend a mixer or a dance or a lecture, what kind of expression is on your face? What do others see when they look at you? What would you see if you caught your image in a mirror?

I ask because my experience indicates that many people, like the aforementioned despots who think of themselves as being particularly warm and loving, appear to others as just the opposite. I can't tell you how many dinners and parties and pubs I wandered through in my midtwenties searching for a woman who looked as if she might say, "Yes, I'd love to dance with you"; or, "Yes, I'd enjoy talking to you." What I saw mostly were faces that appeared cold, hard, guarded, discouraging. And I, like most men, am a coward. I have absolutely no appetite for walking up to a woman I am fairly certain is going to turn me away. Would you want to walk up to a man who looked as if he were going to send you packing?

Let me tell you about a particular phenomenon I uncovered recently. Before I was married, I would always look for a woman with a particularly warm and accepting face, even if she weren't the prettiest woman in the room. My reasoning went like this: All the other guys will be competing for the obvious beauty. I won't stand a chance. Let me look for the diamond in the rough, someone who appears sweet and kind and accepting, even if on the surface she isn't all that attractive. At least I won't have to win her away from a horde of other men.

I can't tell you how many times this strategy backfired. The competition for the woman I'd singled out was often more intense than for the woman who looked like, or really was, a model. But it's only been in recent years that I've fully come to understand why.

Not long ago I mentioned to a friend the strategy described above. He drew back in astonishment. As a young man he, too, had pursued the accepting, less attractive woman rather than the *Penthouse* Pet type. We queried other friends. They, too, had pursued the less obviously attractive but more accepting-looking woman and had been equally shocked at the stiff competition they'd encountered.

The moral? Men respond to women who look as if

they're going to accept them. If you indeed are as warm and accepting as you think you are, make sure it's apparent to the men around you.

Let your inner warmth surface. Men will respond to it as bees to pollen.

## *Your Inner Creativity*

When my wife was a teenager she says her father referred to her and her sister and her mother as his "three dumb girls." He did not refer to himself and his two sons as "three dumb guys."

This all-too-familiar construct suggests why so many women, to this day, squelch their own intelligence and energy and creativity. Women were supposed to be pretty and noncompetitive. To men fell the role of sage, entertainer, wit, and wag.

And yet one of the things that attracted me most to my wife was her rather elaborate and theatrical miming of cats. We had known each other for only about six weeks and were out to dinner with a large party of people. Joanna was down at one end of the table, I at the other. Suddenly I sensed everyone's attention being drawn her way. I looked up from my linguini. Joanna's teeth were chattering, her eyes crossed, in imitation of her cat, Albert, watching two other cats making love outside on the driveway. The crowd howled with laughter. Joanna went on to do Albert opening doors, Albert napping, Albert staring at her mother's canary.

When she finished, our friends broke into a round of applause. Joanna's face was flushed with embarrassment and excitement. She never looked more beautiful to me than she did at that moment. My chest swelled with pride that this clever, attractive, talented woman was *my* date. Who knew that she was so artistic? Why hadn't I discovered it sooner, on my own?

The point, of course, is that men—healthy men, anyway—respond to women who are vivacious and alive and loving and talented. If you've been hiding your inner talents because you're afraid of turning men off, stop. Now. Let the creative, energetic inner you out. You'll attract a lot more men than you'll drive away. And isn't it so much more of a natural, zestful way to approach life than to wait around to be appreciated for your beauty?

# Rediscover
# the Old You

Often, in the aftermath of a divorce, people experience more grief and depression than they anticipated, the leaver as well as the person who has been left. In a conventional, monogamous society such as ours, being unbonded, a single, can trigger all kinds of negative feelings that play havoc with one's sense of self-esteem. *I am worthless, I am inferior, I am different* are not uncommon thoughts among the newly, and even not so newly, divorced.

Now in many self-help books feelings of diminished self-esteem are treated with what I consider much too much casualness. "Learn to love yourself," prescribes one author. "Think positively," counsels another. That done, let's get on with the business of living life to the hilt.

Fine and noble goals indeed, learning to love oneself

and thinking positively. To some extent I recommend them myself in this book. But at the same time I think it's important to address a few words to those whose negative feelings cannot be so easily quieted, whose grief and depression won't let go as graciously as all that. Understand that you are not alone. Even for those whose lives are going swimmingly, feelings of self-love ebb and flow. An optimistic outlook suddenly fades and reappears and fades again. These are things over which we don't always have as much control as we'd like.

So if you find yourself overwhelmed at times by despair and gloom, don't jump to the conclusion that you are a loser or that there is something drastically wrong with you. You have a right to your grief, to your sadness, to your inertia. It can be as self-destructive to ignore your negative feelings as to wallow in them, for sooner or later they must be expressed. Better to acknowledge them than to try to override them with an hysterical burst of manic activity, only to find yourself suddenly on the verge of a nervous breakdown. Everybody gets depressed at times, even happily married women with wonderful, caring husbands.

That said, let me see if I can't alert you to an aspect of your life that may very well make you feel good about yourself in a healthy, justified way—your past.

In the wrenching process of splitting up with your husband of umpteen years, perhaps you have forgotten the bouncy young woman you once were, or the promising poet your English Lit. professor saw you as, or the good singer, or excellent golfer, or competent librarian you used to be.

Well, maybe you haven't forgotten the "old" (or should I say "former"?) you. But you may very well have misplaced her. Now's the time to remember yourself as you used to be, to rediscover the old you.

Chances are, when you were married, you gave up lots of activities and interests because your old fuddy husband didn't enjoy them. Maybe you're the outdoors type who loves camping, hiking, swimming, and scuba diving, but your ex was a stuck-in-the-concrete city dweller whose biggest athletic feat was walking the dog. Or maybe you adore art galleries, concerts, and plays, but hubby's grandest form of culture was watching *Bowling for Dollars* on the tube. Now's the time to wipe the slate clean, recall how you used to feel and behave, and become like that again.

If you always enjoyed skiing but never ventured onto the slopes after your ex broke his collarbone, go skiing. If you love art museums but your husband thought Klee was a cartoon cat, visit a museum this Saturday. Doing activities you once enjoyed can make you feel jollier and more like you felt before all these troubles rained on you. Rediscovering *you* can buoy your confidence, make your spirits soar, and encourage men to notice you once again.

One thirty-three-year-old freckle-nosed San Francisco woman, Suzanne, for example, found romance when she rediscovered her former addiction for backpacking. "Before Jon and I were married, I'd always liked getting outdoors, especially backpacking in the low Sierras. Jon wasn't the outdoors type, even though we first met on a backpacking trip. That had been his only venture into the great outdoors. After we were married, I never went into the woods or walked through the mountains because Jon didn't want to, and after our divorce I was too emotionally devastated to face all those long trails and high hills. I was already climbing enough mountains in my daily life!

"But, by chance, an old friend, Ginger, and her husband were in town for a convention that Ginger was finding a real bore. She looked me up in the phone book and talked me into going backpacking for a few days.

"From the very first morning, when the early sunlight filtered golden through the trees, it was stimulating to be out in the mountains again. The air was so tangy you could taste it. By afternoon, though I was pleasantly tired, the trails seemed less difficult and the hills lower. By the second morning, old skills I'd forgotten I even knew were coming back to me: I started a fire that morning with one match and remembered how to pack my backpack so it sat on my shoulders just so. There's an art to backpacking many novices don't know. But I'd always been good at it, and by midday my confidence had soared and I was feeling remarkably content and good about myself. I think a lot of my anxieties were caused by just moping around the house!

"Ginger and I met a few other backpackers on the trail, and I'd forgotten how cheerful and friendly fellow hikers are. About midafternoon, we ran into a man sitting exhausted on a granite boulder beside the trail. We stopped to chat and he said he was going to the head of the trail, the same direction we were, but was worried he wouldn't make it. That surprised me because he was a muscular, lumberjack-looking fellow who seemed built to take easy trails like this in long, Paul Bunyan strides. Then I saw his trouble: His pack was slung too low on his back, almost to his waist. You have to carry it high on your shoulders. I wondered if I should say anything, because you know how *macho* most men are when they get out of the suburbs and into the least wild terrain. But he was sitting there puffing and then he said, 'I've never done much backpacking before. Thought it'd be easier than this.'

"I decided he *needed* my help, so I offered, 'Here, let me show you.' He wasn't at all bothered to be rescued by a woman. We invited him to hike with us along the trail, and that night he even gathered wood for our campfire.

"We built a roaring fire, opened a few tin cans, then sat around after our meal singing folk songs and roasting marshmallows. The man told us his name was Dave (funny how long it takes you to learn *names* in the woods); he taught English at a small San Francisco college. That night, sitting around our cozy fire, I decided I liked Dave. Next morning, when he helped me break camp and talked to me on the trail, I suddenly realized that though I hadn't tried to make it happen, Dave had come to like me, too.

"When we returned to the city and Ginger and her husband left town, Dave called and invited me to go with him to a fabulous lobster restaurant down by the pier. The next weekend, we took a picnic and our bikes north of the city and bicycled through the wine country of Napa Valley.

"Since then, when Jon takes the children for the weekend, I often head with my backpack for the Sierras. Sometimes Dave comes with me, but at other times I go alone and I've met other men. I doubt that Dave and I will get serious, but that's fine because I'm not ready to remarry yet. Maybe I never will be."

Would Suzanne have begun meeting men through backpacking if an old friend hadn't looked her up on the off-chance that she might like to go camping? Sooner or later she probably would have. Good ideas do not remain mired in the unconscious forever.

But why not sooner rather than later? How about sitting down right this minute and thinking about your former pleasures. What did you used to enjoy? Playing basketball, water-skiing, sailing, swimming, dancing, or yoga, perhaps? Choose one of those old joys and do it again.

Decide what you'll do *this weekend*—not next week, next month, or six months from now. And rediscover the old you. No excuses. If you always loved bicycling but your bike's now a pile of rust, rent one. (If you know a man you'd like to go biking with, rent a bicycle built for two.) If you loved ice-skating but it's July and ninety-five degrees in the shade, think of another old pleasure you could engage in this week. You'll be surprised how good it will make you feel.

*Yes, but I adored sports when I was eighteen. Now I'm older and times have changed,* you think? Nonsense. It's an old saying, but nevertheless still true: You're as young as you feel and act. You were energetic, charming, pretty, and witty enough once to make a man fall in love with you. Once you rediscover that bright, sparkling *old* you, I'm confident you'll do it again.

# CHAPTER

## 12

## Change Your Living Patterns

Years ago when I was single, I saw a listing in the newspaper for a weekend bus trip to the Rhinebeck Crafts Fair in New York State. I said to myself, "Gee, that sounds like fun," then quickly added, "Oh, but that's just not the kind of thing *I* do. Besides, it sounds like too much trouble." So I spent my Saturdays as I always did, playing touch football with my friends in the morning, going to a bar for a couple of beers, watching a football game on the tube, going to a singles bar that night. Now that I think back, I realize what an unadventurous singlehood I had. All the different trips I could have taken, places I could have visited! What I should have said was, "Forget my friends. I'm going to Rhinebeck this weekend."

Perhaps you, too, are blocking out many opportunities to have fun, get out of the house, and meet people, including men, because you're stuck in a self-limiting groove. A group of friends at the office invite you to go canoeing one weekend and that sounds fun, but then you catch yourself and say inwardly, "Oh, but I've never gone canoeing. What if I looked silly?" So you decline. Or a friend suggests you both sign up for scuba lessons and though you've always secretly wanted to try diving, you feel uneasy (as we all do when trying something new for the first time), so you say, "Sorry, I've got to do the ironing."

Sound familiar? If so, then it's time to break your old routines and try a new adventure. Take a bus some weekend to a nearby art show. Join your company softball team. Go to a horse race. Take a ride in a hot-air balloon. The next time a friend suggests an activity that sounds like fun, or even if it doesn't sound like that much fun, resist the impulse to run back to your safe living room to watch old reruns on the tube. Overcome initial lethargy and *go*.

Even if you don't meet a man, you'll be out there relating to people, extending your networks, keeping your life interesting (which makes you more interesting to others). And who knows? You might meet someone, as Ali did.

A teacher in a small New England elementary school, Ali, told me the last thing she wanted to do last summer was try sailing. "Greg and I had separated, he'd kidnaped the kids, and I was just hanging in there trying to pay the utility bills." Luckily, Ali had a very energetic friend named Beth who had answered an ad in a sailing magazine placed by a yacht owner looking for a crew to sail for the summer in the Caribbean, and Beth insisted Ali come along.

"It turned out that the crew consisted of two men, plus Beth, and me," Ali says. "Now, I *know* what you're thinking: They just wanted us out there for group sex. But that wasn't true. There's a lot of *work* to do on a sailboat. I was the cook, and Beth, who knows all about sailing, helped navigate and steer. Beth did get romantically involved with the captain—a short, dumpy, balding little man named Rob.

But the other man, Frank, and I were just buddies. Sailing people get to know one another in marinas, though, and one night when we were tied up off the Florida Keys, a skipper from another boat stopped by to chat. It turned out Jerry was from Massachusetts, too, not far from where I live, and we got to know and like each other. Nothing big came of it, we explored the Keys together for a couple of days and that was it, but it was nice being treated as a woman again, and when I got home I didn't feel so depressed and lethargic anymore. Beth and I are already trying to sign up on a crew for next summer!"

I'm not suggesting you tackle an entire summer adventure, as Ali did (although if you feel up to that, great). Just try some simple, doable change. If you've always wanted to play tennis, buy a racquet and join a tennis club. If riding a motorcycle or snowmobile sounds like fun, *accept* his invitation when a male friend offers you a ride. If you'd like to go bowling but you can't find a friend to go with you, forget your friends and go bowling alone. Even if you feel skittish about attempting some new activity or going some new place, realize you're not unique. More people than you think are afraid to swim, attend cocktail parties, climb mountains, or sky-dive. I've read about people who fear bicycling, dancing—even badminton.

But the way to overcome a fear is to *face* it. Once you tackle a challenge and succeed, you'll feel more confident and courageous about trying a major change (like switching jobs or moving to a sunnier apartment). But first just try a few simple steps. Seek out a new singles beach. Go to a local crafts fair, summer stock theater production, or concert. Buy a fishing license and go trout fishing. Join a woodworking class. Whatever sounds fun, *do* it! Give in to your impulse to take a chance, to do something different! Gradually you'll shed your outmoded married routines and acquire an active life-style better suited to the sparkling new single woman you now are.

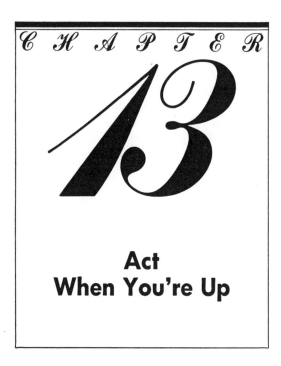

# CHAPTER
# 13

## Act
## When You're Up

Human nature is perverse. Sometimes, for no apparent reason, we wake up and find ourselves in a particularly good mood. We head into the bathroom, look in the mirror, and again for no apparent reason discover we are having one of our good-looking days. Our hair is falling just the way we like it, our complexion looks a touch rosier than normal, and the bags under our eyes are less pronounced and lighter. Why?

Who knows, really? For that matter, who cares? The point is, when you are having one of your up days, there is no better time to get out into the world to see what the day has to offer. If you had planned to repaper the den or curl up with a good book, forget it. It is essential that you venture out among people. Your inner happiness and harmony will shine through. The attractive, well-rested face you encountered in the mirror will be as apparent to others as it was to you.

One woman I know reports that she was recently walking down the street in such a wonderfully heady mood that a passing stranger couldn't help but remark, "Lady, you look like you've got the world on a string."

"I do," she trilled.

And Betty, a forty-two-year-old divorcée who lives in a suburb of Atlanta, describes the results of one of her good-looking days: "I'd just gotten a raise, I'd had my hair (which was always long and bushy) cut in a short, curly style, and I'd lost five pounds. It was a warm, balmy spring day that Saturday, and I felt sensational—better than I'd felt in years. I could have stayed home that day to paint the bathroom or scrub Miss Havisham (that's my collie), but I decided this bubbling energy was just too wonderful to waste on *chores,* so I decided to take a bike ride. I packed a bottle of wine, a few McIntosh apples, and a sliver of Brie cheese and went pedaling into the countryside. The trees were just budding light green that day, the forsythia was blossoming yellow, and I felt almost giddy.

"Then I saw this fellow biker about ready to pass me. He was slim and tall, with perfect posture, and his skinny little butt was incredibly cute as he pedaled by. I could see, though, he wasn't eighteen because there was a lock of hair peppered with gray sticking out from under his cycling helmet. I flashed him a friendly smile and said, 'Isn't it a *gorgeous* day?' He smiled back, and we were suddenly compatriots out here in the spring countryside. Suddenly the craziest idea occurred to me—I decided to *race* him! I would never have done that in my down-and-gloomy days. He was enormously strong and fast and I had to pedal so hard I thought my lungs would explode, but I kept up with him for about half a mile. Then I laughed and hollered, 'O.K., you win, I need a breather.' And he stopped, too!

"I think you can guess the rest. I shared my apples, wine, and cheese with him, and he shared his peanuts with me. It turned out his name was Richard and he was a struggling free-lance artist who often took afternoon bike rides to relax and keep up his energy. For years he'd worked as a corporate executive, but one day he woke up and realized he wasn't ever going to be president and life was too short to spend it all in a stuffy office, so he quit the rat race and was having a great time painting in his studio.

"When we finished snacking, Richard asked me if I'd like to ride with him again on Sunday. I did. Now, we don't go out every night, but we see each other most weekends, and I credit our relationship to that 'up' day when I felt so incredibly good."

While Betty made the best of an "up" situation, Nancy, a Chicago housewife who works part-time as a bank teller, told me how she takes advantage of her best time of day. Although she didn't actually speak first to a man, she found herself responding to his approach because she felt great.

"I always feel good in the morning, and the following experience shortly after my divorce made me realize I should make the most of my morning hours," Nancy says. "Because I'm definitely a lark, I schedule my exercise class (a combination of ballet, jazz, yoga, and gymnastics) for Monday, Wednesday, and Friday at 7:00 A.M. When we're finished, I feel exceptionally lively and thin. My good humor and expansive mood are wasted at work because in the mornings my coworkers are still silent and groggy. I always wish I felt better at night because I believe that's when opportunity knocks the loudest.

"Not always, though. Last month, after my Wednesday class, I showered, washed my hair, put on makeup and a new pantsuit. I looked and felt exuberant. As I walked down the block to the bus, I felt as jaunty and secure as that model in the "Charlie" commercial. As I was stepping

along, an extremely cute guy approached me. He had just
walked out of a small, chic brownstone on this very chic
block, so I knew he wasn't a back-alley type.

" 'What are you doing on my street?' he asked. 'I get
the paper every morning, and I've never seen you before.'

" 'I'm exercising,' I said gaily. 'Do you want to see my
headstand?'

" 'Right *here*?' he answered.

" 'Well,' I said, laughing in my early-morning flirtatious manner, 'to tell you the truth, the sidewalk is a bit
hard for my head, but I'll give you a rain check.'

"Anyway, we chatted awhile and I told him about my
class, and he said, 'Tell you what. I'll meet you at your class
Friday morning, and I'll watch your headstand. Then we
can go for breakfast. How about it?' And that's what we did.
He arrived at my class at 7:30 A.M., just in time to see my
perfect headstand: I sucked in my stomach and kicked up
my legs like a veritable Olga Korbut. When I got dressed,
we ate breakfast—breakfast is the most intimate meal, don't
you think?—and then he walked me to work. We've become
the greatest of friends though not quite lovers—yet. I never
would have met him if I hadn't been feeling so great. If I
had walked along that very street later in the day when I
was winding *down*, I might not have noticed him, and I certainly wouldn't have responded. I'd have stuck my nose in
the air, remembering the words my mother spoke at least
four hundred times since I was three: 'Never speak to
strange men.' If I'm having an ugly day, I won't bother to
talk to anyone unless I'm forced to. I'll wait until my hair
and clothes look good. Since everything I've read on energy
and organization says you should plan your difficult activities for when you feel energetic and concentrated, I plan
anything that requires initiation for up times."

If it worked for Nancy, it can work for you. You doubt
it? Maybe you think you're not pretty and that would never
happen to you. Nonsense. Studies reported in *Psychology*

*Today* have shown that beauty truly is as beauty does, and a woman who *feels* pretty also *looks* pretty to others (no matter how large her nose or how many freckles she has).

So act when you are up to put more men in your life. This may be the perfect time to try some of the suggestions in this book that intrigue you but at the same time seem too bold, not really *you*. Just the smidgen of added confidence that you feel when you are having one of your "good looking" days is often enough to put you over the edge, carry you to victory at a pursuit that only yesterday seemed dangerously beyond your capabilities.

# Learn
# to Flirt

My next suggestion may surprise you because there's been so much talk since the sixties about women being totally up-front, honest, and sincere. But if you want to meet lots of men, learn how to flirt.

*Flirt?????* Isn't that an outmoded ploy used only by coy Scarlett O'Hara types with brains the size of lima beans? Didn't that tactic go out with dropping your lavender-scented hankies and wriggling your bustle?

Not at all.

Smart women, I think, have always flirted. In fact, most loving husbands and wives I know still flirt with each other. At a recent party I noticed one male friend who's been happily married fifteen years. Throughout the evening, I watched his wife, Barbara, laughing gaily at his corny jokes, brushing his arm whenever he came near, tilting her head coquettishly when she spoke to him. Barbara, who happens to earn at least fifty thousand dollars a year as head of her own public-relations agency in New York City, isn't some fluffheaded twit. But she knows the value of flirting, and she still thinks her husband's sexy enough to flirt with. Now, there's one lucky guy!

Despite what you may have heard, flirting doesn't mean you're a tease. It's merely a harmless sport played exclusively for fun. What's wrong with laughing at a man's jokes, giving him an impish look, or telling him he's clever and charming? Nothing that I can see. Flirting is a way to say, "I think you're cute" without getting so deadly serious you have to commit yourself to a long-term relationship. It's simply play.

But let me tell you what Candice, a thirty-three-year-old stockbroker in Dallas, says about flirting. Candice, by the way, isn't a ravishing beauty: She's flat-chested, bony, and has short, cropped, mousy-brown hair. But now, two years after her divorce, she never lacks male admirers.

Flirting, avers Candice, "is neither a skill nor a science. And above all, it is not work. Flirting's just play. You play with a man with your eyes, by the way you touch him, or let him glimpse your thigh. But you're playing not to be cruel. This is teasing he likes. I recall the first time I really flirted with a man at a party. The party had been given for a few of our clients, so I was obligated to go, though I felt about as dynamic as a paper clip. Then I noticed this wonderfully sexy man—tall, with coppery hair, very successful-looking. Several young, cute girls were after him, so I figured I had about as much chance as a bag of potatoes. I concentrated on entertaining this old bald toady in my office who grunts when he sits down. At least *he* thought he was cute. (Sigh.)

"Still, I couldn't keep my eyes off this sexy man. Once he caught my eye and I looked at him intently for about five seconds, then glanced away. When I moved to another part of the room, I met his gaze, then looked away again. The third time this happened, he was talking to a blonde who wears about a 38-C, and I couldn't believe it: When I looked away I saw out of the corner of my eye that he kept looking at *me*. That's when I realized, *He likes this. He's ignoring that adorable blonde to watch flat-chested me.* It was late in the evening before he finally cornered me and said, 'I've been trying to catch you all night.'

"My heart was fluttering so I thought he could hear it, but I played it cool. 'I know,' I said.

"He cocked his head to one side like a playful retriever and asked, 'You weren't running from me, were you?'

" 'Naturally,' I told him. Inside I was telling myself, 'Don't blow this, Candy, you'll never forgive yourself.' But to him I said, 'I wanted to save the best for last.'

"He laughed and we started talking. Never did he leave my side for the rest of the evening. When the party ended, he drove me home. Since then, I've learned some men prefer being touched. You know, just a brief brush of a hand when you're both reaching for a cheese canape on an hors d'oeuvres tray, or a wisp of body contact in a crowded elevator. Your touch has to be light and playful; if you're too suggestive, an uncool man may practically *attack* you!"

Flirting is like breathing. Every woman knows—at least unconsciously—how it's done. The girl who flips back her long, glossy hair, steadies a man's hand with hers as he lights her cigarette, glances seductively over her shoulder, or smiles saucily knows what she's about. Luckily, though, now that women have become liberated, you're no longer confined to subtle flirtatious gestures like shy smiles and lowered lashes. Now you're permitted to be totally outrageous if you wish. And many women take advantage of their newfound freedom.

How? To explain what I mean, let me first tell you about some outrageous tactics men have used. Baseball pitcher Tom Seaver, for example, the first time he saw his future wife on a California college campus, didn't walk up politely and say hi. On a dare, he *tackled* her. And a movie producer, while aboard a yacht, saw a young woman standing on the pier—and pushed her in the water. She emerged from the bay dripping and laughing, and presto! Love at first dunk. Now liberated women are reversing those tactics. One woman I know met her husband-to-be when she went up behind him in a bar and pinched his *derrière*. Another rushed up to her future husband (he was a total stranger at the time) at a party, and feigning mistaken identity, cried, "Oh, Charles!" and kissed him passionately. A second later, she flustered sweetly, "Ooooh, you're not Charles" ... but contact had been made.

Helga, a Chicago divorcée who stands five-foot-ten, flirted with a man in a crazy way—but, oddly enough, it worked. "I was at a friend's wedding reception and noticed this good-looking man—slim and impeccably dressed with hair the color of mahogany. I'd seen him arrive with two other men, so I figured he was fair game. I tried to meet him by mingling with a group he was chatting with, but he walked away before I could open my mouth. Now, to understand what happened next, you have to realize this was a very relaxed, informal party among friends. We'd all had a few drinks, and all my friends are a little kooky, O.K.?

"Anyway, I found a friend—her name's Michelle, but we all call her Mickey—who knew this man. She told me his name was Hank and he was a free-lance photographer. He'd even sold some photos once to *National Geographic*, she said. Then I went into the kitchen, got a paper bag, cut eyeholes in it, and put it over my head like the Unknown Comic. Mickey and I started cracking up, and I was so tipsy I didn't care if I seemed weird. So then Mickey led me back into the party room and introduced me to Hank. I wasn't running around acting loud and obnoxious like those stupid guests who put lampshades on their heads. I was very quiet and polite.

"I had no idea how Hank would react. But I figured if

he thinks this bag is stupid, at least he'll never know who I am. Plainly, though, he was amused, but he, too, acted like everything was perfectly normal. 'So your name's Helga,' he said. 'Do you go to many weddings?' We chatted about five minutes this way, but I could see he was finding the bag funnier and funnier. Finally, just before he cracked up, he said, 'By the way, why are you wearing a paper bag over your head?'

"I was feeling good and said, 'Am I wearing a paper bag? The saleslady told me this was the latest in spring hats!' And both of us started to giggle. Hank was persistent, though: He asked again. Then I said, 'Truthfully, Hank, I wanted to meet you but didn't know if we'd like each other. If we didn't, you'd never know who I was.'

"He laughed and said, 'Well, I don't know how you feel, Helga, but I like you already.'

"I removed the bag and it was the beginning of a lovely romance. After the reception, he asked me to go to a photography show the next evening. And four months later, we were married. When anyone asks us where we met, we always say, 'In a paper bag.' "

Though Helga's paper bag sounds bizarre, perhaps it worked because, like most flirtation, it was so ambiguous. Hank didn't, in fact, know exactly what Helga meant by it. "The essential quality of flirtation is ambiguity," Dr. John Sabini, an associate professor of psychology at the University of Pennsylvania who has done some research on flirtation, recently told a reporter. "Once flirtation becomes explicit, it may be a lot of things, but it's no longer flirtation." In other words, once you say, "You're sexy," or "Let's go to bed," you're seducing or propositioning a man, not flirting with him. Dr. Maury Silver, who teaches psychology at Johns Hopkins University, agrees. He points out that ambiguity is the *essence* of flirtation, because it allows you to test the waters, so to speak, to get a man's reaction without committing yourself. Flirting, if it flops, leaves you a graceful exit. If a man doesn't return your glance, ignores your touch, or thinks your remark silly, you can just drift away as if meeting him were the farthest thought from your mind.

So the next time you have a chance, try some casual flirting. It's lots of fun and a great way to meet men.

# Get a Job

If yours was a traditional marriage in which your husband worked and you stayed home with the kids, I'd advise you to get a job. If you haven't worked before, just getting hired can lift your spirits and make you feel more independent and self-assured. A job also gets you out of the house and gives you a place to go and a schedule to follow, so you're less likely to spend the whole day moping about home in your bathrobe. Working gives you an incentive to buy a new, more flattering wardrobe and lose a couple of pounds if you want to. It gives you money to spend so you'll be less dependent on your ex and can put more fun in your life. As an added benefit, working puts you in touch with men. If you choose your job with care (elementary-school teacher or playground supervisor *aren't* careers I'd recommend), chances are you'll meet dozens of male coworkers.

Maybe you think you have no marketable skills. But I maintain that if you've worked as a housewife and mother, you're probably a lot more employable than you believe. As author Doris Lessing has said, no one is more suited for a career than a middle-aged woman who has run a household—and industry should be putting such women to use. Your pluses: You're mature enough to handle responsibility, you've learned to balance a budget, you know how to organize time and schedules, and you're not likely to quit to have a baby (as a young woman often does).

Or perhaps you think you have no time to work now that you're raising kids by yourself. But the fact is, you can probably find a part-time job that won't interfere with child-rearing. Going off to the office for a few hours a day and having an excuse to dress up can even be a welcome relief from household routine. Here in Tenafly, where I live, many offices hire women with two or three children to come in two or three hours a day to pack books, file, type, answer phones, or do other jobs that don't require you to have an M.B.A. Yet these jobs pay pretty well and allow you plenty of free time. To find a part-time job, just open any local newspaper to the "Help Wanted" section: You'll be amazed at the lists of part-time office help needed.

Another way to work without giving yourself totally over to the nine to five is to sign up with a temporary office-help agency like Manpower, Inc., or Kelly Services. (Just look in the Yellow Pages under "Employment—Temporary" in any good-sized town and you'll find dozens of these agencies listed.) Working temporarily, by the way, doesn't mean you're not "good enough" to work full-time. Writers, free-lance photographers, executives' wives who want to use their excellent skills but still have time to vacation with their families—all these people find temporary work.

To get a temporary job (and you can get a job doing anything, from computer programming to just answering phones), you merely have to go into the agency and sign up. Depending on the type of job you want, you may have to take a few tests (typing, shorthand, spelling, whatever). Then the agency sends you out on assignment for a couple of days, a week, or even a few months. Salaries depend on the going market rate in the city you work in, but just to give you an example, Kelly Services in Stamford, Connecticut, was recently paying temporary secretaries $7.00 to $8.50 an hour.

Secretaries, by the way, are in enormous demand today (and I'm not being chauvinistic; lots of *men* work as secretaries today, too). Each year, an estimated eighty thousand to ninety thousand secretarial jobs in the United States go unfilled, a cumulative shortage that may reach a quarter of a million by 1985. Thanks to that large demand, salaries for secretaries are up. A woman at the placement office of the Katharine Gibbs secretarial school recently told me that in Fairfield County, Connecticut, a good secretary *starts* at an average salary of thirteen thousand dollars a year, and some executive secretaries now earn thirty thousand dollars a year. (That's better than a teacher of the fifth grade I know who just got her first job at ninety-eight hundred dollars a year!) I know typing may sound like dullsville (and I'm not saying that's your only option), but it could be the start you need. If you get with the right company (one that promotes from within and has several top female executives), you can eventually gain promotions to administrative assistant and other higher positions. Anyway, I'm not here to give you career counseling. To help determine which jobs you're best suited for, what skills you have, and how to win the job you want, just stop by your local bookstore and pick up a handy job-hunting guide, such as *What Color Is Your Parachute?* by Richard N. Bolles (New York, Ten Speed Press, 1977; $7.95).

Before accepting a job offer, consider how many men you'll be working with. Forget beauty shops, women's gyms, cosmetics shops, and feminine boutiques. Look, instead, for a job in a field full of men. Get work in a construction company, a trucking firm, a men's-clothing store. Work for an investment or legal firm. Apply for a job pumping gas. Sell Mercedeses or BMW's. If you don't mind standing on your feet in the sunlight all day, work *on* a road construction crew. Most construction outfits, especially those in the West, now hire women to carry the flags (so you needn't become a Caterpillar tractor operator or do other hard labor). If you plan to go back to college, at least *consider* a career in a traditionally male profession such as forestry, math, or engineering (and avoid female-dominated careers such as nursing and teaching, which pay poorly, anyway).

To give you an example of what can happen when you take a job in which you're surrounded by men, let me tell you about a thirty-six-year-old divorced woman in Seal Beach, California. Marcia found her former career as a kindergarten teacher useless for meeting men, so she chucked the whole thing and moved into a totally new job—the kind of situation most women dream of.

"About a year after my divorce, I realized all my suffering was behind me, and it was time to concentrate on a normal life again," Marcia relates. "For me, that means *men.* I hate living alone, and once my anger and bitterness wore off, I realized all men weren't like my ex. I decided to get a job *just* to meet men. I was trained to be a kindergarten teacher, a position where the only males are five years old and wet their pants when they're nervous, so I knew that would never do. Then a friend who works at the naval base here in town told me about an opening at the Enlisted Men's Club. I applied, and with her recommendation, I got the job!

"Though you didn't have to be especially bright to work in this job, I liked it because I got to work lots of different places. Sometimes I worked in the bar, at other times in the bowling alley or restaurant. The fantastic thing was all the

men I met—all ages, from eighteen-year-old seamen to re-
tirement-age chief petty officers. (Retirement in the Navy
isn't what it is in industry: A chief petty officer can retire
after twenty years, so lots of these guys were only thirty-
seven, thirty-eight.) An added advantage of my job is,
unlike working on a construction crew or other male-
dominated area, I wasn't invading the male world, so I
didn't have all the hostilities associated with that. Anyway,
after a while I got to seeing the same faces again and again,
and because sailors seldom see women, they're eager to
strike up a conversation with *any* female.

"One night when I was working in the cafeteria, one
tall, lanky chief who looked a lot like Henry Fonda in *Mr.
Roberts* kept coming through my line with pie and coffee. I
had already spoken to him each time through, so we weren't
total strangers. On his third trip I said, 'You're going to
lose that lanky look if you keep eating pie.' He fumbled with
the money in his wallet for a minute, then gave me an
abashed look and replied, 'I know, and I don't normally
even eat dessert. But I was just transferred here from a car-
rier in the Mediterranean. You're the first woman I've spoken to in six months, and it felt so good I just couldn't stop.'
It was so cute the way he said it. So I told him, 'Well, we
can't have that. Why don't you put the pie back. I get off
work in about three hours, and I could treat you to a whole
conversation.' He laughed, put the pie back, and was standing at my side a half hour before I got off work. How can
you mess up with a guy that eager? We talked three hours
that night and went out the next night. His name was
Randy and he was a really nice man. We see each other a
lot, but not every night because I have to make room for
some of the other great men I've met. I've even had to turn
down dates because I don't have that much time in my life.
Marcia smiles impishly, then adds, "I guess I'm like the Ma-
rines: I'm looking for just a few good men."

Marcia's job, of course, was a dream come true. Few

women are lucky enough to find a position with *thousands* of unattached men available. Still, her story illustrates a good point. When you look for work, try to find a job where the men are. Sell tickets at a baseball park. Work in a men's health club. Apply for jobs in your city's financial district, in a hardware store, or at a marina. God knows, these aren't the most glamorous positions around, but look at the positive side: They're easy to get. Also, you can usually work jobs like these part-time, leaving your mornings free for jogging, shopping, or tennis lessons.

What if you interview for five positions and still haven't been hired? Simple. Try again. I mean it. Who cares if that dodo at the last place failed to recognize your talents and skills? The next interviewer may very well hire you. Your interviewing skills get better with practice, and you may need a few failures at first before you see exactly how to do it. But while job-hunting can be trying, I maintain that the rewards far outweigh the drawbacks. Once you land a job, you'll soon be meeting more men in a day than you'll meet at home in a year.

So get ahold of today's newspaper *right now* and look through the want ads.

# CHAPTER 16

## Take a Trip

If you've just been divorced, separated, or widowed, I realize you may not have all that many pennies in the bank. But if you do have some spare cash, by all means take a vacation. "Travel?" a recently divorced woman I know asked, groaning. "Christ, I'm so immobilized I can't even go to the post office!" Perhaps you, too, feel so hassled or lethargic that vacationing sounds too difficult even to attempt. But just listen to my side a minute.

If you haven't been away since you've been single again, you deserve a break. Escaping from humdrum routine for even a weekend can rejuvenate and energize you, make you feel more positive about yourself. A man is usually more relaxed, approachable, and interested in meeting women while traveling than when he's home, pressured by memos, phone calls, and board meetings. Also, when

you're on the road, everyone's defenses drop. You make
friends in minutes, not days. Not only does traveling offer
endless chances to sit, stand, and eat next to men, but also,
face it, you just seem more provocative and alluring to a
man you've met at a sidewalk cafe in Vienna than you do to
the plumber who comes to fix your toilet.

*Oh, but a man met on vacation is just a one-week stand
at best,* you think? Not necessarily. One Missouri woman
(thirty pounds overweight and not all that beautiful, by the
way) met a millionaire bachelor from Spokane while admiring Michelangelo's "David" in Florence, Italy. Once back
in the States, Susan and Art wrote each other for about
six months, decided they'd fallen in love, and got married.
People you meet in an exotic place just *seem* more exciting—sometimes for life. Besides, so what if you don't meet a
man who will love you forever? Just getting together and
having a few laughs for an afternoon or evening can lift
your spirits, make you feel great, teach you to flirt. A vacation is just too much fun, and too great a man-meeting option, to overlook.

Where to go? Before we get to that (there *are* places in
the world where men outnumber women by the thousands),
let me say this: I don't think you should design any vacation
*solely* to meet men. If you do that and fail to meet someone,
you'll just wind up feeling discouraged, and the whole trip
will be a wash. Plan your vacation first and foremost for
fun. Go where you've always wanted to go. Plan activities
you love.

Now that that's said, let's get down to the nitty-gritty:
great places to travel. I polled dozens of travel agents, editors, travel writers, stewardesses, and single women to see
where their favorite places in the world are for meeting
men. Here they are.

The Hawaiian Islands—especially Maui. One San
Francisco divorcée returns to Maui every summer because
she finds so many bronzed, outdoorsy males there and adds,

"I always meet three or four I'm reluctant to leave." A good hotel for a single woman is the inexpensive Pioneer Inn (a single room is less than $35 a night) in the picturesque historic whaling town of Lahaina. Overlooking the harbor, the inn, with its forty-eight high-ceilinged rooms, is cozy, friendly, and has one of the most popular bars on the islands—the Whalers Saloon, filled on balmy tropical evenings with surfers, beachcombers, and sailors, all stomping their feet to the tunes of a rowdy piano player.

Visit Honolulu, where men under age fifty outnumber women that age by nearly twenty thousand! Many of these available men gather downtown at Jameson's Irish Coffee House, 15 Merchant Street. A watering hole for single upward-strivers but not a singles bar in the traditional sense, this bistro offers a warm, friendly, unintimidating atmosphere for getting together. Or stop by the super-deluxe Mauna Kea Beach Hotel on the island of Hawaii. Several women voted this resort hotel the best man-meeting place on the islands. If you can't afford to stay here (a single room runs $170 or more per night), stop by around noon for the sumptuous buffet luncheon, open to anyone.

No matter which city in the world you visit, of course, you'll always meet distinguished, gentlemanly men in the better hotels. In Hong Kong, just sit in the bar of the Peninsula or Mandarin hotels (two of the best hotels in the city) and you'll see hundreds of British and American businessmen. As one thirty-five-year-old Manhattan woman and veteran traveler told me, "You can't help but meet somebody."

A favorite city for stewardesses is Kuwait, a city teaming with males, including many international businessmen. Because Arabian women seldom leave their house, and when they do, wear those black cloths over their faces, Kuwaiti men go crazy for American women—especially blondes. The best place to stay? Any of the better hotels, such as the Kuwait Hilton or the Kuwait Sheraton. This oil-rich country is expensive these days, though: Be prepared to spend at least $100 a night, probably more, for a single room in a luxury hotel.

Or check out Jamaica. Though the bustling city of Montego Bay is filled with unsavory longshoremen, other parts of the island are populated with many friendly, eligible bachelors. The best place on the island to meet men? The Sheraton Hotel's Jonkanoo Bar in the cosmopolitan city of Kingston. Just go there between 5:00 P.M. and 7:00 P.M. weekdays for a glass of wine and you'll have half a dozen distinguished fellows to choose from. You might also want to check out the local service called "Meet the People," run by the tourist boards of Jamaica's major resorts (Montego Bay, Port Antonio, Kingston, and Ocho Rios). While not a dating service, "Meet the People" will put you in touch with men and women who enjoy what you do—snorkeling, sailing, tennis, Ping-Pong, or whatever. You get together casually, informally—and, of course, you never know whom you will meet.

Or try a week in British Columbia. Single men between ages twenty-five and thirty-four outnumber women that age by seven thousand there. You'll find many of these single guys at the posh Sundance Guest Ranch near Ashcroft, where the ambience is casual and friendly. You're awakened early by the wranglers so you'll have hours to ride the trails. Then at day's end, you and the other guests gather around the great stone fireplace to drink (bring your own liquor) and hear guitarists sing old Western ballads. In such an easygoing place, even the shyest woman could connect. How much? About $1,000 a week. But if that's too steep for your budget, British Columbia has many less expensive guest ranches you may want to check out. (For information, write the British Columbia Government Travel Bureau, Parliament Buildings, Victoria, British Columbia, Canada.)

What about Europe? Some six million American tourists use American Express offices in foreign cities as their summer check-in points, and whenever you stop by any of these offices, you're likely to run into a lonely Texan or a good old boy from Oklahoma. You'll be amazed how instantly friendly all Americans become with other Americans on foreign soil. Just *being* from the U.S.A. makes you feel—and act—like long-lost neighbors. To meet men, most travel agents I talked to agree you're best off avoiding northern Europe (Scandinavian women are too sexually liberated to compete with). And, despite the romantic reputation of Parisians, France also got repeatedly poor marks. As one travel editor told me, "There's lots of picking up going on on the French Riviera, but most of it's a bit seamy. I'd avoid the Riviera—unless you want to bare your breasts." So in Europe, go to other places.

Try Italy, for example. You needn't worry about being shy. Italian men are aggressive enough for both of you. Rome's always great (in fact, you may attract more bottom pinchers there than you'd care to meet). So is Perugia. An intellectual center, home of the *Università per gli Stranieri* (University for Foreigners), Perugia attracts floods of Italian men, many of them doctors from Bologna, who come here just to meet women. As a former travel editor for *Mademoiselle* told me, "Just sit in an outdoor cafe in Perugia for four minutes—you can't miss." High in the Umbrian mountains, Perugia is also idyllically picturesque, and it's the chocolate center of Italy. Oddly enough, *local* Perugians are somewhat cold and aloof, so you'll want to meet students and men who, like you, are just passing through. One good place to find them is around the bulletin boards in Palazzo Gallenga, looking at the posted lists of university events (including English-language films).

Another great country to visit is Greece. In Athens, the big matchmaking spots day or night are the bars on the arcade off Syntagma Square. Just sit there for a few minutes and you're bound to meet someone. Two of the best hotels in town (both good places to meet executives) are the Athens Hilton and the renowned Grande Bretagne, built in 1826. If you'd rather avoid bars and keep your night life more casual, by all means go to one of Athens' many *tavernas*, sociable restaurant-cafes where one or two American women alone will inevitably attract male notice. Every woman I talked to has her own favorite *taverna* in town, but one that sounds special is the very popular Xynou at 4 Angelos Xerondos in Plaka, where guitarists perform Greek songs.

If you feel uneasy about traveling alone, try London. Exotic enough to be exciting yet filled with men who speak English, London's perfect for a single woman on her first holiday. You may imagine Britons to be formal and aloof. That's just a myth. Londoners are, in fact, quite friendly and eager to help an American who's lost or confused about which street to take to Trafalgar Square. London pubs, cozier and less anxiety-causing than American singles bars, are such easygoing, *friendly* places to meet men. As one travel writer wrote, "The English say 'chat-up' instead of 'pick-up,' and the difference in phrasing reveals a whole different *style*—one that's frankly nicer than its American counterpart." One of the most popular pubs in town is Dirty Dick's, where fake bats and spiders dangle from the ceiling, but to find dozens of other great pubs, just pick up any travel guidebook to England at your local bookstore. Other good places for London chat-ups: Trafalgar Square, Regent's Park Zoo, Hyde Park Corner on Sundays, and of course the traditional U.S. Embassy and American Express offices. If wealthy men interest you, look for them at Claridge's Hotel, where heads of state and foreign dignitaries stay when they're in London and you often can't see the hotel entrance for all the long black limousines lined up before the doors. International businessmen also congregate in the posh London Hilton; if you can't afford to stay there, drop by the pub or disco for the evening. Discoing, by the way, is still popular in London. Though the city's disco scene is rapidly changing, you'll still find plenty of popular night spots. Stop by Tramps at 40 Hermyn Street to disco with the chic social set, or try the popular Tiffany's at 22 Shaftesbury Avenue, where you can dance every night until 2:00 A.M. for $2.00.

Then there's Mexico. Since Mexican women tend to stay indoors and even those who do venture forth seldom sleep with a man before the honeymoon, Mexican men go wild when American women come to town. (You needn't sleep with them, of course; just bask in the attention.) Two unassertive southern California women I know, who hate to lie on native beaches trying to compete with all the long-legged, bikinied blondes, go to Mexico regularly for an ego boost. As one said, "Mexican men are so romantic. They give you flowers, serenade you with guitars . . . you feel like a queen!" If Mayan ruins intrigue you, go to Yucatan (scholarly men— archaeologists, Ph.D. candidates, and writers—tend to collect here). Or try Acapulco, with its white-sand beaches, exciting night life (which usually doesn't *begin* until 11:00 P.M.), and hordes of young single men. Barbara Rubin, my travel agent at Trips Away Travel agency in Tenafly, New Jersey, says, "When I book young single men on tours, the three places they most want to go are Acapulco, Hawaii, and the Club Med."

Club Med, the worldwide French resort network, by the way, is terrific for a single woman traveling alone. For about $1,000 a week, you can take a Club tour to any of a dozen or so romantic tropical islands (including Bora Bora, Guadelupe, and Martinique). And you're always traveling in a group, usually with many single men, so you never feel really alone. At most Club villages it's handy, though not mandatory, if you speak French. The greatest thing about the Club is the relaxed, friendly ambience: casual chats around the bar, dancing usually until dawn. Many activities are planned, so before you have time to hesitate you're swept up in a busy day of sailing, spear-fishing, tennis, or excursions to intriguing local sights. If you do try the Club, diet before leaving. The country-style French cuisine (served family style, so it's remarkably easy to chat with fellow travelers) is so delicious you're bound to gain five pounds. That $1,000 price tag, by the way, may sound stiff, but it includes everything: bus fares, tips, and all the luncheon and dinner wine you can drink.

Another good possibility: Take a cruise. I absolutely guarantee you if you take a cruise to Europe you'll meet at least two or three men worth knowing (perhaps even one going to the city you're headed for, so he can show you around). *The Love Boat* atmosphere exists to a great extent on every ocean liner. You'll be seated at a table for breakfast, lunch, and dinner with several people (probably men, since cruise directors tend to be matchmakers), and you'll have ample time to socialize around the bar and at evening shows. Every activity on a ship—the pool, shuffleboard, afternoon movies—is designed to get people together. Though I know of no marriages yet, I do know half a dozen women who've found shipboard romances en route to Europe. As Bev, a forty-eight-year-old dietician who had undergone a particularly ego-shattering divorce when her husband of twenty-two years left her for a younger woman, told me, "Before I boarded my ship for Scotland I felt I was the ugliest woman alive. But one week aboard that ship made me realize I'm not only still attractive, I'm even alluring. I only met men who *flirted* with me, but Lordie, that was nice. I returned home realizing it was Larry [her ex] who made the big mistake—not me."

*That's fine for her*, you may think, *but I have children I can't leave behind.* Then take your kids with you. I mean it. Although *teenagers* can be a drag (they look at you with such dour expressions whenever a man stops to chat), cute younger children can even attract male attention. A man who's too timid to approach a single woman will often feel relaxed striking up a conversation with a five-year-old boy—and, of course, it's easy, then, for him to start talking to you. A divorced dad with kids at home also may like to see a woman traveling with young children. He thinks you'll be more receptive to his kids. To make traveling with kids easy, Club Med now has a parent-child village in Guadelupe. While the youngsters play at the children's camp all day, you're free to go snorkeling, play tennis, swim, and lounge on the beaches.

If you can't afford a major trip, take a short one. If you live in Los Angeles, for example, spend the weekend in Las Vegas (eighteen hundred more men than women under age sixty-five there). Vegas is remarkably cheap, by the way: To attract gamblers, some casinos offer $.49 and $.99 breakfasts, and there's even a Motel 6 in town (reservations a must) for only $13 a night. If you enjoy tennis, go to a tennis camp. Or if you like surfing, rent a cottage and spend a week at the beach.

Getting away from your daily routine and having fun can change your whole outlook on life. Even if you fail to meet a man on your getaway, you'll feel more "up" and ready to meet one when you get home. So the next time you have a few days off, consider a *real* vacation—not one where you just hang around home watching *As the World Turns*, but a trip where you'll see new places, tackle challenges, and meet people. You'll be amazed at how great you'll feel.

## Move to
## San Diego

O.K., admittedly the title of this chapter is a bit tongue-in-cheek—but not entirely. Some parts of the country just naturally offer more eligible men than others. Orlando, Florida, for example, is senior-citizen paradise, and you may look long and hard to find a man in his late thirties. Tampa has the oldest median-age population in the country (nearly four out of ten people there are over fifty, and nearly 60 percent of those older people are women). In Chicago, women outnumber men by 270,000. And in New York City's Manhattan, women outnumber men by 500,000. Definitely not promising statistics. Or take the wooded back hills of Connecticut: full of families. If I lived in any of those places and *really* wanted to meet men, I'd move.

Other regions are just naturally for women who want to reconnect. Stroll along any street in Venice, California, and you'll see beautiful young men everywhere. In California, which caters to singles, you'll find not only singles bars but also singles cruises, backpacking trips, clubs—even singles breakfasts.

I recently did an in-depth survey of American cities to determine where the men are and discovered some mind-opening statistics. First, you can't compare cities across the board because some places have tons of old men and no young ones. Others have thousands of spare eighteen-year-olds but offer sparse pickings if you want a man over thirty. I've already pointed out that you shouldn't eliminate a guy just because he's "too old" or "too young." Let's say, though, that you'd *prefer* a man between twenty-five and thirty-four. Then here are the best places to find him.

### Best Man-Meeting Cities in America
### (Ages 25–34)

1. San Diego—three men for every two women
2. Biloxi, Mississippi—three men for every two women
3. Norfolk, Virginia—three men for every two women
4. Minneapolis, Minnesota—seven men for every four women
5. Charleston, South Carolina—five men for every four women
6. Columbia, South Carolina—thirteen men for every nine women
7. Honolulu, Hawaii—eleven men for every nine women
8. Austin, Texas—thirteen men for every eleven women
9. Anchorage, Alaska—nine men for every eight women
10. San Antonio, Texas—nine men for every eight women

What are the *worst* cities for romance? If you're looking for a guy between ages twenty-five and thirty-four, Raleigh, North Carolina, takes the prize for having fewer eligible young men per woman than any other major city in the country: only three young men for every five young women. Three other cities tie for having rotten man-woman ratios: Sioux Falls, South Dakota; Kansas City, Missouri; and St. Louis, Missouri. All have only four men between twenty-five and thirty-four for every five women that age.

But enough about bad places. Let's get back to the good ones. Are there any cities where *older* men outnumber older women? One is Anchorage, Alaska. (O.K., so maybe that city's too snowy for you, no matter how many men live there.) But Fargo, North Dakota, might not be so bad (you'll find six men for every five women there). And the capital for distinguished older males is balmy Albuquerque, New Mexico, where the sun shines 76 percent of the daylight hours and there are seven older men for every three older women. Nestled over a mile high in the mountains, Albuquerque has its own symphony orchestra, five museums, and two universities—it sounds like a nice place.

What if you want a kind, gentle man in his late thirties or forties? That, unfortunately, becomes more difficult, at least statistically. About the best you can do if you're looking for a guy who's between thirty-five and forty-nine is to go to a city where your odds are even (that is, where there are at least as many men as women). Here they are. (An asterisk marks cities where you'll find a *few* more men than women.)

1. Anchorage, Alaska*
2. Biloxi, Mississippi (about seventy-five hundred more men age twenty-five to thirty-four, too)
3. Charleston, South Carolina (also more men than women in the twenty-five to thirty-four age bracket)

4. Austin, Texas
5. Norfolk, Virginia* (lots of sailors here)
6. Fargo, North Dakota (but North Dakota has the lowest divorce rate in the country, so most of these guys are married)
7. Honolulu* (especially good because there's a surplus of younger men here, too)
8. Raleigh, North Carolina* (but there are lots of extra women between ages twenty-five and thirty-four, so you'll have a lot of competition)
9. Great Falls, North Dakota (the odds are about even stephen for all ages here; it's only when they reach sixty-five that women begin to outnumber men)
10. San Diego* (thanks to the naval base)
11. Boise, Idaho
12. Casper, Wyoming (the population is one of the most evenly balanced in the country—until the old guys start dying off)
13. Las Vegas, Nevada* (but you've got only a slight edge here—only about 925 more men than women)
14. Sioux Falls, South Dakota (this is an odd town—in nearly every *other* age group, women outnumber men)
15. Seattle* (but the surplus of younger women keeps these thirty-five- to forty-nine-year-old men busy)
16. Los Angeles (an idyllic town for singles, too)
17. San Francisco

And, finally, for those of you who could love a man of any age from eighteen to eighty, here are the top five American cities where men of all ages outnumber women (and by how much). Remember, the numbers that follow represent *extra* males left over after every woman in town has one.

| City | Men Outnumber Women by |
|------|------------------------|
| San Diego | 46,491 |
| Minneapolis | 23,201 |
| Norfolk, Virginia | 16,797 |
| Honolulu | 16,764 |
| Anchorage, Alaska | 5,900 |

So if you despair of ever finding a man you like, maybe you're in the wrong house, neighborhood, or city. Move from the very married suburbs into a chic bachelor neighborhood. Get out of the woods and into the whirl of activity downtown. No sense sabotaging all your efforts by living in a female-filled city when you could be in a place where men outnumber women by the thousands!

## CHAPTER 18

## Enlist Family and Friends

You need not find on your own all the new men you meet. Ask for help. Your friends and family (including your children) can put you in touch with dozens of attractive guys you otherwise might never meet.

Ask your sister to introduce you to that cute shoe salesman she works with. Have your best friend fix you up with that newly divorced English professor she knows. (If a date sounds too formal, why not suggest that your friend invite you both to dinner one evening?)

At the very least, friends can help get you out of the house. Even if you don't meet a man, you are out there relating to people, extending your network of acquaintances, sharpening your social skills. And at most, friends can match you up with a man you'll marry. Friends, after all, know you and the kind of man who will be best for you, sometimes even better than you do. I still remember a friend of mine—Lara—who was always picking and losing overbearing *macho* men (like her father) when, in fact, I thought she'd be happiest with a soft-spoken, sophisticated, academic type. When a philosophy professor I knew broke up with his wife, I invited both him and Lara over for a Sunday afternoon barbecue. They've been happily married now for five years.

So cultivate new friendships whenever you can. Just getting out of the house with another *woman* can put you in touch with men at the beach, movies, or in bars—especially if your friend happens to be bold and daring. Margaret, a woman I know, was at Mount Vernon one day with a really outgoing, gregarious friend named Alice when they spied two men in a nearby Corvette. "Oh, those guys have got sandwiches and I'm *starving*," Alice said. "I'm going to go ask if we can have some." Well, of course, Margaret was about to die of embarrassment. But Undauntable Alice marched bravely over and not only got a free lunch but also met both men. One of the men *Margaret* wound up dating for the next three years!

So the next Saturday night or Sunday afternoon you have nothing to do, go out with the boldest woman you know. I realize if you have a friend like this she may bring out your feelings of jealousy and inadequacy. ("How can *she* be so confident when I'm so insecure and chicken-hearted?" you may feel.) But if you can *bear* those feelings, going out with such a woman can really be worth it because she'll bring you into contact with so many different people. (Besides, she's probably not as confident as you think. She may just be covering *her* insecurities under a blanket of bravado. You've got different coping styles, that's all.)

Of course, you can also have friends fix you up with blind dates. (Do I sense reluctance?) Perhaps you've been out on blind dates in the past and found that the men were pretty much losers. This is frequently the case, but not always. And I can assure you that I have known dozens of successful, kind, attractive, lovable men who have gone out on blind dates.

To make blind dates work for you, the secret is persistence—as Maureen, a thirty-one-year-old divorcée in Minneapolis discovered when her friends fixed her up. "At first after my divorce I didn't want to see anybody and I just stayed home weekends and evenings, but that got so depressing I knew I had to get out," Maureen relates. "Several girls at the office who knew I was divorced offered to fix me up with dates, but I refused: All my blind dates had been such *cretins.*

"Then one day I overheard two guys in my office talking about politics. Some local politician had just lost an election, but he'd gotten 10 percent of the vote. 'It figures,' I heard one guy say. 'You know the old saying, no matter how crazy something is, there's always that 10 percent who will go along with it.' That made me think maybe those statistics would work for me. If some dippy politician could get 10 percent, why couldn't I? If you date lots of men, I said to myself, you're bound to meet *one* you like."

So Maureen asked her friends to arrange ten blind dates for the next ten weekends—all on Saturday nights and no two dates with the same man. "I left Fridays open," Maureen explains, "because those were for repeat dates with any man I liked. I was scared, of course, but I told myself these were men my *friends* knew, so how awful could they be? The first guy wanted to talk about duck-hunting all night and made me listen to his duck calls. The second sat in a trance all evening listening to Mozart. But the third was a gem: a thirty-two-year-old accountant, a big lovable bear of a man named Bobby. We enjoyed the same movies, read the same books, laughed at the same jokes.

"He asked me out for the next Saturday night, but I told him no. I was determined to stick to my ten dates . . . who knew what I'd *miss?* The next Saturday, he asked again. I didn't want to discourage him, so I said, 'Gee, Bobby, I really like you and I'm free Friday, but Saturday I have a date.' He said, 'Boy, for a woman just divorced you have a busy social life. The men you knew must have been *praying* for this divorce.' I laughed and told him what I'd done. I feared he'd be disappointed to learn I wasn't the most desirable woman in town, but he seemed secretly *pleased* with my plan and was happy to wait for Friday nights (I reserved all of them for him). I liked Bobby for that. Lots of men would have been too insecure to go along with me. I did meet other attractive guys, including one bricklayer who called back a couple of times. But Bobby was the best, and we've been dating regularly for the past six months."

"That's fine for *her*," you may say, "but I don't have any friends—only kids." Lucky you. Though children may at first seem a handicap to your social life, they can be a marvelous *asset*. Give a birthday party for your son (and make certain he invites all the kids with good-looking divorced dads). Or pick out a girl whose father has custody for the weekend, then ask her to go with you and your daughter to the zoo. Even if the man doesn't take the hint and join you, he will have to pick up his daughter at your place at the end of the day (*don't* offer to drop her by his house on your way home, or he could hide inside and you'd never even see him). When he does pick up his daughter, make certain the girls are having too much fun to stop immediately, then invite him to linger for coffee—or even dinner. Children are actually wonderful pathways to new men because it all looks so *innocent:* You just want to make sure the kids have fun. Unlike never-married men, by the way, most fathers *appreciate* a good mother (remember, his last wife may have screamed at the kids, or refused to cook them breakfast).

Jamie, a lovely thirty-four-year-old from Bristol, Connecticut, at first thought her two sons—Shawn, eight, and

Anthony, eleven—would prevent her from meeting new men. *Then* she discovered Little League.

"At first I thought Little League would be a real drag," Jamie admits. "I mean, that's where all the together families are—and who wants to hang around a bunch of happy families when yours has just gone to the dogs? Anyway, how many available men could there be around a Little League park? As it turned out, *plenty*.

"The first night I took Anthony to practice, two divorced men were there. Anthony wanted to pitch, but he wound up shortstop because the coach said he had a good arm but couldn't throw enough balls in the strike zone. During practice, all the parents just stood on the sidelines with nothing to do, so I started looking the men over. I noticed this one guy standing alone—a tall, muscular, ex-football-player type. And he must have noticed me because he came over and said, 'Which one is yours?' When I pointed out Anthony, he said, 'Yeah? Say, that kid's got a cannon for an arm.' Now, who, I ask you, could feel uneasy around a man who thinks your son has an arm like a cannon? We talked for the rest of the practice. He told me his name was Brad, he was a lawyer, and he'd been divorced about a year (so he wasn't looking for a shoulder to cry on).

"The next practice, Brad was there again, and after practice, he asked Anthony and me out for a Coke. Naturally, we went, and while we were sipping Cokes, Brad asked me, 'Anthony's got quite an arm. How come he's not pitching?' When I told him the coach said he lacked control, Brad said, 'Aw, there's nothing to control but practice. Why don't you let me come over some afternoons and play catch with him? He'll be throwing strikes in no time.' After a few afternoons of pitching practice at my place, it was easy for Brad and me to start dating. Now we're married, and all our sons have graduated to Babe Ruth League. Little League's a great place to meet men. Carol Channing never knew how right she was when she said, 'A diamond is a girl's best friend!' "

Perhaps you believe the myth that men don't find mothers sexy or want a woman with children. That may have been true when you were eighteen—but, then, the men your age were still boys themselves. After twenty-five or thirty, a man usually likes kids and finds mothers appealing. Divorced dads have no qualms about dating mothers. (His last wife was a mother, wasn't she?) So go to a baseball diamond, a soccer field, or a basketball court. Volunteer to raise funds for the Boy Scouts. And do attend parent-child picnics. Single dads are everywhere. And if a man's interested enough in his kids to spend time with them, he's usually a sympathetic, considerate, gentle, loving guy.

So why wait to get off by yourself at a singles bar, tennis club, or party to meet men? You've probably got friends and children. Use them.

# CHAPTER 19

## Singles Bars

About a year ago I wrote a column in *Oui* magazine recommending against singles bars. Yet as you're going to discover in just a few paragraphs, I'm touting them here. Have they changed that much over the past twelve months?

Not at all. They're about the same as they always were. The reason I suggested the readers of *Oui* avoid them is that the vast majority of *Oui*'s readers are men ... and men are what you find a disproportionate amount of in singles bars. In fact, on any given night of the year, there's probably no easier or surer way to find a place where men outnumber women than in the nation's more than twenty-eight thousand singles bars. And unlike football stadiums and bowling alleys, the men here are *looking* for women, almost by definition.

*Sure, they're looking for women, like a fox looks for chickens.* Yes, yes, I know all the myths about men who frequent singles bars. They're only interested in one thing, most of them are married, every other one is a budding young Mr. Goodbar. And there's no question that these myths are not to be taken lightly. There *are* a lot of creeps and sickies who hang around in singles bars. Yet it would be a mistake to rule out all the men, or even the vast majority of those who visit singles bars, because of a few bad apples. The truth is, if approached in the right frame of mind and with your antennae working, singles bars can be fun, festive, upbeat, and, most important of all, a plentiful and continuing source of available new men, a well that never runs dry, so to speak.

Let me see if I can shed some light. Toward the beginning of the book I tried to explain just how fragile and vulnerable many men are. Here I'm going to expand on that theme. When the average woman walks into a singles bar what her eye usually encounters first is a tableau out of *Cabaret,* dozens of slickly dressed, sexually gymnastic, confident, swaggering revelers, most of them male. It's hard for her to believe that any one among them could be sensitive or warm or tender.

But let me assure you, this is a case where outward appearances couldn't be more deceiving. I know. Not too many years ago I was a habitué of singles bars. Every Friday and Saturday night, and often several weekday nights as well, I and many of my friends wandered Manhattan's most popular singles bars, ostensibly looking for sex but really looking for acceptance, for a woman who would really like us.

Men don't like to admit this, of course. But I know in my bones and my cells and brain and my heart that it is undeniable. Some evidence: I have *never* heard a man describe a one-night stand with genuine excitement, only *macho* bravado. I have heard hundreds of men recount meeting a new woman, one they liked and who liked them back, with exaltation, bubbliness, the same kind of enthusiasm more frequently ascribed to women.

Close friends have confided their loneliness, their feelings of inadequacy and shyness around women a hundredfold more than their horniness, their desire to love 'em and leave 'em. Believe me, without love in it, a man's life is as incomplete and barren as a woman's, maybe more so. Countless studies indicate that single adult males have a significantly higher incidence of depression, suicide, morbidity, and health problems than adult single women.

What does all this mean? That the terrifying tableau of lechery and wolfishness that confronts you the moment you step into a singles bar is a chimera. Look deeper. Don't accept surface impressions. Realize that approximately four out of every five men you see will *not* get up the courage to even approach a woman tonight, that a greater ratio will go home alone, feeling dejected, rejected, and unloved.

And, as with any random segment of the population, there are no more psychotics nor liars nor thieves here than there are among other groups. In fact, if you choose a nice pub, the clientele may very well be superior to other groups in income, profession, educational background, and cultivation. I know scores of dentists and doctors and lawyers and successful business executives who frequent singles bars on a regular basis because they just aren't connecting with women in other arenas. To look at and speak to them, one would assume that these men would have no trouble at all. But as I indicated before, men are often a great deal shyer and more self-effacing around women than you'd guess. I've met scores of men who are charismatic leaders among their business colleagues but are thoroughly lost and rudderless in the company of women.

Now, does all this mean that you should wade right into the thick of things, walk up to the man who appeals to you most, and ask him back to your place? Absolutely not. Singles bars may be full of willing men, but just as you would anywhere, you should use restraint, judgment, patience, and good manners. You should also understand that there is no need to violate your own sense of morality and style, no need to compromise yourself just because you're in a different milieu than you ever expected to be. Believe it or not, when the dust settles, the people in singles bars are the same kind of folks who work in your office or go to your church or live on your block.

Now, if you're about to confront the singles bars scene for the first time, you're probably a bit tense. Here are some tips. First, appearance counts. Forget the "I want to be liked for myself" approach. Surface is all he sees at first, so you might want to dress a bit sexier than usual. Wear clothes that drape, cling, and move. If you feel like showing off, wear a glittery jumpsuit, metallic T-shirt, or satin knickers. If you'd rather dress simply, that's O.K. too, but wear your hair loose and free. Second, don't expect too much. The most exciting man next to Clark Gable may be here, but probably not. Best to keep expectations realistic.

How to behave? Find a spot at a table or the bar, order a drink (Perrier or soda if you dislike hard stuff), and look around. Suppose a debonair guy with chiseled features wearing Calvin Klein jeans and a red silk shirt seems to be looking at you. Underneath that glittery façade he may be a sensitive, caring man; don't be afraid to catch his eye. (Tonight is eye-contact night.) Gaze, don't stare. Smile. Most of all, look friendly, warm, interested, and approachable, not as if you'd rather be home washing underwear or balancing your checkbook. You'd be horrified if you knew how many men *didn't* approach you in the course of your life because you looked as if you were going to rebuff them.

If the man ambles over, say hello. Pretty easy so far, right? Tell him you noticed him. He looked nice.

Don't fret about witty one-liners or how little you know about OPEC. Discuss the mundane: your names, where you

and he work, what you both like to drink. Suppose you like
him and he says, "Your place or mine?" (although this is a
lot less likely to happen than you've fantasized). Don't feel
you'll lose him if you decline. He's probably just as timid as
you are and is coming on *macho* because he thinks *you* expect it. If you like him but prefer not to sleep with him—
just yet—reply, "Not yet, but I like you a lot and would like
to know you better. Why don't we have lunch sometime
soon?" Then pin him down to a definite day—tomorrow—so
he'll know you're not rejecting him. Again, men feel shy and
fret about rejection, probably more than you do.

Here's a sample conversation:

YOU: Gee, that's a terrific shirt.

HIM: Say, it's kind of crowded in here. What say you come
to my place for some brandy?

YOU: That sounds like fun, but I've made it a rule not to
go back to a man's place when I've just met.

HIM: I'm a nice guy. I won't do anything you wouldn't
like.

YOU: I know, it's just a personal rule that makes me feel a
little better, but I would love to see you again. I'd
love to have lunch and get to know you better.

HIM: Gee, won't you change your mind?

YOU: No, I'm sorry. I have to get to know you better
first—and I'd like to.

If all goes well, you can then exchange cards and phone
numbers, perhaps make a lunch date. You can say, "Tell
you what: I'll take you to lunch."

O.K., that's if a man approaches you. What if he
doesn't? Then take a deep breath and approach him. Be
straightforward, not cute. Here are a few prosaic but absolutely workable bar banalities that even the shyest woman
can master:

- "Hi."
- "Do you come here often?"
- "What are you drinking?"
- "May I join you?"
- "I've been wanting to meet you."
- "Boy, what a crowd. It's not usually this noisy during the week, is it?"
- "What other bars do you go to?"
- "What kind of music do you like?"

Keep your openers light and friendly. If he just sits there like a rock, move gracefully on. But don't think his lack of response means you're ugly, boring, witless, or too fat. Maybe he's gay or his wife beats him. Remember, Mother was right when she said, "You can't please all the people all the time." (Or was it Abe Lincoln who said that?) Anyway, it's true.

If the singles bars scene sounds too intimidating even to attempt, then try a downtown cocktail lounge at 5:30 P.M. when executives are just stopping for drinks after work. I have a divorced woman friend who swears that this is the best time of the day because the clientele are more likely to be businessmen unwinding than rakes looking to conquer. Or try a neighborhood piano bar in the evening. Whatever bar you choose, practice smiling, reaching out, risking, making contact. Here are ten more basic rules for barhopping:

1. Think positively.
2. Try different bars.
3. If you dislike hard liquor, drink Perrier.
4. Go solo.
5. If you don't find the man of your dreams, don't give up. Try again next week.
6. Keep your expectations realistic. Consider the man who isn't a "10."

7. Take the initiative.
8. Don't go into a depressive tailspin just because some guy rejected you. Everybody gets rejected sometimes. It's part of the life process. On a purely biological level, Darwin points out that species that survive are species that have it tough.
9. Go home with a man or take him to your apartment *only* if you're sure he's O.K. Usually, it's best to suggest a second date first.
10. Be yourself—but be the best you can be.

Before signing off on singles bars, I'd like to make one last point. Some of you may have tried them once or twice and decided they're simply not for you. You felt out of place, too old, too out of step; repulsed, even, by the noise and the brazen searching for partners. So be it. I would feel awful if I thought that any of the advice in this book were causing you to do things that made you genuinely uncomfortable.

On the other hand, I would feel wonderful if I knew that something I wrote was helping you to stretch, to go beyond yourself. Some of you, I suspect, have been tempted by the notion of visiting a singles bar but have allowed all the facile negative publicity ("They're just meat markets") or your own shyness to stop you. If that's the case, I urge you to pick out the nicest singles pub near you and give it a whirl. Sure, you're going to be nervous at first, and sure, you're going to feel out of place. I wish I could adequately communicate to you just how overwhelmed I felt the evening I entered my first singles bar, Malachy's on Manhattan's Third Avenue (the site of the bar is now an antiques store). The sensation of being an alien, of being out of my element, was as intense as passing through customs on my initial trip to Europe, stepping into Brussels airport, a twenty-year-old college junior, without friends, fluency in French, or a place to stay.

Yet as with many of life's new experiences, time somehow soothed my nervousness, my resistance, the unfamiliarity of it all. Before long I was mastering the art of edging my way through the crowd to order a drink at the bar, learning how to smile and make small talk with strangers. My second visit was less anxiety-causing than my first; I knew what to expect. My third and fourth visits were almost comfortable. The sixth or seventh time I went to Malachy's, I met a lovely young woman from Connecticut who three years later became my wife.

Abraham Maslow, the psychologist, tells us that true personal growth is achieved most significantly when we allow ourselves to be in those situations where we feel out of control—when someone who fears heights, for example, takes an elevator to the top of the Empire State Building, when we invite a person whom we feel is above us socially or professionally for a dinner party at our home, when we take a job interview for a position whose criteria we worry we do not meet.

For some of you, visiting a singles bar will be downright scary, will make you feel out of control. Yet if you can endure your feeling of discomfort for an hour or two, or through a second or third visit, I predict that you will soon feel quite at home. True, you may conclude you don't like the environment of these bustling, crowded meeting places for the unattached. But at least you will have come to this decision firsthand . . . and you will be a stronger, more experienced person for it.

# CHAPTER
## 20

# Detecting
# the
# Available Man

For much of this book, we've been concentrating on *you*, how you can change your life-style, attitudes, and living patterns in small but significant ways—to bring more men into your life. Now it's time to talk about *him*. Let's face it: Lots of men you meet are totally wrong for you. They're married, gay, living with women, or just so peculiar they never think about women. How do you find men you'll like who will like you?

The first step is weeding out available men from those already taken. That sounds hard, but it's easier than you think: You can do it without saying a word.

Once you think about it, you'll realize men constantly give you availability clues. The classic but unfortunately least reliable clue is that old standard: the wedding ring. Lack of the traditional gold band, of course, means little (many happily married men go ringless these days). But if he does wear what looks like a wedding ring, he's probably quite married. Look elsewhere (unless, of course, you enjoy flings with married men).

A man skiing alone, doing his own laundry, or anywhere on vacation by himself is probably unattached. If he's in a bar alone at 9:00 P.M. or at a party by himself, chances are he's unmarried (or soon will be). In fact, anytime you spot a solitary man in a place he'd normally bring his wife or girl, he's probably available. Places men rarely go alone—unless they must—include beaches, museums, movies, theaters, concerts, parties, and picnics. Social places, after all, are for socializing, usually with the opposite sex. If a man's alone anywhere people normally go to have fun, he probably lacks a woman in his life.

When traveling, look for the man standing in the airport lines with only one small suitcase or *one* ticket in his hand. True, he may be married and on a business trip, but he's at least available for this flight, isn't he? Once you're cozily seated beside him, you can learn at your leisure how eligible he actually is.

The eligible man, by the way, is especially easy to detect at parties. If he arrives alone, talks to several different women, and has a roving eye, he's fair game. At a party, you can also tell a man's interested if he's primping. A man who sees you watching him and reflexively smooths his hair, straightens his tie, or adjusts his cuff links may be telling you, "I'm concerned about *your* opinion."

The most conclusive availability signal, of course, is eye contact. For every situation, there's what psychologists call a *moral looking time.* In an elevator, for example, that time is zero. You look at the buttons, then up at the indicator lights. Seldom do you meet any elevator companion's gaze. There's also a length of time you can meet a man's eyes before becoming *intimate:* about three seconds. If you meet his eyes for less than three seconds, you're merely saying, "I no-

tice you and recognize you're a person." Gaze at him longer
and you signal, "I'm interested and available." If your signals are seductive enough and accompanied by sexy eye
play, you may even communicate, "You turn me on." Next
time you stride down the street, play the eye-contact game. I
think you'll be amazed at your results.

Eye signals, by the way, differ from one culture to the
next. So while traveling abroad, don't try using the same
signals you use here in the U.S.A. Latin Americans and
Arabs have longer looking times than we do, while northern
Europeans look at each other for briefer periods. A Japanese man may pay no attention at all to eye contact.

By the way, there's something body-language books
usually don't tell you but I think you ought to know: Body
language is *relative*. In other words, what one man means
by a long, deliberate stare another might not mean at all. To
avoid embarrassing predicaments, don't take a man's tie
straightening, for example, as absolute *proof* he wants you
to talk to him. He could just have an itchy neck, or maybe
he's getting ready to talk to his boss, whom he just spotted
across the room. Or though it seems as if a man is meeting
your eye with a "come hither" look, he could, in fact, be
nearsighted (myopic types without their glasses will meet
other people's gazes for *hours*), or he may only be checking
the clock above your head. Body-language signals are strong
*indications* of availability but not absolute truths. Once you
notice that a man seems interested in you, walk to another
part of the room. Are his eyes still following you? Pause to
see if he starts your way, if not by actually following you
then by turning or twisting his body in your direction,
"cheating" toward your side of the room. If he does so, now
may be the time to go up to him and say hi. If you were
reading his signals correctly—and you probably were—
great: Perhaps you and he will soon begin dating.

You, of course, also send out subtle availability messages of your own. Some of them you have no control over. They well up from your unconscious. But others you can affect considerably, and they are well worth thinking about. The reason is profoundly simple. You know you are available. You know it so well, in fact, that perhaps you go through long stretches when you can think of nothing else. But do others?

Earlier we discussed the importance of letting out your inner warmth. Now I must ask this: Is the true nature of your availability going begging because you've assumed that it's as obvious to others as it is to you? You're a divorcée. Or separated. Or widowed. You don't have a man in your life. It's written all over your face, isn't it?

Maybe not. Sometimes we get so used to acting a certain way that when our life suddenly changes we don't totally adapt. When you were happily married you probably made certain adjustments in your behavior. You didn't return the glances of strangers. You stopped wearing perfume to the supermarket. You made little effort to maximize your attractiveness when running errands about town.

Now that you no longer share your life with one man, have you continued to act as if you still do have a loving and reliable mate? Have you forgotten or neglected to adjust? Yes, you know you would love to go out to dinner with the man who owns the laundry where you used to bring your husband's shirts. But does he have even the vaguest sense of your availability?

Several years ago I coached a Little League team. Quite a few of the parents used to show up for the games. One of the boys' mothers always wore perfume and outfits that seemed perhaps 10 to 15 percent dressier than the other mothers'. One day not too far into the season it hit me: *Mrs. Levin is divorced.* My wife corroborated my instinct, for she knew Mrs. Levin from the PTA. Had I myself been a single parent I would not have had the slightest difficulty picking up the woman's message. *I do not have a husband. Do not overlook me.*

Now some readers may be thinking with self-righteous indignation, *Of course you'd pick up her message. She's a tramp.*

I beg to differ. To project to those about you that you are available to date is not to act promiscuously. It is simply to announce to those who might be interested in you that you might be interested in them as well. There is little difference in what you are doing from what a never-been-married woman in her early twenties does: She looks her best when she goes out in public.

There may be dozens of men in your daily routine who are dying to meet and romance you. But if they mistakenly assume you are happily married, most of them will make no attempt to so much as strike up a conversation with you. They'll think, *why bother?*

Don't let this happen. Without violating your basic nature, see if it isn't possible to splash on perfume a little more often, to make sure your hair is neatly combed when going out (if only to buy a newspaper), and to dress with a bit more sex appeal.

Men notice and respond to these things, perhaps only on an unconscious level; but respond to them they do. Don't be surprised if all of a sudden men seem to be looking at you in a different light as you stand in line at the supermarket or search out the right-sized bolt at the hardware store.

Once you know how to spot him, you'll find the available man everywhere. Soon you'll be able to weed out potential dates from dedicatedly married men in a matter of seconds. Of course, once you learn how to signal your own availability, single men will also begin finding you.

# Look for
# the Shy Man

I occasionally teach a course in New York City for men. The course is titled "How to Meet New Women." Invariably I notice two or three attractive, well-dressed, prosperous-looking men in the class who seem as if they should have no trouble at all meeting women. Then these men get up to ask a question and I see why they've come: For some inexplicable reason, they're painfully shy. Speaking in front of the class turns them into blushing stutterers, men who can barely keep their poise.

Chances are, you don't consciously seek out men who are shy. They are difficult and wooden to talk to at first, often so much so that you assume that they are arrogant ... or worse, don't like you. Yet I maintain that even with these problems, the shy man may be an untapped source for romance and fun and companionship.

First of all, the shy man is usually sensitive and compassionate. He really listens when you've been hurt (he *knows* the pain of rejection). He won't chatter mindlessly all through *Gone with the Wind*, doesn't press you to sleep with him on the first date, and may even be *grateful* to stay home from a party when you've got the flu.

Also, there's usually much less competition for shy men. Other women, too, find them as difficult to get to know and give up prematurely.

Finally, shy men are plentiful. Zimbardo, the expert on shyness, claims there are about eighty-four million shy people in the United States. If a mere 15 percent of them are single and male, that means there are close to thirteen million men out there who are having trouble meeting women.

Helen, a short, plump, thirty-four-year-old divorcée from Keokuk, Iowa, says, "I love to talk, and shy men like to listen. After my divorce, I went back to graduate school for my master's degree, and during Christmas vacation, two girlfriends and I lined up a car ride to Vail, Colorado, to go skiing. The driver turned out to be about thirty with a thick, bushy red beard, really very sexy. (I've always had a weakness for bearded men.) At first, this man, whose name was Alan, seemed cold and aloof—a real *macho* guy—and I hated him. But after sitting beside him for about two hours, I realized he was just terribly shy. Whenever he looked at me, he'd even blush! So I went into my chattering routine. I just talk about whatever pops into my head: the weather, what I ate for lunch, my eccentric aunt who paints carrots, how I twisted my ankle trying to rescue a canary. I learned years ago that we all have interesting stories in our lives— it's just how you tell them. By the time we reached Vail, Alan had relaxed enough that I asked him to join us for drinks at a little Austrian café we'd heard about. Anyway, he accepted, and we dated for the next eight months—until I graduated and got a teaching job in Missouri. A quiet man is the only type I feel bold enough to ask out. With the

Burt Reynolds types, I'm always afraid they'd laugh and say no."

A mother of two in Galveston, Texas, prefers the shy man for exactly the opposite reason—because you *don't* have to talk incessantly to him. "A bashful man will sit with you quietly and watch a sunset, won't interrupt every thirty seconds when you're reading the last chapter of an Agatha Christie mystery, and doesn't wear lampshades on his head at parties. Extroverted, loudmouthed men who want to be constantly in the limelight bore me. I mean, how many women would really like to live with Don Rickles? I'm just not much of a talker and I deplore two-hour monologues from men who fear a minute of silence."

An added advantage of the introvert, says Marian, a twenty-five-year-old nurse who lives in a small Kansas town of five thousand people, is that once you've pulled him out of his shell, he's yours forever. "A shy man is ideal if you fear, as I did just after my divorce, that any man you like will leave you. Unlike a self-confident Lothario, a shy man doesn't have twenty names in a little black book."

Marian met a gentle, considerate, but incredibly bashful man one Sunday afternoon while washing towels in the laundromat. "I didn't have to say anything terribly witty to impress Ernie. Just, 'Hi, is this dryer free?' was enough. Pretty soon, we were swapping comments about detergent and bleach, and he was helping me fold my towels. By the time our clothes were dry, I felt comfortable enough with him that when he asked me to stop by the Dairy Queen with him, I said sure. I mean, how can you mistrust a man who offers you an ice-cream cone? That was two years ago, and Ernie and I have gone out several times a week ever since. At first it was slow going. I mean, Ernie tended to mumble so much I could hardly understand him, and I did have to prod him to take me to a movie the first time. I remember I must have told him twenty times how much I was dying to see that flick (whatever it was). But now Ernie's totally relaxed with me, though I can see he's still uneasy around other women. Once I jokingly teased him about dating this new teacher who came to town and he said, 'You're kidding. What would I *say* to her?' I like knowing he feels most at ease with me."

Some women I've talked to admit a shy man can at times be silent to the point of madness or be socially inept. ("I once dated a fellow named Jim, so shy he would hardly talk. He always used to buy two beers, even though I told him I hated beer, then drink them both himself!" says one exasperated woman.) Still, if you're patient and understanding, the bashful man will eventually relax and talk freely. Will he ever get *beyond* the talking stage? Many women interviewed for this book agree that he will. Though a Detroit secretary says it took her six months to coax her shy lover into bed, once there he was worth waiting for. "A reticent man has all these deep passions that are all the more explosive because they haven't been *used*," she confides.

Take my word for it, there's nothing wrong with the shy man—except that he has a few insecurities. (Don't we all?) So look for him. He's the quiet guy in the corner of the room at a party, the one in the back row of your adult education class, the man in the bar looking furtively in a mirror because he'd rather not watch the goings-on *directly*. He may not meet your eyes at first. He may even seem indifferent because he fears letting his feelings show. But chances are underneath he's a kind, gentle, compassionate man who will be grateful that you cared.

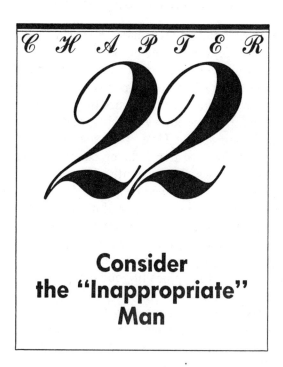

# CHAPTER 22

## Consider the "Inappropriate" Man

When you were twenty-two and fresh out of college, chances are you wanted the man you loved to be perfect. Ideally, he'd be, say, a Wall Street financial whiz who lived in the upper East Sixties in Manhattan, played squash in the afternoons, sipped Chablis by candlelight at night, and flew with you on romantic weekends to Aruba. Also, he'd look like Robert Redford.

And how could you miss? All the men you knew were young, eager, single, and full of promise. Every man you met was going to make it someday. The premed student was possibly the next Dr. Barnard. The sensitive English major in the back row would be the next T. S. Eliot. The blond Adonis pumping gas to work his way through night school had dreams of studying law and becoming F. Lee Bailey II. Any man you knew could go on to be a U.S. senator or president of AT&T. Nobody was bald. Fat still looked like muscle. And failure was for the old guys.

I maintain you've got just as many men to choose from today as you did when you were twenty-two. You just may be failing to consider them because they *look* inappropriate. Some are bald, others have paunches, and they may manage McDonald's stores, not IBM. They may have suffered business failures, have bratty kids, or be struggling anxiously with midlife crises. But despite all their flaws, many of these "imperfect" men are lovely, gentle, wonderful people who can offer you love, consideration, companionship—and romantic evenings at home, if not in Aruba. And furthermore, many "inappropriate" men can bring out the best in you if you'll only give them the chance.

I'd like you to explore in your own mind what's *wrong* with a plumber, a truck driver, or a guy who pumps gas? Nothing. Good men are where you find them, and I know many executives' wives more miserably married than one friend who shares life with a farmer and another whose husband sells shoes.

So look around you. Chances are you may be automatically eliminating some men you should consider. Diana, a thirty-three-year-old divorcée in Memphis, for example, found love behind the wheel of a taxi. "I rarely splurge on taxis, but one rainy day last May I was so exhausted I couldn't face a ten-block walk in the rain to the bus and a soggy bus ride home, so I hailed a cab. I was so wrapped up in my problems with work and the kids that if the cab driver had been Siamese twins, I wouldn't have noticed. I mean, how often do you notice the *driver*? However, when this driver insisted on talking to me and wouldn't accept my monosyllabic replies, I looked up. He was young, muscular, and very good-looking in a swarthy, brooding Zorba the Greek sort of way. I could tell he was bright from his conversation.

" 'How come a bright guy like you is driving a cab?' I

asked. He told me his whole story. He liked being his own boss, enjoyed having time to read and paint and not be cooped up in an office. By the time we got to my neighborhood I'd learned that he came here from Argentina and started driving a cab to work his way through law school but then got to *like* driving because of the freedom and flexibility. When he asked if he could buy me a cup of coffee, I hesitated for a minute because I was brought up very middle-class, meaning you marry up—not down. I knew my mother would faint at my taking up with a cab driver. But the truth is I've always been attracted to Latin men. We stopped for coffee at a neighborhood coffee shop—and now we see each other at least several times a week. He has the charm and gentleness you don't find in these upwardly mobile urban types, and my kids just love him."

A thirty-year-old friend of mine, recently separated from an ambitious college professor, is now dating a sweet but terribly shy and insecure man who works as a civil servant. "I know Joe isn't most women's idea of the ideal male," says Samantha. "He's divorced with three kids and he takes me camping in Maine, not to glamorous nightclubs. But I was so demoralized after John left me that I just needed a man to be *nice* to me. When I feel depressed, I can call Joe and I know he'll come over. On a cold winter morning, he'll stop by to help me start my car. I don't need a high-powered executive type to take me on rendezvous to Capri.... I need a guy who will stop by on Saturday with a bag of *groceries*."

As Diana and Samantha found, and millions of other women are discovering as well, hooking a high-powered, ambitious executive just isn't as crucial as your mother told you. Mother may have been right—for her time. Years ago, a woman's whole *identity* was defined in large part by her man's success.

In the 1980s, though, women have their own careers and their own pursuits, which are often as important to them as a man's is to him. Women no longer have to live in a man's reflected glory. So consider the man who's not president of Xerox—and never will be. He still has a lot to offer.

Perhaps that is why we are seeing so many women who are looking down and parallel in their search for a man. Social lines are more blurred than they once were. Once-rigid criteria for selecting a mate are softening. Women are becoming more healthily selfish in choosing a man who turns them on instead of one who is supposed to turn them on. Who needs a doctor for a husband when you're a doctor yourself? Better to find a man whose looks or personality are just what you wanted instead of one whose career is what you wanted.

Consider, for example, how many women have begun dating and marrying younger men. I suspect you've felt healthy, sexual impulses toward men who are younger than you. But have you thought of pursuing one? Older men date younger women all the time. What about turning the tables?

A younger man is eager, energetic, very potent, and impressionable. He seldom asks you to plan a dinner party for twelve, doesn't expect you to have read every page of *War and Peace* (and is impressed when you have), thinks you're clever because you can bake a soufflé. Admit it: Even on your worst days you can cope with life better than a twenty-two-year-old can. And on your best days, you'll dazzle him with your knowledge of the world. Ellen, a thirty-eight-year-old divorcée in Minneapolis, is now dating her twenty-seven-year-old hairdresser. "And he's a *young* twenty-seven. He's absolutely gorgeous, he never went to college, and we have *shaving cream* fights in the bedroom. I adore him. Young men are wonderful. They're so flattered to have your attention."

Of course, you may have fears that a younger man won't *know* he's younger. How to tell him you're ten years his senior and have three kids at home? Lucille, an attrac-

tive thirty-nine-year-old from Chicago, handled the problem in an interesting way. She met her younger man, Tracy, one night when she and a girlfriend were coming out of a movie theater and Tracy happened to be standing in front of the theater reading the reviews. Tracy asked them if the movie was any good, then invited them to have a cup of coffee. The next day, he asked Lucille out to lunch. "Tracy was charming, bright, funny—but, alas, ten years younger than I was," Lucille recalls. "Since I look years younger than my age, I knew he'd be surprised—even shocked—if I confessed I was thirty-nine and had three teen-age kids. I knew I had to tell him the truth. After all, if we dated and he came to my house, I couldn't exactly stuff my kids in the refrigerator or under the sofa. Still, I couldn't bear seeing his face fall when I told him my age. So when he asked personal questions, I said cheerfully: 'I'll send you my résumé.' "
And she did, complete with the facts under "Personal"—divorced, three children. "He wasn't the least perturbed," Lucille says, "so we went out and had a delightful affair for about two years. What, you ask, could I possibly see in a man so much younger than I? He was so energetic and fun to be with. He was also freer and more sexually experienced than many men my age or older who suffer from the Simultaneous Orgasm obsession."

By now, if you're over thirty, you may say, "I could never make love to a younger man." I know it sounds scary to undress in front of a young, muscular male when your breasts are less firm than they once were and your bottom's maybe a bit droopy, but if he doesn't care, why should you? Besides, when lovemaking's wonderful and the lights are out, *everybody's* eighteen.

We're getting ahead of ourselves, anyway. You make love only when you feel at ease with him. Right now, we're just talking about one or two *dates*. Believe me, the younger man is worth a second look.

And so are a lot of other men you may be ignoring.

Look around you. The world's full of unattached men. So what if he's two inches shorter than you, or wears garishly flowered Hawaiian shirts, or thinks Brahms is a brand of chocolate? If he's sweet, kind, and considerate, he can help you through this tumultuous time and make you feel good about yourself again. As that lusty, platinum-blond bombshell Mae West once said in her throaty, bedroom voice, "Honey, I agree with Will Rogers: I *never* met a man I didn't like." I think all women could take a lesson from Mae.

# CHAPTER 23

## Seize the Moment

All this advice about appropriate and inappropriate men is fine, but perhaps you believe that nobody—eligible or otherwise—*ever* approaches you. I'll bet you're wrong. I think a lot more men probably make passes at you in a week than you realize, but you overlook them. You fail to seize the moment.

*Nonsense,* you think? *Why would I do that?* For a number of reasons.

Probably the No. 1 reason for missed opportunities is emotional insecurity. Maybe you're feeling especially dull, chubby, or unglamorous on a particular day. So when a man looks you in the eyes or says "Good morning" to you in the elevator, you dismiss his overture as just your imagination. I'm not saying you reject him consciously, but unconsciously your reasoning may go something like this: *He*

*looks interested. Ah, but that's silly. Why would a tall, in-*
*telligent, handsome man like that want poor, mousy, boring*
*old me?* And out of the elevator you step.

At times when you're feeling less than perfect, you may
ignore the most blatant advances. Lila, a newly divorced
woman in her midthirties from Atlanta, once turned down a
dinner invitation from an incredibly sexy friend of her ex-
husband's because "I just thought he felt *sorry* for me."
Only later did Lila realize she may have missed the chance
of a lifetime. (Shortly after that, the man started dating
another, more receptive mutual friend.)

Another woman, who once owned a brilliant red dress,
actually recalls *ignoring* a man who approached her with a
friendly smile and said, "Red means you're passionate." "I
just thought he was being silly," Susie recalls. How absurd.
That man was probably really turned on.

At other times, you may notice the advance—at first.
But two hours later at home when you're tired or fretting
that you'll never escape your underappreciated job, you
talk yourself out of your original feeling. Plagued by doubts
and insecurities, you tell yourself, "Oh, I'm probably mistaken. Why would anyone that great be interested in *me*?"

You may also overlook men's advances because they're
too subtle. It's been my experience that many women (and
men, too, by the way) are victims of Romantic Movie Over-
sell. Result: You may think a man's not making a pass unless he whispers breathlessly in your ear, "Come with me to
the Casbah" or some contemporary version of that line.
Most men are seldom that direct. Dozens of men, in fact,
may be extending overtures you fail to recognize. The man
in the garage who says he likes the color of your car, the guy
in your apartment building who asks you the time whenever
you meet in the hallway . . . both these men could be sending
out feelers.

Do these advances seem inept? Well, maybe they are.

But most men aren't Charles Boyer, so have pity. They're doing the best they can.

The point is, whenever a man makes an overture—even one that seems less than overwhelming—make the most of it. Seize the moment. Virginia, a thirty-year-old mother of two girls, reports, "There was this man in my office I wanted to meet named Curtis. But I was too insecure just to go right up to him, and ours is such a large office that we seldom saw one another. Then one day I had a chance to talk to him in the company cafeteria. It was just before I was leaving for Acapulco for five days (my ex had custody of our two daughters that month). Curtis was sitting with a group of people, including my friend Vivian, who stopped me as I was on my way out. She told everyone at the table that I was going to Mexico, and it was a particularly gray, smoggy day outside, so Curtis said, 'Well, you'll have to drop us a card so we can see what sunshine looks like again.'

"And that's just what I did. During the five days I was gone, I sent Curtis two postcards. The first was a simple photo showing a couple dancing on a veranda by moonlight. On the back of the card I scribbled, 'Having a wonderful time—wish you were here.' A couple of days later, I followed that up with a card showing an old mansion in Mexico City and on the back I wrote, 'It's really a lovely old place. And to think they say it used to be one of the most expensive brothels in Mexico.'

"Well, when I got back to Torrance, Curtis couldn't wait to ask me out. The first day back at work, he even saved a table for me at lunch in the cafeteria. We've been living together for seven months now, and we're thinking of marriage."

So look again at that guy who's always offering you joking propositions. Keep an eye open, too, for the men offering even subtler signals. What about that man who always seems to arrive at the coffee machine the same time you do (and even knows you take your coffee black)? Or the guy who says you look happy today? Or even the man who seems to have forgotten his cigarettes and asks for one of yours? (He did ask you, not some other woman, didn't he?) Maybe these men are using the only icebreakers they know, and with just a hint of encouragement from you, a romance could blossom. Believe me, most men won't take the trouble to ask "How was your weekend?" unless they feel a spark of attraction to you. The most perfunctory banalities are often much more of a signal than you realize.

Whatever you do, pay attention to that man who says he likes your hair, your scarf, or your smile. *Oh, he's just being polite,* you think? I say, So what? A man who notices you enough to be polite today could be in love with you six months from now. Most great romances, despite what nonsensical romantic novels dish out, *do* begin with just a kind word or a friendly nod. Once you're attuned to men's overtures, I'll bet you'll find a lot more men than you ever imagined are sending you vibes.

# Confide

Now, this next advice is a little tricky, so listen carefully. Sometimes when you're feeling particularly gloomy, broke, overweight, or lonely, some thoughtful man may approach you and say something like, "Hey, you look like you just heard World War III's been declared. What's wrong?" Usually you'll be so preoccupied with your worries or be so afraid of seeming pathetic, you'll just mumble, "Oh, nothing," and the man will move on. But maybe, if this guy really does seem concerned, you should confide.

There's nothing wrong with saying simply in a matter-of-fact, unwhimpering tone, "Oh, my landlord just raised my rent two hundred dollars a month and I don't know what to do," or "My son came home from third grade with a black eye yesterday, and I feel awful because I've always told him not to fight and then this bully beat him up." It's not necessary to go into ancient history about how your husband was a twerp and your apartment's dismal and you hate your whole screwed-up life (even if it is one of those nightmarishly bleak days when you really do feel that way). But by sharing your problems in a simple, unpathetic way, you may make a kind, considerate man decide you need a little help—and he may decide he's just the guy to give it.

Now, as I said before, confiding is a bit tricky because some people act concerned just to be polite, not because they really care. Certainly, if you're at a bustling party and some jovial hail-fellow-well-met comes up and says, "Hey, you look low," you shouldn't instantly dump all your miseries on the poor guy's head. I'm also not suggesting that if a man says, "Hi, how are you?" that you whimper, "Oh, Josh, just *awful.*" People who ask, "How's it going?" or some variation of that line usually don't want to *know.*

On the other hand, if you see that a man really is offering a strong shoulder to lean on, accept it graciously. Letting a man help you can be the beginning of a beautiful romance.

One of the best places to confide, by the way, is in a group. All kinds of self-help groups have sprung up across the country for normal people like you and me who happen to be facing some trying times. At Parents Without Partners meetings, for example, you can confess to partnerless dads how lonely and confused you sometimes feel—without appearing pitiful. (Your listener, after all, understands because he's dealing with the same fears and uncertainties.) Encounter groups, too, can offer a way to unburden yourself without looking as if you've really gone bananas. Though you may not meet a man at group sessions, you may make new matchmaking friends who will wind up introducing you to all the eligible men they know.

For example, Lacey, a shy twenty-nine-year-old woman from Chicago, learned she could tell her deepest secrets and, instead of thinking her pathetically helpless, one man admired her for it.

"Whatever hang-ups I had before I was married and divorced became worse," Lacey confides. "I'm not outspoken or brash, and I've always had a lot of difficulty relating to people. People think I'm standoffish, but that's just the form my shyness takes. I was really a mess for months and months after my separation—a burden, I'm afraid, to my girlfriends. After all, my shyness was compounded by being abandoned: My husband left me.

"Barbara, a friend who'd just completed *est* training, insisted that *I* take the training to stop playing the victim and transform my life. She used all the *est* jargon, which I hate, but I thought maybe she was right. I was most impressed that Valerie Harper and Cloris Leachman were *est* graduates; after all, I'm not just shy, I'm starstruck, too. So I borrowed $350 from my parents, filled out the forms, and went to the guest seminars, where I felt harassed by their sales pitch but became determined to go through with it.

"There I was one weekend in March three years ago, sitting on a stiff-backed chair at the Hilton with 250 other misfits. The trainer, named Ron, was brutal! He's calling everyone an asshole and a turkey and telling us that no, we can't go to the bathroom except on breaks, and those are the rules. As the morning goes on and I'm dying to go to the john, he starts telling a man who's crippled from polio that he's responsible for his polio; then he tells an attractive young woman who's describing the pain of her extramarital affair that she's putting on the woman act. Both are crying—and the badgering, threatening, and mocking go on. *What am I doing here?* I'm wondering, me a shy woman who hates authoritarianism and crowds?

"So it goes all weekend—process after process. During the Fear Process, I'm conscious only of a bloated bladder; during the Danger Process, I'm writhing with discomfort. Acute discomfort and fear of getting up and speaking in front of all these people plague me. Ron has been talking for some time about how you have to lay your ass on the line. I'm so terrified of this public abuse and laying my ass on the line that I lose all inhibition and finally get up and say, 'I've always been self-conscious about the gap between my front teeth, which isn't attractive like Lauren Hutton's gap.' Then I say my teeth protrude and my childhood nickname was Bucky. I tell him because of this I've always been nervous about kissing men. Ron tells me *I'm* responsible for my teeth, that I intellectualize everything and fail to experience things, and that I'm sleeping through life. I feel very self-conscious and humiliated in front of all these people. Finally it's time for a bathroom break, and after I get out of the ladies' room, I'm composing myself in a corner of the hotel lobby when an attractive man whose name tag says "Mike" approaches me.

" 'I was very moved by everything you said,' says Mike, 'and I'd like to join you for dinner during the next break if it's okay with you.'

" 'Thank you,' I say, 'I'd love to.'

"So we met at the door during the next break and walked to a small Viennese restaurant in the neighborhood. I had the most wonderful time I'd ever had on a date. We both expressed our reservations over this grueling experience and said it wasn't necessary to go through all this humiliation. We both hated the techniques that were used and agreed not to go back for the next weekend, even though we wouldn't get our money back. So you see, I met the man who has turned out to be my dearest friend by confessing my deepest pain. Oddly enough, though *est* was gruesome, it did put me in touch with my feelings, and a lot of my shyness just seems to have evaporated. What I learned is that you don't have to do what was drummed into me as a child: Put your best foot forward. Sometimes you can reveal your insecurities, unburden yourself. You'll not only feel better, but also some men will actually *like* you for it. Mike enjoys helping me. And while I'm beginning to realize I can do more for myself than I ever imagined, it's still nice to know I have a broad shoulder to cry on when I need it."

I'm not suggesting you put yourself through the ordeal Lacey endured. But if a man seems concerned about your problems and interested in helping you, I say let him. Lacey could have been so preoccupied with her own emotional wounds that she might have ignored Mike's thoughtfulness. Instead, perhaps because of the *est* ordeal she'd just faced, she was open and willing to accept sympathy from a friend.

Confiding, by the way, also works in reverse. If a man looks especially dismal or upset, perhaps he's looking for a confidante. And if you go up to him and ask honestly and gently, "What's wrong, Harry?" and let him know you really care, he may tell you secrets even his mother doesn't know. Sharing genuine hurts and pains can make people feel intimately close to one another. And sometimes those confidential bonds, which can blossom into love, can begin to form the minute you say hi.

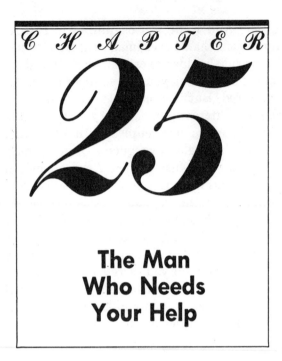

## The Man Who Needs Your Help

When you were a girl, Mother taught you that a "gentleman" always helped a lady. He held the door for her, held her coat, held her chair. And what were you to do in return? Smile and say, "Thank you." That kind of chivalry may have been fine back in King Arthur's day or when Sir Walter Raleigh dropped his cloak in a mud puddle for a lady to cross. But today, now that women are liberated, it's time for a little reverse chivalry, don't you think? After all, men need help, too.

I don't mean you should start holding doors for muscled he-men. That would seem a bit silly, wouldn't it? But what I am suggesting is this: Look for a man who needs your help. If you spot a man with seven packages in his arms, offer to carry a few of his bundles to his car. If he's standing at the meat counter looking baffled, see if he needs any help selecting a roast. If he's sitting in a restaurant reading a guide book to your city, offer to show him around town. Be chivalrous and you'll get his gratitude as well as his attention. He won't feel offended; he'll just think you're thoughtful and considerate.

Sometimes a man needs help through a genuine *crisis* in his life. Yet, ironically, just when he needs a woman most, he's most likely alone. Dozens of women may seek out a man when he's at his money-earning, creative, and carefree-bachelor peak. But when he's down-and-out, facing bankruptcy, or he just lost his job, nobody cares. That's when you can give him a great psychological boost. A man may *like* a woman when he's flying high, but he *loves* one who sticks by him when he's down on his luck.

Consider, for example, the case of Lucy and her second husband, Gregory.

"My first wife, Linda, had committed suicide," reports Gregory. "She was compulsive about her self-destruction and had been seeing a psychiatrist for almost two years. The doctor warned me she might try suicide. I did everything to prevent her from doing it. I flushed all her sleeping pills down the toilet and wouldn't even allow a sharp knife in the kitchen. You can imagine the nightmare we lived. But one day, while I was at work, Linda left a note and walked in front of a bus. I couldn't bring myself to tell our daughter, Melody, the truth, that her mother had been suffering from mental problems for years. I thought it might tear her up even more than she already was.

"Unfortunately, Melody started blaming *me* for the suicide. She thought it was my fault Linda went to pieces. To get even, she started messing up in school, running around with a bad crowd, and smoking marijuana. I knew I should tell her about Linda's mental history, but I just couldn't. I was afraid she'd think I was making it up and hate me even more.

"That's when we met Lucy. She was thirty-seven then,

my age, and divorced with a daughter away at college. Lucy
lived in an apartment next to ours. Anyway, I was so distraught and worried and feeling powerless over Melody that
I never even noticed Lucy had developed an interest in me.
She even invited me over to dinner one night, but I just
said no in an abstracted way and walked on. Then one
night I came home to find a note on the door that Melody
was at Lucy's place. When I went there, I found Melody
stoned out of her mind and asleep on the sofa. Lucy said
she'd found Melody and a boy trying to break into my
apartment so she could get her clothes and run away. Lucy
chased the boy off with a threat of the police and took Melody to her apartment, where Melody unburdened herself for
about an hour, then broke down and cried for another hour
before falling asleep. I didn't know what to do. I figured this
was the end of my daughter, and I felt lost and helpless. So
when Lucy asked me to let Melody stay with her the night, I
said O.K.

"The next day when I came home from work, Melody
was waiting for me at the door. She ran to me, threw her
arms around me, and cried. I finally found out what had
happened. Once while talking to Lucy, I'd told her about
my wife's suicide and that she'd been seeing a psychiatrist
for years. I must have mentioned the doctor's name. Anyway, the day I left Melody with her, Lucy had taken Melody
to see the psychiatrist, who explained everything, how
Linda had suffered from deep psychological problems and
that suicides are nobody's fault. It was something I should
have done myself, but I was just too mixed up and confused
to think, and I was so grateful to Lucy for sticking out her
neck for me that way. I mean, some men might have gotten
angry about her butting in, but I was grateful. So was
Melody.

"It was Melody, about two days later, who told me I
must be blind not to see Lucy liked me. Thinking about it, I
realized she was right. So the next time Lucy picked up her

mail, I went out and said, 'If that dinner invitation's still open, I'd love to do it.' It was, and we started seeing each other regularly. Once we started dating, I found out what a great woman Lucy is. I had no problem getting Melody to accept her. God! After that, Lucy was her best friend. Still is."

Lucy wasn't trying to "trap" Greg into matrimony. She was just helping him because he needed her. And that's one of the best ways for a relationship to begin.

I can't guarantee, of course, that if you help a man he'll fall madly in love with you. But there's a possibility he will. Besides, helping a man (or a woman, for that matter) can get you out of yourself and make you feel more positive about the world.

You needn't help a man solve a *major* crisis, by the way. Maybe he only needs to borrow your car for the morning or to have the elevator button pushed because he's carrying two bags of groceries. Perhaps he's been living on frozen turkey pies for six weeks and would love a loaf of your freshly baked homemade bread. Or it could be his lawn's getting brown and crackly, and he needs to borrow your sprinkler. Look for ways to help a man, to be there for a man, and you'll begin finding needy fellows everywhere. And when you find one, give him a hand. He won't think you're pushy or sexually aggressive, he'll think you're just friendly and nice. After that, love may just naturally follow.

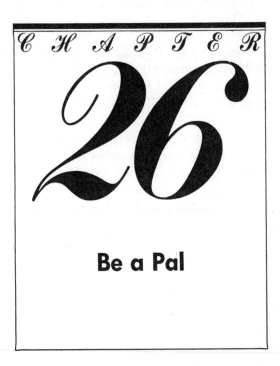

# CHAPTER 26

## Be a Pal

When I was seventeen I fell deeply in love with a girl named Marybelle. She seemed to like me well enough, calling me when I hadn't called her for a while and suggesting we study or go ice-skating together. But whenever I tried to steer our relationship onto a romantic or sexual level, she discouraged me. She was content to be my pal but wanted no more than that.

I was not content. True, I enjoyed being with her for her company alone. She was funny and interesting and lively to be around. But it constantly irked me that she did not find me attractive or charismatic enough to be boyfriend material. My role as just "pal" felt emasculating. A real man, I reasoned, doesn't have girl *friends*. He's got girl-friends, several of them. When he wants platonic companionship he hangs around with other males, fellows he plays football and pool with. So as much pain as it caused me, I stopped seeing Marybelle altogether. And oh, what a void it left in my life.

Now, over twenty years later and after much research on the subject, I've discovered that many relationships that start out platonically, or with only one half of the couple feeling romantically inclined toward the other, wind up as bona fide love relationships. It astonishes me that it's taken me so long to realize this. How could I have been so foolish as not to observe that where there is mild affection there may one day be genuine passion?

The point of all this is to alert you to the importance of nurturing your existing friendships with men . . . and to encourage you to seek out additional friendships with men. Just because a man doesn't fall in love with you at the very start doesn't mean that one day he won't wake up and realize that he's slowly been growing deeply in love with you. And just because you don't feel tingles and chills when in the company of a male friend doesn't mean that at some time in the future you won't.

One of the nice things about making pals with a man is that it is so much easier for you than trying to find a lover. It's a lot less scary bringing a slice of your birthday cake to the new man next door than it is asking him to the Christmas party at your office. You can return again and again with gifts and favors, even with very little active encouragement from him, without feeling you are compromising your dignity. Who can find fault with a friendly, giving neighbor?

Kimberly, an artist from Iowa City, describes how a friendship with a man evolved into something much more than that:

"After my divorce, I was just twenty-three, and my mother offered to take care of my daughter, Cindy, so I could go back to the University of Iowa for a degree in art history. To pay the rent, I took a part-time job at a shoe store. That's where I met Wade. He was working his way through college, too, majoring in English Lit. I sold hose, he sold shoes. Wade was one of those bright, witty, well-dressed men women go crazy over, so I knew I could never compete and automatically dismissed him as a possible lover. But we became friends. Just buddies.

"One night we were walking back toward campus together (he had an apartment, I lived in a dorm) and I started telling Wade about the awful cafeteria food. He said any time I wanted to come over to his place to fix an old-fashioned home-cooked meal, I could use his stove. That sounded so great, I said, 'How about tonight?' So that's what we did. After dinner that evening, Wade's roommate Larry showed up, and we all sat around joking, listening to records, having a good time—the way pals do. But when I went into the bedroom to get my coat, Wade followed me. And as he was helping me on with my coat, he kissed me. I was stunned. *My buddy kissed me!* That night, back in the dorm, my real feelings welled to the surface. I guess I'd been crazy about Wade all along but had been too afraid to admit it because I was sure he could never fall for me. Thank God, I kept our friendship up. After that night, Wade and I saw each other almost every evening. About a year later we got married."

Now, what about you? You probably have a male friend in your life—or at least a potential one. Have you ever thought of him romantically? Have you been neglecting the relationship because you were convinced it was going nowhere? Or because you just never found him attractive enough?

Perhaps now is the time to pick up the phone to suggest an afternoon in the park, a jog down at the track, something simple and low-key and brief. Platonic relationships are well worth working at. You never know when either one of you is suddenly going to start looking at the other in an entirely different light.

# Maybe It's Good to Sleep with a Man

Sometimes, when speaking to groups like Parents Without Partners, I'll meet a woman who has gone out on ten to fifteen dates with the same man but still feels they are strangers. Yet the woman feels that to sleep with the man would destroy their relationship. I maintain that just the opposite may be true. Sleeping with the man may be the very path to intimacy she needs. Sex can bring people closer.

One of the great divisions between men and women comes about, I suspect, over a common misconception about sex. Most women think that most men are sexually active. Not true. Not true at all, in fact. A few men are *very* sexually active. But about 80 percent of them are not. (It's sort of like selling insurance. About 10 percent of the salespeople sell 90 percent of the policies.)

Because women think that most men they meet are

hopping in and out of bed whenever they care to, they are afraid of being used, of playing themselves cheaply.

In reality, because so many men find it difficult to meet a woman who is attracted enough to go to bed with them, they are often terribly grateful when finally they meet a woman who does want to have sex with them. They can't quite believe it. *She cares. She found me attractive. She didn't mind my bald spot.*

While some men have contempt for a woman who accedes to their charms—*à la* Groucho Marx's quip, "I wouldn't join any club that would have me"—most men feel pleasure and warmth. In fact, some of them will try never to let you get away. You have blessed them with your company *and* your body. This is much too special and wonderful to let go of. Don't be surprised if in some cases you are the one who wants to let a relationship end as a one-night stand.

I know there's that old cliché that if you sleep with a man who's not your husband, he'll look down on you, think you're "loose," all those old ideas your mother may have passed down. But I don't believe that. Rather than look down on you, most men I know would think you're even more special. I can sincerely say I've never known a man to say, "Oh, God, that awful woman, she slept with me last night!"

From my experience, if a woman sleeps with a man, he feels more affectionate—in some cases almost grateful— toward her. I know, as a man, that I always felt *flattered*, not offended, when a woman liked me enough to make love. In truth, I was a bit awed by a woman so confident and capable she could initiate lovemaking. I said to myself, "This woman really knows what she wants and is willing to go after it no matter how society frowns. She's pretty extraordinary. I wonder if I can handle a woman like this."

Let me tell you a secret men seldom admit: Sex scares us, too. We fantasize about it and look forward to it. But we also have our fears. That first time with someone new can be more unnerving than most guys care to admit. Look at it from the man's point of view. He wants to be terrific—not just good, but the best lover you've ever had. He hopes you'll have an orgasm (and he's afraid you won't). He worries he won't be able to last long enough, or you'll think he's a klutz. Maybe you'll think he's too fat or too hairy or too soft or his penis is too small. What if you laugh at his paunch or suddenly notice he's knock-kneed? We guys worry that we don't look so great naked. Maybe his wife left him and told him as she slammed the door that he was the lousiest lover she'd ever had—and she'd had *plenty* of them.

So picture this poor guy going to bed with you for the first time. He's eager to please, but his palms are sweaty. He's intensely aroused, but he's had one too many Bloody Marys. And with dozens of doubts and insecurities floating through his brain, he has to maintain an *erection* besides! You know, it's ironic: Just when he's most worried about being terrific (his first time with you), he's also most likely to fail.

Most men, of course, would rather be celibate for the rest of their lives than admit what I just told you. But believe me, it's true. We men put on a brave, *macho* act (because we think that's what you women expect), but inside we're as jittery about that First Time as the shyest woman.

So how does this man feel when after you've made love together you smile and tell him how wonderful he was? Let me tell you, he feels *sensational!* Also grateful, loving toward you, happy. Life is never sweeter for a man than when a woman he's drawn to says he's good in bed. So is this guy going to give you the brush-off the next morning? I doubt it. He's going to appreciate you all the more.

Carolyn, an advertising copywriter from L.A., is a divorced woman who slept with a man on their second date. Her reaction? "Jack and I had known each other only about six weeks, and one night we went to this very romantic seafood restaurant on the pier—candlelight, soft music, cocktails, wine. Though it was only our second date, I felt as if we'd known each other for years. When we went back to my apartment for a margarita and Jack leaned over to kiss me, a voice inside (I think it was *Mother*) whispered, 'Don't do this . . . you'll be sorry. He'll think you're cheap.' But I was so turned on, I couldn't resist, and that night we made love. It was beautiful—not lightning-flashing *great*, but tender and nice—and I didn't regret it one bit afterward.

"But in the cold, stark light of morning, what I'd done hit me. Jack was still asleep and I lay there thinking, *Oh, my God, he'll despise me. He'll tell everybody at work. How will I ever face him again?* Just then Jack woke up, looked at me, gave me the sweetest smile, and said, 'Morning. You look pretty. Want to go to Denny's for breakfast?' And I could see it was O.K. Jack really was as kind as I'd thought, and nothing bad at all happened. Now we're living together. I'd read that all those clichés about men hating women who were 'easy' were old hat, but I didn't really believe it until I found out for myself."

Maybe you think that won't happen to you, that the man you meet will be an overbearing clod the morning after. I say, so what if it's a one-night stand and it doesn't work out? You shouldn't let that cast a pall over your life. So maybe you made love and he didn't like it (or you didn't) or he never called you again. You've been liberated, and you're an adult. If the man's too rude or inconsiderate to call back or was just after a quick romp in the hay, forget it. You don't want him, anyway.

As I see it, the drawbacks of sleeping with a man aren't as terrible as the old clichés say. And the potential *rewards* can be great. Sex is fun, of course; that's a big plus. But it's also healthy. It's good exercise, good for your hormonal system, makes your complexion glow, and relieves tension. Despite what you may have heard of the joys of celibacy, doctors say the idea that if you go without sex you'll somehow free your energies to be more creative, athletic, or imaginative is poppycock. While some women can go for years without sex and be quite content, others feel awful during celibacy: They feel irritable, anxious, depressed, phobic, and have other unhappy reactions.

Some women have told me they just never felt close to a man until after lovemaking. "I was always careful about who I slept with," said Jane, a thoughtful, forty-two-year-old widow from Fort Lauderdale. "In fact, other than one very inept one-night stand, I'd never done it with any man but my husband. Maybe it was moral values—I grew up in a very strict Catholic family—or maybe I was just scared of men. But I wanted so badly to feel close to Roy and have him feel close to me. Our relationship was smooth enough, except there was this distance thing. He always seemed a little reserved, and that made me feel reserved with him. Then one night after we'd had a couple of drinks, it happened. I can't say the experience was that fantastic, not the act itself, but we had been totally intimate with each other, and that reserve between us was just gone. Later, Roy told me he hadn't been any more sexually active than I'd been, and I figure maybe it was the worry about our eventually making love that kept us from really relaxing with each other. Once we made love and it wasn't as bad as either of us feared, everything was O.K. When you have sex with a man, you can't hold back. You *have* to feel intimate. At least I do. And once you let yourself be vulnerable and find out you don't get hurt, that the other person is trustworthy, you can let go and feel close to each other. All I know is that before we had sex, we felt a little uncomfortable with each other, and afterward we were able to feel close."

I'm not advising you to hop in bed with every Tom, Dick, or Frankie who asks. All I'm saying is, if you meet somebody at a dinner party or bar and the evening swells to a romantic crescendo, maybe it's O.K. to sleep with him. If you've known a man for several weeks or months and you like each other but really can't seem to relate, maybe you should go to bed. Only you can decide.

If you do decide to go ahead and sleep with a man, I have one final word of advice. Although I can't speak for *all* men, most guys I know aren't really looking for a *femme fatale*. You don't have to do anything exotic, like wear bunny fur underwear, to turn a guy on. Just be yourself. Just try to make your first night *friendly*. If he's at your place, offer him lemonade or a chicken-salad sandwich. Tell him how great he was. Be *nice* to him. That's better in the long run than being lusty. Believe me, if you're sweet, warm, and caring—if you just relax and be yourself—that's the most any man could want.

# More Great Places (and Ways) to Meet Men

By now you've probably mastered the basics. You're out of the house, you've rediscovered the old you, you've learned to start and carry on conversations, make eye contact, and smile. You also know how to detect the available man, change your daily habits in small and subtle but significant ways to bring more men into your life. Now let's get down to the nitty-gritty: where to meet men.

We've already lightly brushed over dozens of places to meet men (at work and parties, on vacations, in bars), but now let's get down to hard-core specifics. What follows is a list of great places and ways to find men. In some cases I'm suggesting places that offer a relaxed, easy, sociable atmosphere—just the mood you need for romance to blossom. But most of the following suggestions will show you how to find places or situations where men outnumber women by two, five, ten, even a hundred to one. In short, here's the final guide to make all your man-meeting efforts succeed.

## *Advertise*

If friends and family have fixed you up only with men you have nothing in common with and the situation seems hopeless, advertise. Yes, I mean run an ad in the personals section of your local newspaper or regional magazine and advertise for the kind of man you'd like.

I know advertising sounds scary at first. What if you meet a con man—or worse? But look at it this way. If the replies you receive scare you off, you don't have to answer. List only a box number in your ad, and you'll be able to screen applicants at your leisure. If you phone some guy who just wants to talk dirty, you can hang up without revealing even your name. But if he sounds nice (and I'll bet some men you call will be too intriguing to resist), make a date to meet in a public place. (Later, if he's as marvelous as he sounds, you'll have time for private tête-à-têtes.)

Of course, you may feel too hesitant ever to contact a strange man on your own. One of the best solutions I ever saw to this problem of meeting a stranger alone was in a recent personals section of *Connecticut* magazine. Three imaginative young women had gotten together and written this ad: *"Attention: Single, Handsome, Professional Men. 28–40. Three very attractive ladies—business writer, teacher, travel agent—invite you to dinner. We cook—you bring wine. Reply: P.O. Box* [etc. ] *..."* That seems a perfect solution to me. No pervert is going to confront three women together. In fact, barring some extraordinarily bold male who decides to answer by himself, the man who answers that ad will probably have at least two friends (which assures you he isn't a total social outcast). So if you feel too shy to advertise by yourself, persuade a couple of divorced, separated, or widowed friends to advertise with you.

If you feel confident going solo, what should you say in your ad? Any personals section will give you ideas. Describe yourself, your interests, what you'd like in a man. Be honest but positive, as if you were writing a résumé. Also, to receive the most answers possible, don't "require" that the man fall into a certain age range: Some perfect-in-every-other-way man may be just a year older or younger than you specify.

How many men can you reasonably expect to hear from? That's impossible to say, but some women have received thirty, forty, even fifty or more replies to a single ad. If you fail to round up enough suitable applicants, just reword your ad or try another newspaper or magazine—perhaps one with wider readership. It's at least worth a try.

## Ball Games

One of the best places I know to meet men is at a football, baseball, or basketball game. Just the price of a ticket admits you to a world of masculine sports fans—most of them in a happy-go-lucky, ready-to-meet-you mood. Men generally go with each other to sporting events, so take a girlfriend with you. Don't buy a reserved seat. Opt for the cheaper and more flexible grandstand or bleacher seats. Arrive early so you'll have time to look over the available men and choose your seats accordingly. If you arrive early *enough,* you can even move to another seat if the guys you sit beside at first turn out to be drips.

If you know nothing about the game, ask the men near you to explain. Or if you'd rather appear knowledgeable, go to your bookstore and pick up any of dozens of sports guides, such as *The Baseball Catalog* by Dan Schlossberg ($7.95) or *How to Watch a Football Game* by Frank and Lynn Barrett ($7.95).

Another possibility: The next time you winter in Florida, go to a baseball training camp. Some two hundred exhi-

bition games are held by major-league teams from about
mid-March to mid-April. Tickets are cheap ($3.50, or even
just $1.00), and the stands are filled with men. I'm sure you
can find your favorite team's winter vacation home (if
nothing else, just call the box office), but here's a quick rundown on where some major-league teams (or their farm
teams) have their Florida spring-training headquarters:
Atlanta Braves, West Palm Beach; Boston Red Sox, Winter
Haven; Cincinnati Reds, Tampa; Los Angeles Dodgers,
Vero Beach; New York Yankees, Fort Lauderdale; Philadelphia Phillies, Clearwater; Minnesota Twins' farm teams,
Melbourne.

## Bicycling

Buy a bicycle and pedal to work. Not only does bicycling
firm thighs, stomach muscles, and *derrière*, but cycling
through the city also attracts male attention. Want to lose a
few pounds? At an average pedaling speed of five miles per
hour, you burn five calories a minute—enough in one hour
to destroy the fattening effects of a veal cutlet, a baked potato, and a cup of green beans.

But isn't commuting by bike scary with all the cars
zipping around you? Though biking in city traffic can be a
bit hairy at first, it's fairly simple once you get the hang of
it. The most important thing to remember in city traffic is
that when riding your bike, you're operating a slow *vehi-
cle*—you're not a fast pedestrian—so you must obey all
traffic signals and other traffic laws. Once you're biking
daily to work, you'll meet fellow two-wheeled commuters.

Later you may even want to take an organized group
bike tour to Pennsylvania Dutch country, along Cape Cod's
bike paths, even to Copenhagen or to Melbourne, Australia.
American Youth Hostels, Inc., plans many good, inexpensive group tours (for information, contact American Youth

Hostels, Inc., National Campus, Delaplane, Virginia 22025). Some local organizations also cater to touring cyclists. Vermont Bicycle Touring, R.D. 2, Bristol, Vermont (802-388-4263), for example, plans weekend and longer tours through the wooded New England hills and even rents bicycles. On a group tour, you'll *inevitably* meet—and talk to—all the men in your group.

Or you may want to join a bike club. (Most cycling enthusiasts in clubs are men.) *Bicycling* magazine provides information on bike clubs (look for the magazine on your local newsstand or write *Bicycling,* P.O. Box 3330, San Rafael, California 92902).

If you have no bike but want to buy one, you can pick up a cheap three-speed for about $80, but if you think you'll be doing any serious cycling, plan to invest $180 to $250 for a good, trouble-free machine. When buying a bike, the secret is to choose a reliable one. To do that, pick up a how-to-buy-a-bicycle guide, such as *Richard's Bicycle Book* (New York: Ballantine; $5.95 in the United States, $6.95 in Canada).

## Take a Class

Sign up for a course in some typically male subject, such as carpentry, auto mechanics, wine appreciation, accounting, woodworking, oil painting, sculpting, or portfolio management. Typically you will find five to ten men for each woman in courses such as these.

Or you can do something really different and take a course such as the one I occasionally teach called "How to Meet New Women" at the Network for Learning. There you will really be outnumbered.

Not long ago a pleasant but far from pretty woman attended a session and was the hit of the evening by giving us the woman's point of view ... and by just being a friendly, caring person. During coffee breaks the men swarmed

around her as theatergoers do a leading lady. At the inter-
mission I told her I was surprised but delighted to have her
there because she was the first woman to show up not in the
capacity of lecturer or journalist. She replied that she'd
seen my course listed in the Network's catalog and that it
sounded interesting, fun, and like a good place to meet men.
How right she was! She left with a handsome fellow in a
three-piece suit.

Men met in classes given at adult education centers,
Y's, university extension departments, and art leagues tend
to be considerate, thoughtful, unstuffy guys.

Rhoda enrolled in a painting class at an arts center
near Hartford, Connecticut, for example, and met Larry. "I
don't generally like *crafty* men," Rhoda says. "Guys who
make leather billfolds and little toy wooden cars have this
weak, anemic look that just reeks of impotence. Or at least
that's what I thought. (Lately I've noticed some pretty
*macho* men hanging around our art center.) But anyway,
I've always liked artists because I think you have to assert
yourself strongly to create any form of art. Also, oddly
enough, artists seem to like me. I'm an artist's type, don't
ask me why. Anyway, while I was at this painting class,
Larry was about two easels away. As I walked over to a
table to clean my brushes, I glanced at Larry's still life and
said, 'Hey, how did you get that perfect red on that apple?
Could you teach me to mix colors like that?' It was the most
natural comment in the world because I really did want to
know how he did it. Larry looked up, gave me a warm, sincere smile, and said, 'Sure, anytime, be glad to.' That was
the beginning of an affair that lasted two years."

Classes are great for meeting men because you all share
a common interest and it's easy to swap notes, start conversations. So next time you can't decide how to spend your
Saturday afternoons or Tuesday nights, take a class—*not* in
jewelry-making, macramé, or crochet, but in a subject *men*
usually enjoy.

## Coach a Boys' Baseball Team

Local athletic and recreation departments always need volunteers to coach boys' baseball teams, and usually a team will have three or four male coaches to help you, so sign up. The younger the team, the better off you are. All you have to know to coach a bunch of eight- or nine-year-olds is how to hold a bat and catch a ball with both hands (your brother or father can show you at least that much). Divorced dads hang around Little League diamonds and are only too eager to help pitch batting practice or act as umps. Madge, whose team of ten-year-olds last year won all but one game, says, "Mostly what you need to coach young boys is energy. Try to instill team spirit, and that will carry you far. Most teams of little boys look like the "Bad News Bears" anyway. My secret for coaching my team to victory? I just kept up my boys' confidence by patting them on the backs and praising them for the slightest achievements (a good catch, a great throw, a little grounder). And I *fed* them: apples and peanut butter sandwiches after the third or fourth inning. Most opposing coaches never think of food, so come the fifth inning their kids are exhausted and yours are still high in blood sugar and going strong. Did I meet men? Are you kidding? That's all I did meet. Only about two mothers showed up all season. Two of the men I met I'm still dating."

## Conventions

If you're in a field where you have conventions and if you've always avoided going to business conferences in the past, now you should go. Men away from home at business or trade conventions look for tête-à-têtes, and many times convention delegates stay in the same hotel, allowing for easy room-to-room visiting.

Suzanne found romance at a St. Louis teachers' conference. "I was an editorial assistant on a state teachers' publication, and all of us had to attend the education conference," Suzy recalls. "I was literally surrounded all day by men, but I guess I was too insecure to think any man would be interested in me. Besides, I think of teachers as being *married*, which, of course, isn't really true. While one speaker was at the podium, a crowd of people was milling around toward the back of the auditorium. I was standing among them taking notes when a dark-haired man of average build came up and, holding out a shiny red apple, said, 'An apple for the teacher?' I suppose you'll think me naïve, but I didn't know he was making a pass at me. I just said, 'Oh, I'm not a teacher,' and I went back to my notes.

"That night I was lying in bed in my hotel room reading *David Copperfield* or some such thing when the phone rang. I figured it was my six-year-old daughter, Jessie, who was spending the week with my mother, but it turned out to be this apple man, who told me his name was Tom. He asked if I'd let him come over to my room for a drink! That sounded like fun, but I could hear my mother saying, 'Never ask a man back to your apartment' and I knew she would faint if I had him to my hotel room! So I said, 'Gee, Tom, I think you're cute, but my room is a bit too much right now. I'll meet you in the bar in fifteen minutes?' That night I decided I liked Tom and I did go back to *his* room, where we spent a torridly passionate night. I never saw him again. But I know now that if you go to a conference and look, you'll find available men everywhere. One day, maybe, I'll meet one who lives closer to me, and we'll have more than a one-night stand."

Suzanne's story reveals one problem of conferences: Most men there are from cities far from yours. So if you want only a relationship that will last forever (none of this ships-that-pass-in-the-night stuff for you, you say?), then keep that in mind while conferring.

## Dating Services

*Try a computer dating service? Never!* you think? Why not? Granted, it's unlikely a dating service will hook you up with the perfect mate, but you might enjoy yourself and you'll at least be dating again.

Besides, who knows? You could meet some fabulous man, as Sally did. A sparkling, outgoing woman who went back to school for her master's degree in industrial psychology after her divorce, Sally says, "I was looking for a man who'd be *consistent*. I wanted him to have a good sense of himself, humor, intelligence—and a profession. Since I've always been a risk-taker, I thought, Why not? A dating service is certainly a faster, more efficient way to meet men than most other methods. And do you know what? In six weeks (and for $350), I met not just one, but three, mind you, three utterly delightful, caring men."

As Sally discovered, dating services aren't just for losers. Many successful, career-oriented people who've been working so hard they have no time to look for love use dating services to connect. Few of them marry, but you never can tell. According to a recent *New York Times Magazine* article, of twelve hundred "hopeful hearts" who registered with Godmothers, a dating service that brings together people with similar fantasies and has offices in New York, Washington, D.C., and Philadelphia, a dozen couples started living together, one pair got engaged, and countless numbers had romantic flings.

Matchmaking agencies come in more varieties than you might think. In New York City, for example, you can dial such organizations as "Compatibility Plus," "Dateline," "Club More," "Crossroads," "Video Dating," and "Tiffany Select," the latter for "only single millionaires and beautiful women." So if the first dating service you contact seems too slick, phony, mechanical, or otherwise unsuitable, try another.

## Dude Ranches

Consider spending a week or two at a dude ranch. Dude ranch operators pride themselves on being friendly folks, and soon guests are all on a first-name basis. At a ranch, you'll enjoy barbecues, evening bonfires, and outdoor cowboy breakfasts together, and you eat family-style so everyone chats freely. Dude ranches, which have sprouted throughout the West, vary from bare-bones working ranches that offer only horseback riding and a swimming pool (about $120 to $140 a week per person) to full-fledged resorts ($250 a week and up per person) with tennis courts, masseuses, and golf courses. (When you write for reservations, be sure to ask what the price includes, as some ranches include all meals in their weekly rates, while others charge extra for food.) If the worst happens and all guests are married, you can always flirt with the ranch hands and wranglers who saddle your horse.

If a guest ranch is friendly and chatty in summer, should you go in the off-season, when rates are lower and the pace is even more laid-back? If you like cowboys, the answer is yes. My gut feeling is that few of them are the type to settle down to a life of domestic tranquillity with one lone woman. But you never know. And when you visit a dude ranch off-season, you can be sure that the ratio of men to women will be stacked in your favor, most of the staff being male.

Lists of dude ranches are available from most state and some local tourist commissions, including: the Montana Travel Promotion Unit, Helena, Montana 59601; the Wyoming Travel Commission, Cheyenne, Wyoming 82022; and the Bandera Chamber of Commerce, Bandera, Texas 78003.

Another excellent source is the book *Farm, Ranch and Country Vacations* (a Dickerman Guide, New York, Adventure Guides, Inc., $6.95). Or you might write for *Farm and Ranch Vacations* (about $10 postpaid from Farm and Ranch Vacations, Inc., 36 East 57th Street, New York, New York 10022; 212-355-6334).

## *Fighting*

Men still outnumber women at classes in the martial arts—jujitsu, aikido, judo, karate, and tai chi. So take a course in self-defense. You'll meet strong, athletic, self-disciplined, muscular men with whom you can *wrestle*. (Take care not to sign up by mistake for an all-woman class.)

Marylin, who took a judo class given nights at her local high school, gives some pointers on meeting men in a self-defense course. "My class was virtually all men—only two other women besides myself," Marylin says. "I thought that would be great, with all of us flipping each other and rubbing bodies together, but it didn't work that way. I saw one of the other women sitting astraddle one guy's chest and rubbing herself against him, and *he* seemed to notice. But I was too shy to do that. So I just kind of practiced my 'fits,' as they call the preflipping exercises, and tried to be friendly.

"There was one man, a writer named Sam, who was taking the course just for exercise. Most of the other guys were machinists, industrial painters, very *macho* blue-collar workers. But I liked Sam because he seemed more caring and sensitive. Gradually, I chose him more and more as my partner. One night after class, Sam and I walked to the parking lot together, and he'd left his car lights on and his battery was dead. Luckily I had jumper cables, so I helped him start his car. Then spontaneously, I asked if he'd like to come to my place for coffee. He accepted—and we started dating regularly. Not long after, we both dropped out of judo.

"Now, here's the thing: I'm not sure Sam and I would ever have gotten together by pummeling each other on the mat (though I have read that fighting with women does arouse some men's lusts). I'd suggest that if you meet a man you like in a martial arts class, try to get him off to a *quieter* place if you want him to see you as a woman."

To see which martial art is best for you, you might want to read *The Complete Martial Arts Catalogue* by John Corcoran and Emil Farkas (New York: Simon & Schuster, $8.95).

## Fishing

If you live near the shore, can bait a hook, and like to feel pollack tugging on your line, go deep-sea fishing—with a whole boatful of men. Party boats ranging from 40 to 100 feet long carry up to 120 people (the vast majority of them men) onto the ocean to fish for blues, bass, cod, and other fish.

I can't even begin to explain what a rare and refreshing vision you will be in an atmosphere like this. Men who love to fish often feel guilty about their passion, for it takes them away from home and hearth. You can imagine what a godsend a like-minded woman would be, one who won't recoil with squeals of disgust at the prospect of putting hook into bait, one who will enjoy accompanying men on their unending search to find great new fishing spots.

The atmosphere on a party boat soon becomes relaxed and friendly, particularly if the fish are biting. It's as easy chatting with the fishermen on either side of you as if you and they had been friends for years.

Party boats head out around 6:00 A.M., and though prices vary from boat to boat, you usually can fish for the day for $15 or $20. (Rods often can be rented.) To find a party boat in your area, just go down to the shore and look for lobster and fish markets (most lobster sellers catch their own wares, and many pick up extra money by taking out fishing parties), or ask some man at a local marina where the party boats dock. Once you get into the fishing world, you'll also hear about tuna tournaments and other fishing contests that attract mostly male crowds.

There are also many fly-fishing schools now open across the country (all attended mostly by men). Three in the Northeast include: Orvis Fly Fishing School, Orvis Company, Manchester, Vermont (802-362-1300); Orvis Shop of Boston Fly Fishing School, Boston, Massachusetts (617-653-9144); and Trout Unlimited Fly Fishing Camp, P.O. Box 117, Auburn, Massachusetts 01501. If you can't find a fishing school in your area, the men at these places should be able to steer you toward one.

## *Flying*

If you can fly a plane or want to learn, you'll find a connection to dozens—even hundreds—of men. Once a pilot, you can sign up for flight breakfasts, flight luncheons, and aviation conventions—eventually even give lessons. Plane flying, of course, requires much moola. The FAA requires that you take thirty-five to forty hours of dual and solo instruction, so you can plan on spending anywhere from $1,600 to $3,000 for lessons, depending on how quickly you learn, the number of lessons you take each week, and the school you attend. To hire an instructor and fueled plane costs from $35 to $70 an hour. If you decide to *buy* a plane, that will cost at least $15,000. Still, most pilots are men, and if you've got the money and have always wanted to fly, this would be a great time in your life to learn. Flying clubs are located around the country, and you can find out all about prices, lessons, and other details at smaller airports in your area.

If real planes sound too pricey or hair-raising, you might consider model planes. Every summer weekend in many large parks, you'll find crowds of men flying the model crafts. If even *motors* sound too complicated, how about a kite? You can buy a decent kite for less than $10, and most kite fliers are kind, gentle, thoughtful—and male. (If you can't locate a model plane or kite club in the Yellow Pages, ask about clubs at any hobby or kite shop.)

## Gambling

The next time you're near Las Vegas, Reno, or Atlantic City, go into a casino. Casinos are full of big spenders and high rollers. Gambling men tend to be so absorbed in five-card stud and blackjack that it's hard to get their attention, and dealers, at least at Las Vegas, discourage nonplayers from standing near the tables. But if you're persistent, you'll find many men interested and worth pursuing. Wear something glittery (it's always after dark in a casino). Then get yourself a cupful of quarters and sit down at a slot machine beside any cute guy. Slots are wonderful because you're *expected* to move around, putting in a nickel here, a nickel there. Also, slot-machine players tend to be amateur gamblers, hence more easily distracted by a winning smile. Just put a few nickels in your one-armed bandit, then turn to the man beside you and say, "Oh, I lost again. Having any luck?" or "This is my first day in town—do you play here all the time?" Any question about luck or money will work in a gambling town. Also, you're expected to talk. In casinos, liquor flows like water (some places serve free cocktails), so everybody—except the losers—feels sociable and in a party mood.

## Gaming

Most players of board and table games that demand concentration or skill are men. So learn a game of skill. Join a serious chess club, for example—either a private club (where you'll pay an annual fee) or a public club (which will cost you about a dollar for each hour you play). Public clubs, by the way, not only cost less but also offer a greater turnover of players.

Or try the five-thousand-year-old game of backgammon. This highly sociable game combines skill and luck (a toss of the dice determines which piece you move) and offers a chance to play with up to five other players (hopefully men) on one board. If none of your friends plays, you'll probably want to join a backgammon club (about $75 a year plus $5.00 or less for each time you play). Some clubs draw as many as 150 enthusiasts, and the management will match you up with other players, so it's possible to meet several men in one evening. Once you tire of the game, you can retreat to the club lounge or snack bar for more socializing. To locate a backgammon or chess club near you, check your Yellow Pages. Some health clubs (the San Francisco Bay Club near that city's financial district, for example) also offer bridge and backgammon games.

Of course, there's also bridge. If you're available as a fourth for this highly social game, you'll never lack for bridge party invitations, and your partner will likely be a serious, intellectual man. Some bridge clubs are even set up for singles only (avoid those filled with only blue-haired ladies). Once you become proficient at bridge, you may even want to play in a tournament, where you'll find eligible men everywhere. For information about bridge, pick up any of a dozen or more how-to-play books, or write the American Contract Bridge League, 2200 Democrat Road, Memphis, Tennessee 38116.

## Golf

I'm an avid golfer. For every twenty men I see on the golf course, I see one woman. The cliché is that male golfers don't like to play with women. The truth is, it's always fun to catch up to a woman, or have her catch up to you. It makes the game more festive, more glamorous, even if romance or sex, love and dating are out of the question.

One of the nice things about golf is that when you do hook up with a stranger or a couple of them to form a two-some or threesome or foursome, you are automatically thrown together on intimate terms. Golfers root one another on, commiserate over bad shots, and generally wind up getting pretty close after just a couple of holes.

If you'd like to learn to play well, you might want to check out one of the many golf clinics now located all over the United States. Golf Digest Instruction Schools, for example, which has been called the "Harvard of golf schools," has golf resorts all over the country. (For information, contact Golf Digest Instruction Schools, 495 Westport Avenue, Norwalk, Connecticut 06856; 203-847-5811.) Or you could take a short clinic at a club. Ball Flight Teaching Systems (707 Lake Cook Road, Suite 300, Deerfield, Illinois 60015; 800-323-5770, toll-free; or 312-948-0450), for instance, offers clinics at clubs in large cities throughout the country. (Be sure to sign up for a coed clinic, as some courses are for women only.)

## The Great Outdoors

Rugged he-men and sensitive environmentalists spend weekends in the woods. To meet one of these men, go hiking, riding, rafting, canoeing, mountain climbing, or backpacking. If you were born knowing how to survive in the woods, great. But if you're timid, you'll probably want to tackle the wilds first with an expert. Outward Bound offers a number of wilderness treks designed to make you more self-reliant. (For information, contact Outward Bound, 384 Field Point Road, Greenwich, Connecticut 06830; 203-661-0797; or 1-800-243-8520, toll-free). Ask your travel agent about wilderness trips, or look up the Sierra Club or Wilderness Society in your local phone directory. The Wilderness Society

(4260 East Evans Avenue, Denver, Colorado 80222; 303-758-2266) sponsors more than a hundred trips on which you can ride, raft, camp, or backpack through the Smokies, Adirondacks, Everglades, or other national parks or deserts. Or you could try one of many field trips (from $3.00 to $200 or more) conducted by the Audubon Society. Once outdoors, you'll find that the woods breed camaraderie. Even if you're shy, a couple of nights beneath the stars will generate intimacy without your realizing how you went from silent outsider to one of the gang.

If wilderness treks sound too rugged to tackle, consider bird-watching. Today an estimated 20 million Americans watch birds, and of the 343,000 hard-core watchers who belong to the Audubon Society, 52 percent are men. As a recent *Life* magazine story points out, birders are also better *educated* than other nature lovers. Birding clubs are perfect for meeting men. You rise at dawn to look together for aeries—and may spend all day stalking through the forests. You can also go on Audubon Society-sponsored bird walks or weekends to picturesque Block Island, Rhode Island. So borrow a friend's binoculars and get started. All you need is a bird book (Roger Tory Peterson's *Field Guide to the Birds,* Boston, Houghton Mifflin, at $9.95 is the birder's bible) and a club (contact the national office of the Audubon Society at 950 Third Avenue, New York, New York 10022; 212-832-3200, or obtain a copy of *A Guide to North American Bird Clubs* from Avian Publications, Inc., P.O. Box 310, Elizabethtown, Kentucky 42701).

Other wilderness organizations are:

- National Campers and Hikers Association, 7172 Transit Road, Buffalo, New York 14221.
- American Camping Association, Bradford Woods, Martinsville, Indiana 46151.
- Appalachian Mountain Club, 5 Joy Street, Boston, Massachusetts 02108.

Books to read include:

- *Rent-a-Canoe Directory* and *Learn-to-Canoe Directory,* two booklets offered free from Grumman Boats, Marathon, New York 13803. (The latter lists camping and canoeing clubs.)
- *Wilderness Expeditions* by Heinz Sielmann (New York: Franklin Watts, $30).
- *Wilderness U.S.A.* (National Geographic Society, $9.95 cloth).
- *A Guide to Paddle Adventure* by Rick Kemmer (New York: Vanguard Press, $6.95).
- *Woman in the Woods* by Kathleen Farmer (Stackpole Books, Cameron & Kelker Streets, Harrisburg, Pennsylvania 17105, $3.00).
- *L. L. Bean Guide to the Outdoors* (New York: Alfred A. Knopf, $14.95).

## Health Clubs

If you tend to do your exercises at home with Richard Simmons, change your routine and join a health club. I belong to a gym, and the atmosphere is extremely sexy, but unlike a singles bar, in a very relaxed, natural way.

Everybody is stretching and grunting and sweating in the briefest, most revealing of outfits. One's mind can't help but turn to thoughts of an amorous nature. And it's so darn easy to start talking. Not only do you see many of the same people day after day, you also have plenty of chances to connect while sitting around the whirlpool tub or doing sit-ups. Many health clubs have not only exercise rooms, pools, and tennis courts but bars, restaurants, and lounges as well. You may even find a club that has a social calendar listing bike rides, ski-touring trips, dances, and other mating events.

If you see a sexy man at your health club, what to say? Opening comments come easily. How about:

- "I'm new here. How do you like it?"
- "Ooooh, my thighs are killing me. Do you think a massage would help?"
- "Would you mind holding my feet while I do my sit-ups?"

It doesn't take long to figure out some good-looking guy's schedule so you can show up at the same times he does. And when the time is ripe, you can invite him to play a game of racquetball or tennis.

## Investing

"When recently widowed or divorced women ask me how to meet a man, I give them two suggestions," says Dr. Joyce Brothers. "The first is to buy stock (and you should probably plan to buy at least ten shares if you want a broker to cooperate with you) in a number of major corporations. And then attend their annual meetings. The majority of stockholders at these meetings are male, and they tend to be intelligent, concerned, and financially stable. It is easy to start conversations with other stockholders. You have something in common."

So follow Dr. Brothers' suggestion and invest. Enroll in an investment course at a local community college or university. Check the local want ads and try to land a job in an investment firm. Wall Street types are usually quite willing to give you "inside" tips on the market, and it's easy to ask questions because he doesn't *expect* you to know as much as he does.

## Jogging

While jogging in the park between 6:00 and 8:00 A.M. on weekdays, or any time of day on weekends, you'll probably meet plenty of fellow joggers. (Even if you don't, you'll improve your circulation, increase your energy, and lose weight.) One of the cheapest sports around, jogging requires no training or equipment; you only need a good pair of running shoes.

Though some joggers run every day, you needn't become a running maniac to stay in shape or meet men. Just fifteen minutes a day three times a week are enough. Don't run after dark, or you may meet a mugger. Informal running clubs which gather for both weekend races and daily runs have sprung up all over the United States. Join one.

If jogging sounds just too strenuous, you can also meet running enthusiasts at high school and college track meets. While standing or sitting by an athletic man, say, "I know so little about running, but I'd love to learn. Can you tell me what this race is called?"

For more information on running:

- Road Runners Club of America, c/o Jeff Darman, 2737 Devonshire Place, N.W., Washington, D.C. 20008.
- *Women's Running* by Dr. Joan Ullyot (Mountain View, Calif., World Publications, $4.00). Although dozens of books have been written about running, this one's especially good for women.

## *Join a Club*

Chances are you're tired of hearing this, but join a club. Yes, even if you're not a joiner. People join clubs mostly with one thought in mind: to meet others. So any single man in your club will likely be looking for a woman, and she might as well be you. Most club members share some common interest, so choose a club according to the type of man you'd like to meet.

If you like intelligent men and you're quite bright yourself, for example, you might take a test and join Mensa, the club for people with I.Q.'s of 130 or better. Mensans can be eccentric (I know one who speaks Old English incessantly and another who lives underground to avoid the bomb), but they're also usually clever, witty, successful, and male. If you think you might be Mensa material or you'd like to receive membership information, write to Mensa, 1701 West Third Street, Brooklyn, New York 11223. Or if you like rich, goal-oriented men, check out the Millionaires' Club. (Annual dues range from hundreds to thousands of dollars, depending on the type of membership you choose.) Most members aren't exactly millionaires (their median income is just under $40,000). Still, the guys in the group are hard-working upward strivers and *want* to be rich someday. Once limited only to Californians, the Millionaires' Club is opening branches in twenty-three cities, including New York and Denver. (For information, write: The Millionaires' Club, 4500 Campus Drive, Suite 300, Newport Beach, California 92660; 714-545-7666).

Another kind of club to consider is your college or university club. Once mostly all-male bastions, these have become increasingly coeducationalized, although women still haven't come to utilize them nearly as frequently as men do. Perhaps a few or many years back you went to a college where you made lots of good friends, but after you graduated you drifted apart. You might be surprised to discover how many of these old pals would be delighted to hear from you. More than you expect may be in the same boat as you, divorced and looking to meet new people to date. Alumni organizations as well as actual clubs with headquarters exist in all areas of the country, and it might be a great boon to your social life to check with your school to see what kind of alumni activities are going on near you.

To find other great clubs, go to your local library and leaf through the 1,456-page *Encyclopedia of Associations* (Detroit: Gale Research Company), a guide to more than thirteen thousand nonprofit groups. You're bound to find *one* you like, even if you're not the clubby type.

## Military Academy Tours

If visiting a military academy sounds dull, think again. Men outnumber women there by about a thousand to one. Academies expect citizens like you simply to show up for a tour. So the next time you're near West Point, New York, or the Air Force Academy in Colorado Springs, stop by for a friendly visit. At the Coast Guard Academy in New London, Connecticut, you'll be invited by clean-cut uniformed men to board the sailing vessel *Eagle* and to watch the battalion reviews, while at the U.S. Naval Academy in Annapolis, Maryland, you'll not only get to watch dress parades, but you can even tour a *dormitory*. Cadets and midshipmen are trained to be polite and responsive toward guests. After that, you're on your own.

## Museums and Galleries

There are more than seven thousand museums in the United States, most of them inexpensive and perfect for the cultural pickup. The man met in a museum is often sophisticated, educated, and intelligent. He's at least *curious*. And if he's browsing through a museum alone, he's probably also available.

You might want to take in a typically "masculine" museum like the National Baseball Hall of Fame in Cooperstown, New York, or the National Pro Football Hall of Fame in Canton, Ohio. Or you may want to stick with museums of art, science, or natural history. In any museum, opening remarks are a cinch: You simply comment on any nearby exhibit. While standing before the bones of a *Tyrannosaurus rex*, for example, you might say, "How many pounds of meat do you suppose he ate a day?" Or while near a Picasso painting, you might remark simply, "I adore Picasso, do you?" If you're dismayed, even disgusted by a work, say so.

In a museum that exhibits contemporary, often freaky art, many men feel grateful to find a fellow skeptic. Most museums also have cozy coffee shops, cafeterias, or fountained gardens where you can meet men.

Consider, too, the art galleries, where you might meet a rich collector. Since in most cities galleries cluster in a single district, you can spend a Saturday afternoon browsing through a dozen or so galleries. If you find you like the art crowd, try to get invited to the champagne parties and gallery openings at which new artworks are presented (and where there's often more phone-number swapping than art buying going on). Send every art gallery in your city a letter on good, *personal* stationery, saying you're an art collector and would like to attend openings. You'll be invited.

Going to an opening alone if you don't know a Stella from a Warhol sounds formidable, but it's easier to get by than you might think. Let's talk in some detail about how to carry it off. Most important, try to look relaxed. Act as if you've been hobnobbing with the artistic elite for years. Commenting on a work really isn't necessary. If anyone approaches you and says, "Remarkably like Dali, don't you think?" reply noncommittally, "Hmmmm. Do you really think so?" Answer any question with a question. Don't be drawn into an artistic discussion that's over your head. Even if you don't drink, carry a glass of Perrier so you can sip during a conversational lull.

Look poised. Contemplate a painting. Read a press release. If a man interests you, stroll over and say, "Hello," then tell him your name. If he responds with his name, chat a while. If he looks blankly over your shoulder, don't indulge in self-pity or feel rejected. Just find another prospect. Talk to men who seem total bores (you'll find plenty of *those*). Practice your small talk, then move on.

Above all, remember it doesn't matter if a man seems unentranced by you. These things happen to everyone, including, I'm sure, Elizabeth Taylor. If you fail to meet someone in about forty-five minutes, leave. You have too many other options to fret about one missed chance.

## Hold a Party

If the only time you go to parties is when your friends invite you, it's time to change: Throw a bash of your own. I know everybody tells you to throw a party to meet people, so this advice may sound old hat. But parties are set up especially for men to meet women, and vice versa. Partying is just too good an option to ignore. So give a party and invite all the men you know (even those you know just casually, or the man you met only yesterday).

What's the occasion? Use your imagination. Hold a birthday, a Halloween costume, or a let's-paint-my-doghouse party. Celebrate your raise, your new job, or your cat's baby kittens. If you hate cooking and fear your appetizers will look like shoe leather (and taste worse), keep your menu simple. Try a backyard barbecue complete with hot dogs, beer, potato chips, and homemade ice cream. Or throw a pizza party and let your guests make their own pizzas.

Too broke? No excuse. Try a rent party and ask your guests to chip in five bucks each. I know a rent party may *sound* pathetic, but it's not. Singer Helen Reddy met her husband at a rent party she gave when she was down and out. Being a bit low on cash is nothing to be ashamed of. If you carry it off right, you can make your pennilessness seem *chic*.

If a party sounds just too overwhelming to attempt alone, use your children as waiters or throw a bash with a friend. The last thing you need after a divorce is to sit around feeling mopey and sorry for yourself. So celebrate! After all, you're starting a new life (and how many women you know can say *that*?).

## Politicking

Working together for a favorite political candidate creates an *esprit de corps* hard to duplicate elsewhere. And the victory parties, with everyone hugging and kissing, are sensational. So find a local or national candidate you believe in and back him or her all the way.

Forget typing, filing, and stuffing envelopes—too officey and confining. Volunteer to canvas door-to-door in your apartment building or neighborhood or to throw a wine-and-cheese party for your candidate (another great excuse for a party, and the organization will pay for the food). If you've got a head for statistics or fund-raising, offer your services. Or run for office *yourself*.

Even if your candidate loses, all is not lost. Brenda, an Iowan who worked for Jimmy Carter in the last presidential election, recalls, "We were working our hearts out, and the night he lost, I felt awful. There was this sweet guy named Nick who'd been working harder than any of us, and I suddenly realized he must be feeling as rotten as I was. I figured he'd probably be out with friends, but I dialed his number anyway, and he answered. I said, 'Wanna share an old bottle of 'victory wine'? He did. So we got together at my place, consoled each other, and have been going out ever since."

If politics has no appeal, you can also volunteer for other projects—at work, for instance. If you volunteer for office projects nobody wants, you'll meet coworkers you normally wouldn't meet. Collect blood donation pledges. Carry around a coworker's birthday card for everyone to sign. Join the company volleyball, baseball, football, or bowling team. Offer to organize the next wine-and-cheese party to celebrate a promotion. When you volunteer for politics or any worthwhile project, you just naturally meet new people, including men.

## Sailing

Looking for a skipper or a tanned deckhand? Sailboat owners always need able-bodied men and women to crew. You can learn the ABC's of sailing at a sailing school ($200 or $300 for a five-day course). Or, if you can't afford the fees sailing schools charge, you may be able to take sailing lessons from your U.S. Coast Guard flotilla for free.

Although you may think boat owners want to stick just with their friends, they're actually willing and eager to hire hardworking, skilled "sailors" who share their love for the sea. Patty, an outdoorsy third-grade teacher and sailor from Eugene, Oregon, advises joining a sailing club. "I've always loved sailing, but when my husband and I split up, *he* got the boat," Patty says. "I decided that wouldn't deter me, so I joined a sailing club. They hold regular meetings at which you get to know fellow members. There's no national organization of sailing clubs, but you can get information through friends or from a local marina." Patty also suggests that you check the classified sections of sailing magazines for ads placed by boat owners looking for crews. "I flew to Miami last year and crewed on a sail to the Bahamas," says Patty, "and I met lots of terrific guys who love sailing as I do. I also look at notices on the bulletin boards of yacht clubs in my area. You'll often see a man or a woman who's looking to hire crew. Sailing works for me because I genuinely love it, but I wouldn't advise anyone to invest in sailing lessons until she's sure she loves the water. It wouldn't warm the cockles of any skipper's heart if you upchucked from Miami to St. Thomas."

## Scuba Classes

Most scuba and diving shops and even some gyms and pools offer lessons in snorkeling, scuba, underwater photography, and wreck diving. Years ago, only athletic young men tackled this sport, but now scuba diving's safe enough that even a grandmother can do it. Mostly, it's a wonderful way to meet male divers. You can usually rent diving equipment (fees range from about $18 to $30 a day), and a basic thirty-two- to forty-hour course costs about $100.

## *Shopping*

Anytime you can, shop where men shop. Stop by the pipe store to buy your ashtrays. Buy your cooking wine at a wine shop. Pick up measuring cups not at the supermarket but at your local hardware store. You may even want to buy yourself floppy (and very comfortable) men's p.j.'s at a men's clothing store. Of course, you needn't buy. You can just browse. Pick your shops according to the type of man you like.

If you fancy intellectuals, zip down to your Barnes & Noble, B. Dalton, or Doubleday bookstore and wander until you spy an intriguing man. If you want an adventurer, head for the travel section. If you want him horny, stay near the erotic books. To break the ice, just comment on any book he's or you've picked up: "Have you read this yet? Is it any good?" If you're petite, you have a definite advantage. Wait till a tall stranger comes by, then ask, "Pardon me, but could you please reach me that book on the top shelf?" (The title matters not: It could be *257 Ways to Cook Albatross*, for all you care.)

Audiophiles, of course, frequent record and stereo shops. If you fancy a highbrow, head for the Mozart and Beethoven sections. If you prefer a more Bohemian man, linger near the Pete Seeger and Kingston Trio albums. Select an album, ask if he's heard it, if he liked it. Or remark, "If you enjoy Puccini, I think you'll love this new *Madame Butterfly* recording."

Browse through a showroom featuring BMW's, Jags,

or Mercedes-Benzes. If you like yachting types, shop at marine supply houses. If equestrians appeal, go to the tack shop. Once you settle on the type of man you'd like to meet, shop for him in all likely places.

## Squash

Once an Ivy League sport for men, squash is now played by men and women of all ages. If you're thin, wiry, fast, competitive, and look good in shorts, you'll love it. Squash courts are often located in downtown business districts, so you and male executives can play on your lunch hour. After a fast game, retire to the squash club restaurant or cocktail lounge to meet fellow aficionados. Club membership fees run as little as $25 to $50 a year (you pay extra for time spent on the courts).

## Tennis Camps

Men also play a lot of tennis. So the next time you have a few days free, don't spend it sitting at home watching soap operas. Consider a tennis camp. Tennis camps, which have sprung up all over the country, offer a variety of programs—from grueling eight-hour-a-day training sessions after which you can barely lift a newspaper, to more leisurely paced camps where you have time off at night to play bridge or see a movie. Most tennis camps are run by former tennis pros, and many are held at private schools and universities. God knows, the accommodations aren't posh (often you live in a dorm), but the price is reasonable enough: $50 to $70 a day, all accommodations, meals, and lessons included.

If you'd rather have ritzier lodging, you might prefer a tennis *clinic*. Clinics cost about twice what you'd pay for a camp but usually are held in spiffy resorts. There's the World of Tennis Resort in Austin, Texas, for example, where you live in town houses (for information, contact World of Tennis Resort, Austin, Texas 78734; 512-261-6000; or 800-531-5001, toll-free). Or, if you want the ultimate, most complete and professional tennis resort in the world, most experts agree it's John Gardiner's Tennis Ranch (5700 East McDonald Drive, Scottsdale, Arizona 85253; 602-948-2100). There's also a Gardiner tennis ranch in Carmel Valley, California, but the Scottsdale resort is considered the *crème de la crème.*

If you can't afford a tennis camp or clinic this year, don't despair. There's always your local tennis club—even the free public courts. Men who hang around waiting for courts are easy to chat with and often looking for partners. You might even reserve a court at your club early, arrive to look over the available men, then ask your choice if he'd like to play with you at two. Getting a court is so tough he'll probably be delighted you asked.

For a complete, current list of tennis camps, go to your library and check the latest January issue of *Tennis* (or send $1.25 to *Tennis* magazine, 495 Westport Avenue, Norwalk, Connecticut 06856). For more information on tennis, read *World Tennis Magazine* and *The Tennis Book* (New York: Arbor House, $23).

## Theater Groups

If you can act, join an amateur theater group. In the South and West especially, you'll find outdoor theater in which huge casts of amateurs (plus a handful of pros per show) put on historical musicals dealing with some story from local lore. In an outdoor amphitheater in Hemet, California, each spring, for example, actors and actresses stage a dramatization of Helen Hunt Jackson's romantic novel *Ramona,* and in Beckley, West Virginia, thespians put on yearly productions of *The Hatfields and the McCoys.* You may find similar productions in your area. If not, look around for an amateur theater society, or find a private club or church group that produces plays.

Theater groups are hubs of camaraderie (which often leads to romance). After working in close quarters until the wee hours of the morning, you and your flamboyant actor friends (as well as the prop men and stage crew) will often retire to a Bohemian cafe for coffee. Some groups travel, so you could even wind up on tour. I have only one warning: Avoid groups planning to stage *Little Women, The Women,* or any play with an all-female cast.

If you don't know how to act but want to learn, you might want to take an acting, mime, or puppeteering class at a local college or university. Or you could get into the publicity or production side of the theater—or even film. You can take a course in motion-picture production, for example, at the Danny Rouzer Studio (7022 Melrose Avenue, Hollywood, California 90038). For $750, you receive forty-eight hours of instruction over a two-week period. Classes are given evenings, leaving your days free for sightseeing and going to the beach.

This concludes my list of man-meeting places. But where I stop is just where you begin. Once you start brainstorming, you'll think of dozens of places to meet men on your own. Finding men is really just a matter of shaking up your old mental sets and going not where you want as a married woman, but where the single men go. Once you start doing that, you'll meet more men than you ever thought possible. That I guarantee.

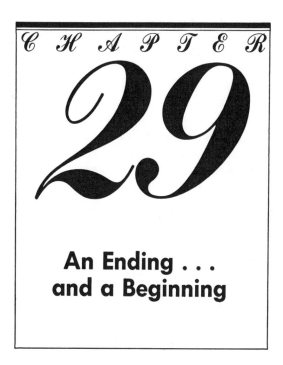

# An Ending . . .
# and a Beginning

Well, it's been fun. In a curious way, I somehow feel I've gotten to know some of you. And I hope that some of you feel you've gotten to know me, at least a little bit.

But now it's time, for you in particular, to move on. Toward that end, I would suggest that you place aside *The Divorced Woman's Guide to Meeting New Men*, temporarily anyway, to begin implementing some of its ideas. 'Tis intoxicating and delicious to get excited by something you've read in a book—*Oh, my God, all the men I'm going to have in my life!* It's another thing to get yourself out of the house and down to the local high school track to do a little "passive" man-hunting while you jog.

But that is what it takes, all right. Getting out of the house and *beginning*. Of course, not all of the dozens of ideas and approaches in this book can work for you. Some may turn you off. Some may inspire not a jot of confidence. Some may sound good in the abstract but just not be something you see yourself pulling off. That's perfectly O.K. If only one of the ideas contained herein has intrigued you just a little ... well, that's all it takes to change your life. One idea. In fact, maybe that's the most effective way of all to use *The Divorced Woman's Guide to Meeting New Men*—pick out the one strategy that moves you the most and make it your banner, your *modus operandi.*

We know one woman who made it a practice to introduce herself to men at parties and gatherings. "Hello, I'm Joyce," she'd say, extending her arm to shake hands. One night at a tennis party for singles she walked up to a young lawyer who had been keeping himself off to the side, seemingly too shy to mingle. "Hello, I'm Joyce," she said. Two weeks later they were engaged. Today they have three attractive, healthy children. All because the woman followed a simple, executable idea.

We are acquainted with a divorced woman named Helene who for some reason became fixated on the old notion that the way to a man's heart is through his stomach. Neighbors, coworkers, casual acquaintances—sooner or later, all were treated to one of her culinary creations. One morning Helene brought an extra brownie from home to give to the attractive new man in the office adjacent to hers. That afternoon Mike, for the very first time, stuck his head in her doorway and asked her to lunch for the following day.

It is difficult to say if it is because the brownie tasted so good, or because the overture of having been offered it was enough of a sign to Mike that Helene was interested. Whatever your interpretation, the result was that after several months of dating, Helene and Mike moved in together. And one idea did it. One simple, modest action on Helene's part (by the way, something almost any one of you reading this book could do) brought about a relationship that was to make two people's lives vastly more complete than they had been.

Now, what idea or ideas are you going to follow? To sum up, here are the major themes put forth in the preceding pages:

1. Get out of the house. You can't meet men while curled up in front of the TV set.
2. Change your living patterns. Follow an instinct to take a trip, do something "crazy" you've always wanted to do. Or rediscover something great from your past.
3. Learn to enjoy light friendships with men. If you can't find a lover, be a pal.
4. Keep your standards realistic. Some men who are only "3's" or "4's" may be sweeter than you think. And with your love, perhaps they can become "10's."
5. Stay open and approachable. Don't miss opportunities to meet men just because you're feeling fat, boring, or gloomy that day. Any time a man makes an overture, respond. Seize the moment.
6. Watch your body language. No matter how bashful you feel, stand straight, make eye contact, and *smile.*
7. Be kind. Help the man who's down and out. Compliment a man you like.
8. Become a flirt. It's fun.
9. Make the most of your up times. Whenever you're having a terrific day or you feel absolutely beautiful, meet as many men as you possibly can.
10. Remember, men are lonely, too. When you're having trouble connecting, realize that some guys are as shy as you are, so keep trying.

I believe any of the above ideas is powerful enough to bring several, and in some cases many, new men into your life.

But I should caution you not to expect instantaneous magic. If you like the idea of going bowling, for example, but the particular night you choose to go turns out to be Women's League Night, don't leap to the conclusion that bowling is an awful way to meet men and you'd better hurry up and find another approach. Maybe, in fact, you should go bowling the very next night, or for that matter, the same night but at a different alley.

I don't mean to sound like a Pollyanna, but the point is, life begins to change for the better only when we stop giving up. One doesn't necessarily have to *believe* in what one is doing. If you sparked to the idea of making lots of male pals but your first few attempts to befriend a man are rebuffed, or involve you only with men who depress or bore you, that doesn't mean you should jettison the procedure as pointless. It simply means you've got to keep trying.

And don't assume that to keep trying means you've got to feel optimistic or joyful about what you are doing. Often success descends upon us suddenly, out of the blue, when we least expect it. But descend upon us it does only when we are out there pitching, trying, *engagé*.

Thus, I guess my concluding message is rather a conventional one. If the ideas I've presented don't work a first or a second time around, try them a third and a fourth and a seventeenth. Years of experience and research in the field of human interaction have proved to me that these ideas are easy to execute and that they do work to attract new men. If you don't abandon them prematurely, sooner or later they will help to bring a wonderful new man into your life. Of this I am convinced.